The Philosophy of Conspiracy Theories

The Philosophy of Conspiracy Theories

Matthew R. X. Dentith

palgrave
macmillan

First published 2014 by
PALGRAVE MACMILLAN

Palgrave Macmillan in the UK is an imprint of Macmillan Publishers Limited, registered in England, company number 785998, of Houndmills, Basingstoke, Hampshire RG21 6XS.

Palgrave Macmillan in the US is a division of St Martin's Press LLC, 175 Fifth Avenue, New York, NY 10010.

Palgrave Macmillan is the global academic imprint of the above companies and has companies and representatives throughout the world.

Palgrave® and Macmillan® are registered trademarks in the United States, the United Kingdom, Europe and other countries.

ISBN: 978–1–137–36315–2

This book is printed on paper suitable for recycling and made from fully managed and sustained forest sources. Logging, pulping and manufacturing processes are expected to conform to the environmental regulations of the country of origin.

A catalogue record for this book is available from the British Library.

Library of Congress Cataloging-in-Publication Data

Dentith, Matthew R. X., 1977–
The philosophy of conspiracy theories / Matthew R.X. Dentith.
pages cm
ISBN 978–1–137–36315–2 (hardback)
1. Conspiracy theories – Philosophy. I. Title.

HV6275.D46 2014
001.9—dc23 2014025888

Contents

Foreword

Consider the following argument (call it the Cecilia/Nixon Argument):

(1) Cecilia subscribes to the theory that Nixon and his henchmen conspired to cover up the Watergate break-in, which was itself instigated at their behest.
(2) Hence Cecilia subscribes to a theory that posits a conspiracy – a secret (and sinister) plot to influence public affairs by partly secret means.
(3) Hence Cecilia subscribes to a conspiracy theory.
(4) Hence Cecilia is a conspiracy theorist.
(5) Therefore Cecilia subscribes to theory that is intellectually suspect and irrational to believe.
(6) Therefore Cecilia herself is irrational, if not mad – at the very least a practitioner of the 'paranoid style' in politics.
(7) Therefore it would be silly to accept or even investigate Cecilia's theory.

What are we to make of this argument? Well, obviously it is valid enough up to step (4), but after that it goes violently off the rails. If (1) is the case, and Cecilia subscribes to the theory that Nixon and his henchmen conspired to cover up the Watergate break-in, then (2) she subscribes to a theory that posits a conspiracy. And if Cecilia subscribes to a theory that posits a conspiracy, then it presumably follows that (3) *Cecilia subscribes to a conspiracy theory* and therefore that (4) *Cecilia is a conspiracy theorist.* But does it follow from the fact that Cecilia subscribes to a conspiracy theory that (5) she subscribes to a theory that is intellectually suspect and irrational to believe? Obviously not. For the theory to which Cecilia subscribes is nowadays regarded as an established historical truth. Since premises of the form (3) can be true and conclusions of the form (5) can be false, it is clear that (5) does not follow from (3). But if (5) does not follow from (3), (6) does not follow from either (3) or (4), though we might be willing to grant that it follows from (5). (If it is irrational to believe in conspiracy theories, and Cecilia subscribes to a conspiracy theory, then it seems that Cecilia is thus far irrational.) Much the same goes for (7). If it is irrational to believe in conspiracy theories, then it is irrational to investigate them, since there is not much point in investigating a theory that would be irrational to believe. But (7) does not follow from (3). The fact that Cecilia's theory is a conspiracy theory does not imply that it is irrational to believe it and hence does not imply that it would be irrational to investigate it (though in the present case investigation would be a bit redundant, since the facts are already in).

Well, so what? The Cecilia/Nixon Argument is obviously a dud, but defective arguments are a dime a dozen, so why should we worry about this one? Because arguments of this form, and every bit as bad as this, are insinuated and suggested day-in and day-out by politicians and pundits, often with an intolerably smug air of intellectual sophistication. Furthermore, despite their obvious fallaciousness, they often convince the voting public. The panjandrums start with the premise that somebody has posited a theory involving some conspiracy and conclude (reasonably enough) that the person has posited a conspiracy theory and is thus a conspiracy theorist. But they then go on to suggest that *therefore* the theory is crazy and not worth considering and that the theorist herself is several sandwiches short of the full picnic. Thus, perfectly plausible theories don't even get discussed. Tony Blair was a noted practitioner of these dark arts. Here, for instance, he manages to complete the inference in a few deft words. He had been asked about a leaked memo recording a conversation in which he had supposedly talked George W. Bush out of bombing Al-Jazeera's studios in Doha, presumably because Bush took exception to Al-Jazeera's news coverage of Iraq. 'Looking tired, [Blair] appeared to lose his cool when asked about reports claiming that the memo showed him talking Mr Bush out of mounting an air raid on al-Jazeera. "Look, there's a limit to what I can say – it's all *sub judice*," he said [it was all *sub judice* because the leakers were being prosecuted, presumably at his behest]. "But honestly, I mean, conspiracy theories..."' (*Daily Telegraph*, 27 October 2005). One cannot but admire Blair's talent for sophistry even when under stress. The inference appears to be that *because* what was being suggested was a conspiracy theory it did not deserve to be discussed. So the Prime Minister was able to avoid answering or even discussing the allegation that his friend and ally, the President of the USA, was the kind of moral monster who would regard the murder of a bunch of journalists as a serious option because he did not care for the content of their news coverage.

So common is this tactic of arguing that a conspiracy theory is not worth discussing simply because it *is* a conspiracy theory that journalists investigating or hypothesising such theories feel compelled to deny either that the theories they are suggesting *are* conspiracy theories or that they themselves are conspiracy theorists, even when they are obviously propounding theories featuring conspiracies ('I am not a conspiracy theorist but....').

But surely arguments along the lines of the Cecilia/Nixon Argument cannot be as crudely fallacious as I have suggested. There must be *some* way of turning the Cecilia/Nixon Argument into something valid. And, of course, there is. We simply add in an extra premise between (3) and (5):

(3′) All conspiracy theories are such that it is irrational to believe them.

This would restore the argument to validity all right, since if, as (3) concedes, Cecilia subscribes to a conspiracy theory, and if all such theories are theories that it is irrational to believe, then it follows that (5) *Cecilia subscribes to a theory that is irrational to believe*. And if Cecilia subscribes to a theory that is irrational to believe, then this suggests that she is thus far irrational, and that the theory she believes is not worth investigating.

The problem is that (3′) is clearly false. Not all conspiracy theories are such that it is irrational to believe them. For example, it is not irrational to believe Cecilia's theory that Nixon and his henchmen conspired to cover up the Watergate break-in.

I am not suggesting, of course, that there are not plenty of conspiracy theories that it *is* irrational to believe. For instance, it is (at least now) irrational to believe the theory that constituted the pretext for the invasion of Iraq – that Saddam Hussein had successfully conspired to acquire weapons of mass destruction that posed a significant threat to the US and the UK. It is also irrational to believe that he was in cahoots with al-Qaeda and was in some way responsible for the events of 9/11. But, irrational as they may be, it is irrational to believe these theories not simply because they *are* conspiracy theories but because they are *bad* conspiracy theories that are not supported by the evidence and that have now been refuted by counter-evidence. (Despite Donald Rumsfeld, when it comes to WMDs, if you search the desert *really thoroughly*, absence of evidence gradually metamorphoses into evidence of absence.)

But perhaps I am doing an injustice to the pundits of the conventional wisdom. Perhaps the arguments that they insinuate are not fallacious deductive arguments like the Cecilia/Nixon Argument, but probabilistic arguments of something like the following form:

(1*) Cecilia subscribes to a theory X that posits a conspiracy.
(2*) Hence Cecilia subscribes to a conspiracy theory.
(3*) Hence Cecilia is a conspiracy theorist.

[So far, so good!]

(4*) It is usually irrational to believe or even investigate conspiracy theories.

(5*) Therefore [from (4*)] it is usually irrational to be a conspiracy theorist.
(6*) Therefore *probably* Cecilia subscribes to a theory that is irrational to believe or even investigate.
(7*) Therefore *probably* Cecilia herself is irrational, if not mad – at the very least a practitioner of the 'paranoid style' in politics.

Call this the Non-Deductive Argument. Here the weight of the inference rests on premise (4*), that it is usually irrational to believe or even investigate conspiracy theories. But, since (5*) follows from (4*), if we can show that (5*) is false we can show that (4*) is false too. And, as it happens, we can indeed prove that (5*) is false. Here's how. First I shall demonstrate that you, Dear Reader, are a conspiracy theorist, as is every other politically and historically literate person:

Premise I: Unless you believe that the reports of history books and the nightly news are largely false, you are a conspiracy theorist (since history and the nightly news are choc-a-bloc with conspiracies).
Premise II: If you *do* believe that the reports of history books and the nightly news are largely false, you are a conspiracy theorist (since you presumably believe that somebody has conspired to fake them).
Conclusion: You are a conspiracy theorist.

The only people *not* impaled on the horns of this dilemma are idiots in the Greek sense of the word – people who take so slight an interest in public affairs that they have no opinion as to whether history and the nightly news have been systematically falsified or not. We can therefore conclude that every politically and historically literate person is a conspiracy theorist. This gives us the following argument:

(a) Every historically and politically literate person is and must be a conspiracy theorist (since to be otherwise is to abandon any claims to historical and political literacy).
(b) It is not usually irrational to be what every politically and historically literate person is and must be.

Therefore

(c) Thesis (5*) is false and it is not usually irrational to be a conspiracy theorist.

Since the Non-Deductive Argument hinges on Premise (4*), and since if (5*) is false (4*) is false, the Non-Deductive Argument collapses.

'Aha', a proponent of the conventional wisdom might reply, 'the problem with your argument, Professor Pigden, is that you are implicitly defining a conspiracy theory as a theory that posits a conspiracy. If we were to employ your ridiculously tendentious definition, then it would indeed be false that it is usually irrational to believe or even investigate conspiracy theories, since many such theories are established historical facts. But what *we* mean by a conspiracy theory is a theory (a) that posits a conspiracy and (b) that it is irrational to believe. Given this definition, it is not only *usually* but *always* the case that it is irrational to believe or investigate conspiracy theories.'

The problem with this reply is that it converts the refutable claim that it is usually irrational to believe or investigate conspiracy theories into the empty tautology that it is *irrational to believe those conspiracy theories that it is irrational to believe*. And from an empty tautology nothing of any consequence follows. Moreover, this manoeuvre could not underwrite the many arguments that *start* from the premise that some thesis X posits a conspiracy and proceed via the *subconclusion* that X constitutes a conspiracy theory to the *ultimate* conclusion that X should not be believed or investigated. For instance, if we return to Tony Blair and the Downing Street Memo, and spell out his implicit argument in pedantic detail, it would go something like this:

(1#) The claim that Blair had talked Bush out of his plan to bomb al-Jazeera involves a conspiracy.
(2#) Therefore the claim that Blair had talked Bush out of his plan to bomb al-Jazeera is a conspiracy theory.
(3#) Therefore the claim that Blair had talked Bush out of his plan to bomb al-Jazeera should be neither believed nor investigated.

Given my definition, this argument fails at step (3#). Just because the claim that Blair had talked Bush out of his plan to bomb al-Jazeera is a conspiracy theory, it does not follow that it should not be believed or investigated. But given my opponent's definition, the argument fails at step (2#). Just because the claim that Blair had talked Bush out of his plan to bomb al-Jazeera features a conspiracy, it does not follow that it constitutes a conspiracy theory. For to qualify as a conspiracy theory it must not only feature a conspiracy – it must feature a conspiracy that it is irrational to believe. And for *that* claim Blair offered neither evidence nor an argument.

But surely all this is a bit too swift! Surely the conventional wisdom (which depicts conspiracy theorists as inherently suspect or unbelievable) cannot be as deeply unwise as I have suggested. There must be more to be said on behalf of the great and the good who routinely dismiss conspiracy theories as (in Christopher Hitchens' felicitous phrase) the 'exhaust fumes of democracy'. Yes, indeed, there is. And that more *is* said – and is said at length – by Matthew Dentith, who patiently refutes it point by point. The case for the conventional wisdom is carefully put and convincingly answered in this excellent book, and it is answered in a more detailed and less dogmatic way than I have had space for in this brief foreword. So be warned. If you are prone to defer to the great and the good and to dismiss conspiracy theories simply because they *are* conspiracy theories, this is a book that might change your mind and even change your life. Indeed, it is a book that might change the political climate, in my view for the better. For a world in which conspiracy theories are *not* routinely dismissed will be a world in which genuine conspiracies are less likely to escape detection and hence a world in which they are less likely to succeed. And that would be a better and more democratic world, a world in which the powerful would be less likely to get away with murder – whether figuratively or literally.

Now, read on.

Charles Pigden

Acknowledgements

It is hard to know where, exactly, to start and stop thanking or acknowledging people when it comes to a book which is not just the result of a year's furious writing but also the culmination of over half a decade of study. As such, these acknowledgements are limited to the people who have aided, abetted or hindered me over the last year.

So, particular thanks to: Beverley Ann Dentith (for mothering); Charles Pigden; Daniel Wilson (for a comment in a talk which clarified some thinking about fortunate data); Dan Withers (for not taking me too seriously); David Merry (for an example about grumpiness); Fiona Balchin (who provided much needed other perspectives); Greg Dalziel (for some suggestions about examples); Jacob Bellamy (who made an inspired comment about the moral wrongness of breakfast); Justine Campbell (for portage); Kira Duda (who was always willing to lubricate our intellectualism with alcohol); Lara Strongman (who sent me a leaflet that made me think more clearly about endorsement by association); Lee Basham (who probably wrote more words critiquing this book than I did in writing it; I'm sorry not all of your suggestions made it in); Marilyn Most (for always looking so proud); Megan Jeffries (whose 'But surely...' questions made me come up with a lot of new answers); Nick Withers (who, aside from keeping me in whisky, kept me in good chat); Queen of Thorns (whose disdain for surprise parties was illuminating); Stephen Boswell (whose 'No, the real issue...' statements sometimes meant rethinking my approaches); Te Namu (who mostly laughed) and Tiddy Alexander Smith (for a suggestion about falsification).

I should also like to thank Zac Arnold, Ethan McAulay and Lucas Jensen-Carey at 95bFM for letting me talk about conspiracy theories on the radio week-in and week-out. Many of your interruptions on air really did clarify my thinking. The same goes for Russell Brown, who keeps letting me be on TV, despite the fact I'm a conspiracy (theory) theorist.

Special, special thanks to my legion of proofers: Andrew Withy; David Merry (again); Dylan Reeve; Laura McQuillan; Melanie Rosen (I still have that video); Mike Dickison; Sara Barham; Sonia Fitchett (who writes comments just like mine) and Will Pollard. Some of the typos you spotted I got rid of; some of your suggestions about my use of semicolons I did not.

Tim Denee, who designed the cover for this book, was such a pleasure to work with that I'm not sure that he can be praised sufficiently. As such, I'm not even going to try.

Finally, as is my custom, especial thanks to H. O. Ransome, whose existence and salience to this work are questionable.

1
Introduction

Three putative conspiracies

One: Former American presidential candidate Lyndon LaRouche believes that the psychedelic rock group 'Grateful Dead' were a front for the Occult Branch of the British Secret Service. They were sent to the USA – under orders from the queen of England – to secretly promote drug use and licentiousness in American youth. The purpose of this conspiracy? The destruction of the USA and all it stands for *by its own citizenry*.

Two: In 1774 Adam Weishaupt, a Bavarian philosopher, founded a secret society, the Illuminati. His aim was, ostensibly, to promote equality and fraternity for all men (for in the 18th century the Enlightenment was still solely the domain of the Western male). To do this, the Illuminati starting infiltrating and taking over influential Freemason lodges in Bavaria. However in 1785, when the Bavarian government came to know about the Illuminati's activities, they issued an edict and officially disbanded the society. According to the orthodox histories, this brought about the end of the Illuminati and their plan for equality for all.

Conspiracy theorists claim, however, that they merely went to ground and focused their attentions elsewhere. Some went to France and helped orchestrate the French Revolution of 1789. Weishaupt, meanwhile, emigrated to the Americas and took the place of George Washington (of whom he was the spitting image) at the Constitutional Convention of 1787. By playing on settler antipathy towards the British Crown, the Illuminati brought about the American Revolution and guided the formation of the USA. Focusing mostly on the fledgling nation of America, which was supported by the new French Republic, a set of scandals around the ownership of slaves was created to bring the loosely knit coalition of the States into one federally controlled Union. An economic depression was then orchestrated in the early 20th century, in order to ensure that American-made goods would proliferate overseas. Once the world was reliant on American industry, a global system of financial control was established. Medical experimentation on ethnic minorities quickly followed until, by the late 20th century, a global, American-run pharmaceutical concern was in existence. Its purpose? The introduction of fluoride – a chemical agent known to make humans docile – into water supplies around the world.

Three: In September 2001, 11 Middle Eastern nationals hijacked four flights over the continental USA. Two of the hijacked planes were flown into the World Trade Center in New York, destroying the Twin Towers. A third plane crashed into the side of the Pentagon in Washington, DC, while the fourth plane crash-landed in a field near Shanksville, Pennsylvania. The masterminds behind the attack – members of the Osama bin Laden-led group known as 'Al-Qaeda' – admitted responsibility for the attacks. They claimed that their purpose was to show the government of the USA just how vulnerable it was to external threats.

These are all stories about conspiracies. The first two are what we typically call 'conspiracy theories', while the third – depending on your theory about conspiracy theories – either is also a conspiracy theory or has some conspiracy theories associated with it.

Conspiracy theories are a popular topic in everyday conversation. However, many of us take a dim view of conspiracy theories, deriding and judging those who believe them. If someone accuses of us of believing a conspiracy theory, many of us will splutter: 'But I'm no conspiracy theorist!' (even if we are willing to admit that conspiracies have occurred). Sometimes we even dismiss the arguments and explanations of our friends, family or colleagues as 'just conspiracy theories'. Often this is not because we know the theory on offer is unsound, but, rather, because it goes against the conventional wisdom, or, if the theory were true, we might have to reappraise many of our other beliefs, say about the way our society operates or just how trustworthy certain institutions are thought to be. Other times we might start out by saying 'I'm not a conspiracy theorist, but...' an expression that typically means we want to put forward some conspiracy theory without having to suffer the ignominy of being called a 'conspiracy theorist'.

There seems to be a common sense intuition shared by a great many people that conspiracy theories are *prima facie* examples of irrational beliefs. Conspiracy theories – according to this intuition – are bunk, bogus, irrational, the result of paranoid ideation or, frankly, just weird. The term 'conspiracy theory', many argue, picks out a class of suspicious, possibly paranoiac, beliefs. Certainly, many people think the theory that the Grateful Dead were part of the British Crown's plan to corrupt the youth of America is not worth taking seriously. Most people are also highly skeptical of the claim that the Bavarian Illuminati still exist and control the world from behind the scenes. When it comes to the events of 11 September 2001 (known commonly as '9/11'), things get more heated. Some claim that, despite the conspiratorial nature of the terrorist activity of that day, the well-accepted, official explanation is by no means a conspiracy theory. Others, however, claim that the official theory is a conspiracy theory – but one that we are justified in believing – or that it is the result of a conspiracy covering up what really happened.

Conspiracy theories can be divisive. We might ask: 'Why are so many people skeptical of them?' This question seems all the more pertinent today due to our increasing awareness that conspiratorial (or, at the very least, conspiracy-like) activity happens more regularly than previously thought. From leaks about mass surveillance programmes to pharmaceutical companies hiding trial data that show certain drugs are ineffective, people in influential institutions look as if they are conspiring *here and now*. So, can we tell a story that justifies our dim view of theories about conspiracies?

Philosophising about conspiracy theories

This book is an analysis of what some might take to be a very curious situation: the case in which we think some theory about a conspiracy might be worth taking seriously. While this book is mostly concerned with the philosophical – particularly epistemological – questions about belief in conspiracy theories, the theories we will look at will not be restricted solely to theories by philosophers. As such, in Chapter 2 we shall look at some of the definitions of these things called 'conspiracy theories', including work in history, philosophy, political theory, psychology and sociology. There is much to be learnt from the work of academics of all stripes when it comes to their various definitions of what counts as a 'conspiracy theory', and what belief in them entails.

In Chapter 3 we will analyse whether a general and non-pejorative definition of conspiracy theory – any explanation of an event that cites a conspiracy as a salient cause – helps in the analysis of conspiracy theories. As we will see, certain features of this general definition will turn out to be useful for the development of the analysis of the warrant of *specific* conspiracy theories while also explaining why it is some theorists take it that belief in conspiracy theories *generally* is irrational.

In Chapter 4 we will look at some of the problems faced by a general and non-pejorative definition of conspiracy theory. For example, this definition implies that any account of the organisation of a surprise party would count as a conspiracy theory. This definition also allows that there could be conspiracies of goodness, and, thus, we do not need to consider conspiratorial activity as necessarily sinister. However, as we will see, these are not problems for such a general definition. Rather, they point towards problems to do with certain kinds of conspiracy theories and how we analyse them.

In Chapter 5 we will look at how we talk about the intentions and goals of conspirators and who a *qualified conspiracy theorist* – the kind of expert who can work out the identity or motivations of such conspirators – might be. However, as we will see later in this book, even if we can appeal to qualified conspiracy theorists, there are still worries to do with the kinds of evidence used for and against conspiracy theories.

In Chapter 6 we will look at the question of whether we live in what Sir Karl Popper called an 'open society'. If we live in a properly open society, conspiratorial activity on the part of the influential institutions should be rare. The benefit of living in such an open, democratic society is that it should be a society in which it is hard *generally* to conspire successfully. So, just how open should we think our society is? Is our belief that we live in an open society really justified by the evidence?

In Chapters 7 and 8 we will look at another set of reasons that are often put forward for claiming we have a justified and *prima facie* suspicion of conspiracy theories: such theories often have explanatory rivals with official status. However, it turns out that it is not altogether clear what role 'officialness' plays in the analysis of theories in general, since what we might term 'official status' is a vague and ill-defined concept. In order to work out what role official status might play in the warranting of any theory, we will look at the role endorsements play in the accreditation of theories, and how having official status from one influential institution tells us little about its official status with regard to some other institution.

In Chapter 9 we will examine the role evidence plays with respect to conspiracy theories. Sometimes the evidence used against particular conspiracy theories ends up being what is called 'disinformation': fabricated information put forward to either discredit some explanatory hypothesis or to make some other explanatory hypothesis look plausible. Occasionally the evidence used for or against some conspiracy theory is selective in character: the evidence has been manipulated in order to make it support some explanatory hypothesis. Some evidence, for or against a conspiracy theory, might even be fortuitous, in that the evidence turns out to be too good to be true.

All of these worries about evidence – which are concerns as to when evidence really is evidence – are commonly associated with conspiracy theories. However, as we will see, these worries come up when we are appraising non-conspiracy theories as well. The general lesson is that, when it comes to appraising evidence, there are a lot of issues we need to keep in mind, whether or not the evidence is being used to support or dismiss some conspiracy theory.

In Chapters 10 and 11 we will look at the question: 'When, if ever, is it justified to infer that a conspiracy theory is the best explanation of some event?' As the previous chapters will show, even if there is some general argument that justifies taking a dim view of conspiracy theories, this does not give us grounds for dismissing the possibility that some *particular* conspiracy theory can be warranted. We will look at how sometimes people infer to any old explanation rather than the best, and what it means to infer that a conspiracy is the best explanation of some event. This being said, showing that a conspiracy exists can be difficult: even if a conspiracy theorist can give an argument to the extent that a conspiracy exists, they need to provide some argument that gives us reason to think there is a tight connection, such that the conspiracy *is the best explanation.*

When, if ever, is it rational to believe a conspiracy theory?

The central question which underpins the analysis that follows is this: 'When, if ever, is it rational to believe a conspiracy theory?' As we will see, a case can be made to say that belief in *particular* conspiracy theories can be warranted.

It is important to note that what follows is not a defence of any particular conspiracy theory. Rather, all that is going to be argued here is that the supposed problems with belief in conspiracy theories are really problems common to explanations of complex social phenomena. As such, the argument that will be presented in this volume is:

1. A defence of belief in conspiracy theories *as long as you can tell a good story about why particular conspiracy theories are likely to be warranted* and
2. A defence of the view that the fact that some theories are *conspiracy theories* is not itself a reason for rejecting them.

The underlying question we should always ask when someone proposes a theory is: 'What should I believe, given the evidence?' A proper understanding of how we answer such a question shows that it is sometimes rational to believe *particular* conspiracy theories. The first moral of this book is that we should not automatically dismiss belief in conspiracy theories *merely because they are called 'conspiracy theories'*. Rather, if we are going to dismiss belief in a conspiracy theory, it will be because we have grounds for thinking either that the alleged conspiracy does not exist or that, even if a conspiracy does exist, it is not the best explanation. The second moral is that sometimes we will be able to infer that a conspiracy exists and that it is the best explanation: sometimes belief in particular conspiracy theories turns out to be rational.

2
Conspiracy Theory Theories

We can all cite examples of conspiracy theories: they are the kinds of things David Icke travels the world advocating, or Glenn Beck presents on his own – widely syndicated – American television network.

David Icke thinks that the world is controlled by alien shape-shifting reptiles, whose sole purpose is to control humanity and, occasionally, feast upon our young. Icke argues that there is an all-embracing conspiracy which includes the mainstream media and our governments. Its purpose? To hide the fact that our lives and social institutions are controlled by the reptiles.

The conspiracy theories of Glenn Beck seem much more sober in comparison. Beck *merely* believes in the existence of a large-scale, long-term socialist conspiracy – encompassing elements of both the Democratic and Republican Parties – to deny American citizens their God-given rights to liberty and freedom from taxation. Beck, who follows in the mould of conspiracy theorists such as W. Cleon Skousen and Alex Jones, does not believe in aliens (well, not the extraterrestrial type); the conspirators behind the plots to curtail the liberties of his fellow Americans are either fallible or malevolent human beings.

Beck's claims are not as 'out there' as Icke's. Typically, people take a dismissive view of Icke's conspiracy theories, claiming they are simply the product of extreme paranoia. However, while many people disagree with the specifics of Beck's theories, they will agree that he is, at the very least, on to something, even if his claims of conspirators being in control of the White House are far-fetched.

Icke and Beck are what we might call 'prototypical' conspiracy theorists: their particular conspiracy theories are often taken to be representative of conspiracy theories *as a class of belief*. People tend to distance themselves from such theories, even if they do find them interesting. In part this is because Icke, and to a lesser extent Beck, are considered to have extreme, possibly even pathological, views, and in part it is because 'sensible people' by and large do not believe in conspiracy theories (or, at least, so we are told).

This latter position is a nuanced one, of course. Following the leaks by Edward Snowden about the extent of the surveillance programmes of the National Security Agency (one of the many US intelligence agencies), as well as the various WikiLeaks document dumps, it seems that certain conspiracy theories have gone from 'far-fetched' to 'worth considering'. Governments, it turns out, do hide secret torture/rendition programmes from their citizens, and they routinely spy on everyone, whether or not wrongdoing is suspected. We probably live, here and now, at a crucial point in history. What do we make of the revelations which show that conspiracy-like activity is more common than most of us previously thought? Were the conspiracy theorists right (or mostly right) after all? What does this mean for the analysis of conspiracy theories given that, typically, much of the academic literature on the subject tends towards the notion that such belief is *prima facie* irrational?

Let us divide the academic world in two when it comes to views about the rationality of belief in conspiracy. In one camp we have what we might call the 'conspiracy theory skeptics': they take it that we have good grounds for a skepticism of conspiracy theories *in general*. In the other camp we have the 'conspiracy theory theorists', who take it that belief in *particular* conspiracy theories can be rational. These two positions are not necessarily at loggerheads. For example, you might be a conspiracy theory skeptic who is also a fallibilist: you might claim that, typically, we are entitled to take a dim view of conspiracy theories generally, although maybe from time to time some specific conspiracy theory might turn out to be warranted. You might also be a conspiracy theory theorist who thinks that, generally, people come up with conspiracy theories for all sorts of poor reasons, but, nonetheless, seeks to investigate each and every claim of conspiracy, in case one of them turns out to be true.

So, is conspiracy theory skepticism – which is often taken as being the default view in the literature – justified?

To see whether this skepticism is justified, it is going to be necessary first to look at what arguments have been put forward in support of such a skepticism (which is the task of this first chapter) and then analyse the best arguments for the aforementioned skepticism (which will be the task of subsequent chapters). Let us start, then, by looking at the influential work of Richard Hofstadter and his notion of the 'paranoid style'.

The paranoid style

Richard Hofstadter's *The Paranoid Style in American Politics* is a seminal text for a generation of conspiracy theory theorists, especially conspiracy theory skeptics who want to understand why conspiracy theories are widely believed. Hofstadter's work has been crucial in the development of theories as to why certain right-wing conspiracy theories – like those of Glenn Beck – have proliferated in recent years.

Hofstadter's work on conspiracy theories centres on the intersection of belief in such theories and what he terms the 'paranoid style'. The paranoid style is a political mode of expression, on the part of conspiracy theorists, in which the ills in society are blamed upon the existence of conspiracies. The thesis of the paranoid style characterises conspiracy theorists not as people who see *some* conspiracies here and there but, rather, as people who think that conspiracies are 'the motive force in historical events. History is a conspiracy, set in motion by demonic forces of almost transcendent power' (Hofstadter, 1965, p. 29). According to Hofstadter, belief in conspiracy theories is the belief that conspiracies are behind everything. He writes:

> I call it the paranoid style simply because no other word adequately evokes the qualities of heated exaggeration, suspiciousness, and conspiratorial fantasy that I have in mind. (Hofstadter, 1965, p. 4)

The paranoid style is intended as an *analogy* between belief in conspiracy theories – characterised as the belief that conspiracies are everywhere – and classical paranoid ideation (or paranoia), rather than as a clinical diagnosis that conspiracy theorists are, in fact, paranoiacs (Hofstadter, 1965, pp. 3–4). Hofstadter's analysis is mostly concerned with the beliefs of right-wing conspiracy theorists, who he thought were the most likely to suffer from the paranoid style[1] (Hofstadter, 1965, p. 3). While Hofstadter acknowledges that conspiracies do occur, his interest is in explaining why we might be suspicious of belief in conspiracy theories generally by showing how such claims *resemble* paranoid ideation. If we consider paranoia to be irrational, then belief in conspiracy theories should be, by analogy, irrational as well.

Hofstadter's work has been influential. For example, Stephan Lewandowsky, John Cook, Klaus Oberauer and Michael Marriott, in 'Recursive fury: conspiracist ideation in the blogosphere in response to research on conspiracist ideation', make use of the analysis of the paranoid style when looking at the conspiracy theories which were generated as responses to their own research into belief in conspiracy theories (Lewandowsky, Cook, Oberauer, & Marriott, 2013, p. 12).

Daniel Pipes, in his sympathetically titled book *Conspiracy: How the Paranoid Style Flourishes and Where It Comes From*, bases his analysis of belief in conspiracy theories in terms of the paranoid style. Like Hofstadter, Pipes agrees that conspiracies occur, but he asserts that belief in conspiracy theories is irrational because they are symptomatic of a conspiracist worldview; conspiracy theorists see conspiracies everywhere and think of them as the root of the ills in our society. He writes:

> A *conspiracy theory* is the fear of a nonexistent conspiracy. *Conspiracy* refers to an act, *conspiracy theory* to a perception. (Pipes, 1997, p. 21)

This kind of argument is echoed in the work of Gordon B. Arnold, who also distinguishes between conspiracies – which, he takes it, do occur – and conspiracy theories – which, like Pipes, he characterises as the fear of nonexistent conspiracies (Arnold, 2008, pp. 1–2).

Jeffrey M. Bale also argues along similar lines, claiming that most conspiracy theories are elaborate fantasies (Bale, 2007, p. 48). While Bale admits conspiracies are rife, particularly in the business and political world, he argues that these kinds of conspiracies are not those commonly believed by conspiracy theorists (Bale, 2007, pp. 54–56). This is an odd claim, given the long history of certain conspiracy theorists using the existence of known conspiratorial behaviour in the business and political world to motivate suspicions about alleged similar conspiratorial activity in those same sectors.

It is sometimes not clear whether theorists who utilise the analysis of the paranoid style treat it simply as an analogy with paranoia, or as evidence that conspiracy theorists are actually paranoid. For example, Hannah Darwin, Nick Neave and Joni Holmes, in their article 'Belief in conspiracy theories. The role of paranormal belief, paranoid ideation and schizotypy', regard belief in conspiracy theories as evidence of low-level paranoid ideation in the overall population (Darwin, Neave, & Holmes, 2011, p. 1292). As Peter Knight argues, treating the analogy that underpins the paranoid style *literally* ends up producing a circular argument. He writes: '[W]hat is paranoia, if not a propensity to believe in conspiracy theories?' (Knight, 2003, p. 19). Characterising belief in conspiracy theories as paranoid and then claiming: 'Paranoid people believe conspiracy theories!' ends up not explaining what is, if anything, wrong with conspiracy theories; Hofstadter's analysis of conspiracy theories through the lens of the paranoid style is an illustrative analogy of the kinds of issues that are typically associated with belief in such theories.

Hofstadter's analysis of the paranoid style is certainly interesting, given that it provides us with a reason why we might be suspicious of conspiracy theories *generally* by an analogy between belief in such theories and paranoia. However, whereas in the case of the paranoiac – who thinks they are under threat when they are not – those who analyse belief in conspiracy theories with respect to the paranoid style must admit that conspiracies occur. As such, adopting a paranoid style analysis of belief in conspiracy theories means that we must first define conspiracy theories pejoratively. According to this view, they are a kind of belief of which we typically take a dim view, whether or not some conspiracy has occurred.

Conspiracy theories now and then

Gordon S. Wood, in 'Conspiracy and the Paranoid Style: Causality and Deceit in the Eighteenth Century', argues that, while belief in *contemporary* conspiracy theories resembles paranoiac ideation, historically belief in conspiracy theories was sometimes understandable, if not exactly rational (G. S. Wood, 1982, p. 411). Wood's case in point is the 18th and 19th centuries, a period he believes Hofstadter glosses over in his analysis of the paranoid style. Wood argues that, as the political climate of the Enlightenment saw a turning away from a providential view – which saw God as being behind all human affairs – to a view in which humans were often the authors of their misfortune, it made sense to see at least some political misfortune as being the result of people conspiring behind the scenes (G. S. Wood, 1982, p. 420). However, this conspiratorial mindset was still fundamentally mistaken, because it was based upon a simplistic notion of political cause and effect in which the *intentions* of political actors were taken to be more powerful factors than we believe today (G. S. Wood, 1982, p. 441).

Wood's influence amongst historians can be seen in the work of Thomas E. Kaiser, Marisa Linton and Peter R. Campbell in their book *Conspiracy in the French Revolution* (Kaiser & Campbell, 2007), Joseph Roisman's *The Rhetoric of Conspiracy in Ancient Athens* (Roisman, 2006) and Geoffrey Cubitt's *The Jesuit Myth: Conspiracy Theory and Politics in Nineteenth Century France* (Cubitt, 1993). Victoria Emma Pagán, in *Conspiracy Theory in Latin Literature*, has a similar view – that conspiracy theories are understandable given a lack of information – which is nicely captured when she writes:

> Conspiracy theory meets the challenge of the lack of knowledge with a preponderance of explanation.... Conspiracy surfaces as a response to a particular historical moment, while conspiracy theory is the

> manifestation of the frustration caused by the lack of knowledge at the core of any conspiracy. (Pagán, 2012, p. 5)

Págan's interest is in how narratives about conspiratorial activity spring up as explanations of events. Conspiracy theories, in her analysis, are a suspicious class of explanations because the agents who are blamed for the occurrence of the event are often convenient dupes rather than the real perpetrators. Conspiracy theories, in this view, are *understandable but fundamentally mistaken* because they posit a simplistic explanation – the conspiracy theory – rather than accepting that the best explanation is likely to be messy and complex.

Págan, like Wood, is doubtful that conspiracy narratives, even if they identify some of the factors of why an event occurred, constitute good explanations. However, there is a worry here that we might be confusing either the development of a conspiracy theory *as a putative explanatory hypothesis* or *conspiracy theorising in a rhetorical sense* with the relative merits (or lack thereof) of conspiracy theories *as a class of explanation*. It would be a mistake, for example, to take a dim view of conspiracy theories because they are sometimes used as a rhetorical device to blame convenient dupes or the usual suspects. At best, the rhetorical use of conspiracy theories shows us that such theories can be put forward for reasons other than the evidence, rather than that such theories are unwarranted. Similarly, it would be a mistake to take a dim view of conspiracy theories merely because some of them are simplistic explanations, since that once again potentially confuses the conspiracy theorising of some conspiracy theorists with the entire class of conspiracy theories.

Understandable conspiracy theorising

Volker Heins, in 'Critical theory and the traps of conspiracy thinking', also argues that conspiracy theorising is an understandable response to problems in the political sphere. However, unlike Wood, Heins argues that conspiracy theorising goes awry simply when conspiracy theorists go beyond the available evidence. Heins claims that it is at the very least understandable in the here and now to theorise about conspiracies, even if some of the resultant conspiracy theories end up being unwarranted. He writes:

> [C]onspiracy theorists do not believe that the world contains a great, unfathomable mystery that will defeat all attempts at rational explanation. Conspiracy theorists are rather hyper-rationalists who do not simply proclaim a truth, but actively 'track' it, as epistemologists say. (Heins, 2007, p. 790)

Heins' argument is similar to one offered by Peter Knight. Knight argues that, given the kind of political reality we live in, *contemporary* conspiracy theorising is by no means irrational, even if it does turn out that many of the individual conspiracy theories produced by such theorising are unwarranted (Knight, 2000, ch. 1). In his book *Conspiracy Culture: From the Kennedy Assassination to The X-Files*, Knight looks at the role conspiracy theories play in contemporary society and how they reflect 'a not entirely unfounded suspicion that the normal order of things itself amounts to a conspiracy' (Knight, 2000, p. 3). Simon Locke, in 'Conspiracy culture, blame culture, and rationalisation', has argued along similar lines. Locke, like Heins and Knight, takes it that conspiracy theorising is an understandable reaction to the kind of world we live in.

Locke characterises conspiracy theorising as

> [A]n outcome of the same logic that produces the sciences of general social analysis, which show the same tendencies to interpret reality in terms of collective social processes often ultimately ascribed to the activities of one specific social group – hence, 'they' are to blame. Conspiracy culture, then, is as 'normal' a condition of the modern world as are these sciences[.] (Locke, 2009, pp. 582–583)

Heins argues that we can explain the popular appeal of conspiracy theories with reference to the notion of 'political alienation' (Heins, 2007, p. 796). Individuals who feel they are alienated from social and political discourse (and thus feel themselves to be on the fringe) are liable, according to Heins, to see themselves as the playthings of uncontrollable powers. As such, it is the context of the kind of society in which we live that makes conspiracy theorising understandable in some cases. For Heins, and arguably also Knight and Locke, conspiracy theories are an understandable response to living in our contemporary, Western-style democracies where politics is seen to be a shady business.

Crippled epistemologies

For Hofstadter and Wood, belief in contemporary conspiracy theories is *prima facie* suspicious because conspiracy theorists have an underlying assumption that the world is more conspired than it really is. Cass Sunstein and Adrian Vermeule, in 'Conspiracy Theories: Causes and Cures', examine the suspicion that conspiracy theories are bunk by positing that conspiracy theorists suffer from what they call a 'crippled epistemology'. To say a conspiracy theorist's epistemology is 'crippled' is to claim that typically such theorists are people who do not know much, and much of what they believe is wrong[2] (Sunstein & Vermeule, 2009, p. 211).

As such, Sunstein and Vermeule do not locate the problem for conspiracy theories as being a problem with the theories *per se* but, rather, with the epistemic practices of the conspiracy theorists who believe them. For Hofstadter and Wood, the paranoid style was merely an analogy between paranoiac ideation and belief in conspiracy theories. Sunstein and Vermeule's crippled epistemology seeks to provide a more straightforward diagnosis of the fault of conspiracy theorists by claiming that their beliefs about the existence of conspiracies are the result of faulty inferences.

This kind of view can be found elsewhere in the academic literature on belief in conspiracy theories. For example, Stephan Lewandowsky, Klaus Oberauer and Gilles E. Gignac use Sunstein and Vermeule's notion of a crippled epistemology when looking at why conspiracy theorists sometimes turn out to be skeptical of scientific claims (Lewandowsky, Oberauer, & Gignac, 2013). Fran Mason claims that conspiracy theories are only good explanations to conspiracy theorists; to non-conspiracy theorists such theories are just the conclusions of fallacious reasoning (Mason, 2002, pp. 44–45). Victoria Emma Pagán has a similar view: she defines a conspiracy theory as being 'characterized by an epistemological gap caused by the secrecy and silence that shroud the event' (Pagán, 2004, p. 109).

For such theorists it is, in the end, the inferential practices of conspiracy theorists that are at fault and can be used to explain our dim view of conspiracy theories. If we take it that conspiracy theories are typically the kind of things believed by conspiracy theorists, then, if conspiracy theorists have a crippled epistemology, the theories they generate due to this crippled epistemology are going to be suspect.

Now, the notion that conspiracy theorists suffer from a crippled epistemology might fit nicely with some of our suspicion of the claims of prominent conspiracy theorists like David Icke or Glenn Beck, but it is not a particularly good fit with conspiracy theorists overall (and to say David Icke or Glenn Beck might suffer from a crippled epistemology may very well be doing them a disservice). Sunstein, Vermeule and others are confusing the attitudes of *some conspiracy theorists* with issues to do with belief in conspiracy theories *generally*. This general view – that the alleged suspiciousness of conspiracy theories can be explained by reference to the practices of conspiracy theorists – is a common factor to the theories of Hofstadter, Wood, Sunstein and Vermeule, and is one we will return to in the next chapter when we look at the thesis of conspiracism.

Conspiracy theory theories and philosophy

This book is not just a general gloss over the state of philosophy with respect to belief in conspiracy theories. Rather, it is an attempt to provide an argument to the extent that belief in conspiracy theories can be rational. For a long time, philosophers have wondered what counts as rational belief, and pondered the various errors in logic and epistemology that have underpinned ideas and notions which were once taken to be rational, but are now taken to be irrational. As such, you would think that philosophers would be very interested indeed in conspiracy theories, given that we have indulged in thought experiments about whether psychics can be said to know the truth of future or distant events, whether an object can appear blue today but turn out to be green tomorrow, and whether there exists a special module in the human brain that allows us to know basic facts about the world (and, coincidentally, allows us to know that some god exists).

Strangely enough, the philosophical interest in conspiracy theories is relatively contemporary. While Sir Karl Popper's *The Open Society and Its Enemies* (Popper, 1969), written in the 1930s, touched briefly on the irrationality of belief in conspiracy theories, most of the philosophical literature on conspiracy theories comes out of two papers written in the last decade of the 20th century: Charles Pigden's 'Popper Revisited, Or What Is Wrong With Conspiracy Theories?' (Pigden, 1995) and Brian L. Keeley's 'Of Conspiracy Theories' (Keeley, 1999). It is fair to say that the philosophical literature on what counts as a 'conspiracy theory' and whether belief in them can be rational is comparatively thin on the ground and small compared with the work, say, in the fields of sociology and psychology. As such, while some recent academic work on conspiracy theories has taken into account the recent spark of interest by philosophers on the topic, it is somewhat understandable why the *philosophical concerns* about belief in conspiracy theories have been neglected (or, if you are being charitable, overlooked) by sociologists, psychologists, historians and political theorists. So, let us examine the philosophy of conspiracy theories by starting off with who we might call the 'grandfather' of philosophical views on conspiracy theories, Sir Karl Popper.

The conspiracy theory of society

In what amounts to only a few pages of *The Open Society and Its Enemies*, Karl Popper characterises a kind of approach to explanations of social phenomena which he calls the 'conspiracy theory of society'.

The conspiracy theory of society is the view that

> [A]n explanation of a social phenomenon consists in the discovery of the men or groups who are interested in the occurrence of this phenomenon (sometimes it is a hidden interest which has first to be revealed), and who have planned and conspired to bring it about. (Popper, 1969, p. 94)

The conspiracy theory of society is a view that is very similar to that of Hofstadter, when he writes:

> The distinguishing thing about the paranoid style is not that its exponents see conspiracies or plots here and there in history, but that they regard a 'vast' or 'gigantic' conspiracy as *the motive force* in historical events. History is a conspiracy, set in motion by demonic forces of almost transcendent power, and what is felt to be needed to defeat it is not the usual methods of political give-and-take, but an all-out crusade. (Hofstadter, 1965, p. 29)

Popper admits that conspiracies are a typical social phenomenon, but he also takes a dim view of any general approach that seeks to explain social phenomena *in terms of conspiracies*. Popper poses a dilemma: either history is the product of successful conspiracies or it is not. Clearly, he argues, most events in the world are not the result of successful conspiracies, so belief in the conspiracy theory of society is *prima facie* irrational, because

> [N]ot all consequences of our actions are intended consequences; and accordingly,... the conspiracy theory of society cannot be true because it amounts to the assertion that events, even those which at first sight do not seem to be intended by anybody, are the intended results of the actions of people who are interested in these results. (Popper, 1972, p. 342)

Popper worries that conspiracy theorists ascribe too much causal power to conspirators and their conspiracies and that, once we understand this, we end up being justified in taking a dim view of conspiracy theories.[3] However, Charles Pigden argues that Popper misrepresents what conspiracy theorists believe. Pigden argues that no one – well, no sensible person – believes history is *completely* explained in terms of successful conspiracies. Rather, what people believe – if they think there are some examples of warranted conspiracy theories – is that conspiracies occur and some of them are responsible for or explain the occurrence of historical events. Conspiracies like the Ridolfi plot, the Throckmorton plot and the Babington plot (to name but a few Elizabethan examples) are part and parcel of our orthodox histories (Pigden, 1995, pp. 3–4). As such, we can believe that some – possibly even many – conspiracy theories are warranted without endorsing the conspiracy theory of society (an argument we will return to in the next chapter).

The consequences of belief in conspiracy theories

Brian L. Keeley, in his influential paper 'Of Conspiracy Theories', expresses a worry about the consequences of belief in unwarranted conspiracy theories. He defines a conspiracy theory as

> [A] proposed explanation of some historical event (or events) in terms of the significant causal agency of a relatively small group of persons – the conspirators – acting in secret. (Keeley, 1999, p. 116)

Keeley argues that, as conspiracies occur, we can have warranted beliefs about them. For example, he accepts the Watergate Affair as being an example of a credible, or warranted, explanation of an event that cites the existence of a conspiracy as a significant cause.

However, Keeley argues that there is no easy or principled *a priori* way to distinguish between warranted and unwarranted conspiracy theories: 'There is no "mark of the incredible," as it were' (Keeley, 1999, p. 137). Thus, he leans towards belief in conspiracy theories *in general* being suspicious because he believes that belief in conspiracy theories engenders too much skepticism about the open nature of our society. The presence of unwarranted conspiracy theories taints the class of conspiracy theories in general, and thus our suspicion of conspiracy theories is justified because of the cost of belief in *unwarranted* conspiracy theories (which will be discussed in more depth in Chapter 6).

Juha Räikkä, in 'On Political Conspiracy Theories', makes use of Keeley's argument for a skepticism of conspiracy theories in general to illustrate the distinction between political conspiracy theories and what he calls 'total conspiracy theories', like the claim that the Illuminati control the world from behind the scenes (Räikkä, 2009b). As Räikkä explains in another work, 'The Ethics of Conspiracy Theorizing', there is a difference between what we construe political conspiracy theorists as doing – 'offer[ing] conspiracy theories to explain social events by referring to genuine political conspiracies whose existence is not widely known or presumed' (Räikkä, 2009a, p. 458) – and the problematic class of conspiracy theories, his 'total conspiracy theories'.

Like Keeley, Räikkä is suspicious of a class of conspiracy theories – total conspiracy theories – and the (supposedly) chilling effect these conspiracy theories have on public debate. Räikkä, like Keeley, accepts that there are warranted conspiracy theories. The problem for belief in conspiracy theories is, rather, that *conspiracy theorising* is a morally suspicious activity because 'harsh claims are made in too early a stage of the investigations' (Räikkä, 2009a, p. 466) (a claim we will analyse in Chapter 8).

In defence of conspiracy theories

For Keeley and Räikkä, the reason why we are justified in taking a dim view of conspiracy theories *generally* is not necessarily because such theories are, by definition, false or irrational. No, it is because the consequences of belief in such theories are problematic. We can contrast this kind of view with that of the philosophers Charles Pigden, Lee Basham and David Coady. They argue that belief in conspiracy theories is not *prima facie* irrational, even if it turns out that many conspiracy theories are themselves examples of unwarranted beliefs.

Let us start with Charles Pigden, who rails against what he terms the 'modern day superstition' about belief in conspiracy theories in his seminal article 'Popper Revisited, Or What is Wrong With Conspiracy Theories?' He argues that any historically literate person knows conspiracies have occurred and that some theories about them have turned out to be warranted.

> Conspiracy theories are widely deemed to be superstitious. To suggest, for example, that New Zealand's lurch to the right is due to a conspiracy between leading politicians, the Treasury, and big business is to invite the shaking of heads and pitying looks from sophisticated colleagues. Everybody *knows* that that is not the way history works. Yet, on the face of it, the evidence points the other way. History is littered with conspiracies, successful and otherwise. (Pigden, 1995, p. 3)

Pigden's view is a consequence of taking seriously a perfectly general definition of what counts as a 'conspiracy theory'. His definition of such a theory states that it is

> [S]imply a theory that posits a conspiracy – a secret plan on the part of some group to influence events by partly secret means[.] (Pigden, 2007, p. 222)

If we admit that conspiracies occur, then it is possible that some of those theories about conspiracies are going to be warranted. To tar the general class of conspiracy theories with the mistakes made by *some* conspiracy theorists – as Keeley and Räikkä do – gets the analysis of whether belief in conspiracy theories can ever be warranted back to front.

Lee Basham has argued along similar lines. In 'Conspiracy Theory and Rationality' he defines what counts as a 'conspiracy theory' in very general terms:

[A] conspiracy theory is,

> A causal explanation of events that appeals to the intentional attempt or success at the deception of those involved in, witnessing, investigating or otherwise affected by those events, on the part of a group of individuals cooperating for the creation or perpetuation of such deception. (Basham, 2011, pp. 52–53)

Basham's interest is in the 'extraordinary conspiracy theories that have become popular in recent decades' (Basham, 2011, p. 49) and how we can distinguish between conspiracy theories that *ought* to be believed from those that are unwarranted. He has a particular interest in what he calls 'ambitious conspiracy theories', conspiracy theories that concern momentous events. Basham's interest is centred around questions about just how open we think our society is, and whether judgements about the openness of our society inform our skepticism of claims of conspiracy happening here and now.

David Coady also accepts that conspiracies occur and that many well-accepted explanations are conspiratorial in nature. He defines what counts as a 'conspiracy theory' in 'Conspiracy Theories and Official Stories' as

> [A] proposed explanation of an historical event, in which conspiracy (i.e., agents acting secretly in concert) has a significant causal role. Furthermore, the conspiracy postulated by the proposed explanation must be a conspiracy to bring about the historical event which it purports to explain. Finally, the proposed explanation must conflict with an 'official' explanation of the same historical event. (Coady, 2006a, p. 117)

His proviso that such theories cannot be in conflict with some official explanation is not because official theories are epistemically better than conspiracy theories but, rather, because he is interested in preserving the notion that conspiracy theories are, in some sense, unofficial stories or theories (a position we will examine in Chapter 8).

Coady's definition of conspiracy theory has been glossed upon by Susan Feldman (Feldman, 2011, pp. 15–16), who uses it to talk about a special kind of evidence – counterfacts – often used by conspiracy theorists to support their conspiracy theories (one of the topics covered in Chapter 9). Joel Buenting and Jason Taylor (Buenting & Taylor, 2010, p. 569) use Coady's 'conspiracy theories are never official' proviso to argue that we have grounds to be suspicious of conspiracy theories generally, even though we must appraise individual conspiracy theories on their evidence. Buenting and Taylor's views will be discussed in more depth in the next chapter, as well as Chapter 8.

For Pigden, Basham and Coady, the idea that we should be suspicious of conspiracy theories *in general* does not wash. Rather, we should appraise conspiracy theories on their individual merits, whatever they may be. For Pigden, Basham and Coady, conspiracy theories are – roughly – explanations of events that cite conspiracies as salient causes of events. Although they have some differing views on, say, whether conspiracy theories are inherently explanations of suspicious or even sinister activity, they are in broad agreement with one another that belief in conspiracy theories is not *prima facie* unwarranted. While some, possibly many, conspiracy theories may well turn out to be unwarranted, the unwarranted nature of some conspiracy theories does not tell us much, if anything, about whether we should treat the class of conspiracy theories generally in a dim fashion.

A taxonomy

Philosophers are not heterogeneous when it comes to views on the merit, or lack thereof, of belief in conspiracy theories. However, it is useful to talk about their views with respect to, say, the views of conspiracy theory skeptics like Hofstadter, Wood, Sunstein and Vermeule, because the said skeptics are engaging in an epistemological analysis of why – for them at least – belief in conspiracy theories should be considered suspicious. Philosophers should be interested in these arguments because it is not always clear that the epistemology these skeptics employ is sound. As such, we can fit the various philosophical views into a taxonomy of views about these things called 'conspiracy theories':

1. There is the general view that a conspiracy theory is just an explanation involving a conspiracy.

This view is captured fairly straightforwardly by the *Oxford English Dictionary* definition:

> [T]he theory that an event or phenomenon occurs as a result of a conspiracy between interested parties; spec. a belief that some covert but influential agency (typically political in motivation and oppressive in intent) is responsible for an unexplained event[.] (conspiracy, 2011)

It is also the view expressed in the works of Charles Pigden, David Coady and Lee Basham.

2. A subtype of the general definition, which sets out that such theories are usually considered controversial; there are two different ways in which such definitions can be controversial:

   a) It is built into these definitions that conspiracy theories are controversial *and that we should take a dim view of them.*

Daniel Pipes, for example, defines conspiracy theories as not *merely* controversial, or *prima facie* suspicious, but downright irrational. Cass Sunstein and Adrian Vermeule's 'crippled epistemology' is another example, given that they define conspiracy theories *as the product of faulty inferences*. We can contrast this kind of view with the other subtype:

   b) The definition is neutral on whether the explanations which fit it are suspicious but, when we evaluate them, most of them turn out to be controversial and suspicious.

In cases such as these, the suspiciousness of the theory is less a part of the definition, and more a sad fact about the kind of things it refers to. It just happens to turn out that we typically think that allegations of conspiratorial activity are suspicious, but this is not because it is defined as such. Rather, allegations of conspiracies just happen to be highly controversial and seldom end up being proven as true.

Conspiracy theory theorists like Gordon S. Wood have views of this sort. For Wood, the term 'conspiracy theory' is neutral in character. Rather, it is the context in which conspiracy theorising occurs that is a problem for whether such theories can be considered rational. Brian L.

Keeley's view that belief in unwarranted conspiracy theories engenders a radical and inappropriate skepticism is also an example of this particular subtype.

Conspiracy theories fitting this type 2 definition are typically labelled as pejorative because, in all such cases, the term 'conspiracy theory' denotes something that is somehow different from a normal explanation of some event.

3. The idea that a conspiracy theory is some sort of explanation of a phenomenon that arises out of a more general tendency to think that unseen (and mysterious) agencies have control over a significant proportion of our society.

Conspiracy theories fitting this type 2 definition are typically labelled as pejorative. The theories discussed by Karl Popper and Richard Hofstadter fall under this general type, and they take a dim view of conspiracy theories.

This taxonomy[4] makes it clear that many conspiracy theory theorists are not disagreeing about conspiracy theories *per se*. Rather, they are often talking about different things that happen to share the label 'conspiracy theory' and thus who counts as a 'conspiracy theorist'.

If we are interested in the question of whether belief in conspiracy theories can ever be rational, then the really interesting type of definitions of what counts as a 'conspiracy theory' are going to be of the type 1 variety. Why? Well, because conspiracy theories that fit the type 1 definition are only as good as the evidence that is offered in support of them. If we simply define belief in conspiracy theories as being typically irrational, as advocates of the type 2 and 3 views tend to do, then we ignore the possibility that sometimes it might turn out to be rational to suspect that a conspiracy exists and we might be able to form a warranted conspiracy theory on that basis.

Our analysis of these things called 'conspiracy theories' should start with the assumption that some of them might turn out to be warranted: thus, in which cases would skepticism of such theories be justified? To answer this set of questions, it is now going to be necessary to provide and defend a minimal conception of what counts as a 'conspiracy theory'. So, with that in mind, let us begin!

3
Conspiracies and Conspiracy Theories

What is a conspiracy?

The most minimal conception of what counts as a 'conspiracy theory' is that it is a theory about a conspiracy: conspiracy theories posit that some conspiracy explains the occurrence of an event. For example, some people believe that there exists a shadow world government, made up of political elites, organisations like the Freemasons, and dynastic families like the Windsors and Rothschilds. Together they decide economic policy, engage in war games and generally plot to make the world better *for them* at the expense of making it *worse for us*.

As such, then, the most minimal conception of what counts as a conspiracy must satisfy the following three conditions:

1. *The Conspirators Condition* – There exists (or existed) some set of agents with a plan,
2. *The Secrecy Condition* – Steps have been taken by the agents to minimise public awareness of what they are up to, and
3. *The Goal Condition* – Some end is or was desired by the agents.

These three conditions are both individually necessary and jointly sufficient for some activity to be classified as conspiratorial, so let us now look at what, exactly, these conditions entail.

The Conspirators Condition

Conspiracies are a kind of group activity: people conspire *together* rather than alone, and so it is a necessary condition for the existence of some conspiracy that there exists a set of agents, commonly known as 'conspirators', who desire or intend to bring about some end. While defining the term 'conspiracy' as being the result or the actions of 'conspirators' is circular – since it builds into the definition that such activity is conspiratorial – 'conspirators' is the standard term of art in the literature. As long as we understand that by 'conspirators' we mean 'some set of plotters', we can keep using this particular term to refer to the plotters involved in conspiratorial activity.

The Secrecy Condition

Conspirators like to operate – at least for a time – in secret. Such secrecy is often used to explain why the evidence that satisfies the *Conspirators Condition* might be phrased or presented in a vague way: operating in secret is a good way to ensure that people do not know *who you are* or *what you are up to*. If it turns out that the conspirators have even some limited success in keeping their plots and machinations secret, this could be used to explain why certain details about their identity or goal remain unknown.

The Goal Condition

For some activity to qualify as a conspiracy, the conspirators must desire or intend to bring about some end. What is important here is that the conspirators desire some end, not the end itself. So, there could be a mismatch between what the conspirators desired and the actual outcome of their activity. If there is a mismatch between the desired end of some conspiratorial activity and the actual outcome, this should not be considered a problem *per se* with determining whether there is a conspiracy. The associated conspiracy theory should explain away the said difference, but, as long as the work the conspirators undertook is *in some way* responsible for the actual outcome, this should not be a concern.

Who are the conspirators?

The definition being presented here as to what counts as a conspiracy – or conspiratorial activity; let us take it that these terms are synonymous – is very general. Under this definition, any activity is conspiratorial if it is undertaken in secret by a group of agents who intend some end. As such, one potential problem with this definition is that it might fail to single out what we really mean by both a 'conspirator' and a 'conspiracy'. Such an argument would go like this: the kinds of agents we refer to as 'conspirators' in these things we call 'conspiracies' – at least the ones we are interested in when considering conspiracy theories – are more than just agents working in secret towards some end. Rather, they are the kind of agents whose existence we should treat as being *prima facie* unlikely, and thus we are justified in being suspicious of any theory that relies upon them.

For example, Jeffrey Bale, in 'Political Paranoia v. Political Realism: On Distinguishing between Bogus Conspiracy Theories and Genuine Conspiratorial Politics', claims that belief in conspiracy theories is indicative of a want to explain why bad things happen to good people *by blaming powerful actors behind the scenes* – the conspirators – rather than the inhuman processes which are the most likely explanation of such ills (Bale, 2007, pp. 50–51). Stephan Lewandowsky, Klaus Oberauer and Gilles E. Gignac, in 'NASA Faked the Moon Landing – Therefore, (Climate) Science Is a Hoax: An Anatomy of the Motivated Rejection of Science', go one step further, claiming: 'the presumed conspirators are typically perceived as virtually omnipotent' (Lewandowsky, Oberauer, & Gignac, 2013, p. 623); the power of the suspected conspirators is said to be godlike.[1]

The notion that belief in the existence of conspirators is analogous to belief in the gods (or, at the very least, godlike agents) can be traced back to the work of Karl Popper and his criticism of the conspiracy theory of society. Part of Popper's critique of the conspiracy theory of society is that

> [It] is just a version of this theism, of a belief in gods whose whims and wills rule everything. It comes from abandoning God and then asking: 'Who is in his place?' His place is filled by various powerful men and groups – sinister pressure groups, who are blamed for having planned the great depression and all the evils from which we suffer. (Popper, 1969, p. 123)

For Popper, belief in conspiracy theories is analogous to belief in divine agency. Given that Popper believes that theism is irrational, he takes it that the conspiracy theory of society is similarly irrational in much the same way. However, Charles Pigden argues that the *conspiracy theory of society* ends up misconstruing what conspiracy theorists believe about who the conspirators are. He writes:

> [I]f this is the conspiracy theory, it is obviously false, for it confers god-like powers on the conspirators. It is as if the simple act of conspiring, irrespective of the social situation or the political, economic, or opinion-making powers of the plotters, can have an impact on history.

> Again, if this is the conspiracy theory, it is a theory that nobody believes. (C. Pigden, 1995, p. 6)

This line of argument can also be found in the work of Simon Locke, who, in 'Conspiracy Culture, Blame Culture, and Rationalisation', argues that conspirators often seem godlike, but only because certain kinds of conspiracy theorists see them this way. Martha F. Lee, in *Conspiracy Rising: Conspiracy Thinking and American Public Life*, argues that, while we know conspiracies occur, what they tend to reveal are not godlike agents with supremely executed master plans but, rather, fallible people engaged in the activity of doing bad things (Lee, 2011, p. 14). Dieter Groh, in 'The Temptation of Conspiracy Theory, or: Why Do Bad Things Happen to Good People? Part I: Preliminary Draft of a Theory of Conspiracy Theories',[2] claims that conspiracy theories are explanations that appeal to the actions of godlike conspirators, who just happen to be fallible and thus whose activities are easily detected. According to Groh, belief in conspiracy theories is irrational because it involves believing both that the conspirators are godlike and also that they are also fallible and thus ungodlike (Groh, 1987, pp. 2–3).

It is true that the kinds of conspiracy theories put forward by David Icke and Lyndon LaRouche involve almost infallible conspirators who control things with ease from behind the scenes. LaRouche believes that there is a long-established conspiracy by the British Crown to, amongst other things, pervert American youth with drugs and rock-n-roll music. Icke, as discussed in the previous chapter, believes that alien, shape-shifting reptiles control the world. For LaRouche and Icke, their particular conspiracy theories require that the agents who plan in secret behind the scenes are all-powerful.[3] However, it would be a mistake to assume that the beliefs of certain conspiracy theorists tell us anything interesting about the nature of conspirators *in general*. After all, the kind of conspiracy theories the Dewey Commission put forward to explain the verdicts of the Moscow Trials of the 1930s,[4] and the historians who write about the conspiracy to assassinate Julius Caesar, did not posit godlike entities as conspirators. These conspirators undoubtedly were powerful *with respect to their positions in society*, but they were not omnipotent. So, while it is true that *certain conspiracy theorists* make it look as if the conspirators they are talking about are infallible, godlike agents, this is an artefact of some conspiracy theory *talk* rather than:

a) representative of all such conspiracy theory talk and
b) a claim about what it means to be a conspirator.

Indeed, characterising conspirators with respect to the claims of certain conspiracy theorists seems like an odd move to make. It would be much better – if we are really interested in asking whether belief in conspiracy theories could ever be rational – to work with a perfectly general characterisation of a conspirator. While some conspiracy theories intimate that conspirators are godlike entities which stride the world like a colossus, not all do. Indeed, it is not even clear that the inclusion of godlike conspirators is typical of most conspiracy theories; some conspiracy theory skeptics may well be confusing the theories of notable conspiracy theorists as being representative of the entire class of conspiracy theories.

Conspiratorial success

Another worry some might have with this characterisation of what counts as conspiratorial activity is that it allows that people can act conspiratorially *without achieving much of note.*

Popper, for example, thought you could only accept the conspiracy theory of society if you thought there were lots of conspiracies *and* that the conspirators successfully achieved their intended ends (Popper, 1972, p. 342). So, for example, Popper argues that the Holocaust was unsuccessful because it did not go to plan. The ultimate goal of the conspiracy – the eradication of the Jewish people – was never achieved because the conspirators and their plot were revealed. This seems like an odd example, since, even if the conspiracy did not achieve its ultimate aim of genocide, we can still explain the torture, execution and mass migration of millions of Jewish people with respect to the conspiracy.

Perhaps what Popper was really concerned with was not consummation *per se* – conspirators achieving their intended ends – but, rather, the failure of the conspirators to keep their activity secret. A revealed conspiracy is a conspiracy that is unsuccessful, *if we take it that a successful conspiracy is one that no one other than the conspirators would ever know about.*

We might call this notion 'perfect secrecy', and this view can also be found in the work of Juha Räikkä – whom we looked at in the last chapter – and Pete Mandik. For Räikkä, if the conspiratorial activity of some group is known – such as the involvement of the Nazis in the Holocaust or the CIA in acts of rendition – then these cannot be examples of what he calls 'genuine conspiracies' because a genuine conspiracy is one in which the conspirators maintain perfect secrecy. Räikkä, then, rules out of contention any belief in a conspiracy theory being warranted because, by definition, such theories are not about genuine conspiratorial activity. The kind of conspiratorial activities we claim to know about – such as the assassination of Julius Caesar or the Holocaust – are not genuine *because they are just part and parcel of everyday history.* He writes:

> Large-scale secret actions, such as extensive military operations, should not be confused with genuine conspiracies. The Holocaust was planned and conducted with the connivance of many people and many organizations, as was the Great Terror of 1934–1939 in the Soviet Union, but it is contestable whether these should be called genuine conspiracies, as it was generally 'known' what was going on. What was not known was who was responsible, how extensive the action was, and so on. (Räikkä, 2009b, p. 193)

It is important to note here that this distinction seems problematic. For one thing, it relies upon an unfalsifiable notion of secrecy – given that no secretive activity under this definition could ever be known about – but also because it is odd to say that the Holocaust *was* generally known about. Generally known about to whom, you might ask, given just how well it was kept secret from the Jewish people in Nazi-occupied Europe *at the time*. We will return to Räikkä and the notion of the 'genuine conspiracy' in Chapter 8.

Pete Mandik has a similar view. In 'Shit Happens', he argues that the kind of secrecy required for belief in a conspiracy must be perfect: conspirators must maintain silence about their activities even if being tortured. Otherwise, 'conspiracy theorists would not be believing in a conspiracy, since, in a sense, they do not believe the secret has been kept' (Mandik, 2007, p. 214).

These views of Popper, Räikkä and Mandik are problematic for two reasons.

First, they rule out of court the possibility that belief in a conspiracy theory could ever be rational, which means our analysis is askew from the outset.

The view that conspirators must keep to some 'perfect secrecy' for some belief in a conspiracy theory to be warranted is incredibly idiosyncratic; no matter what we believe about the warrant of conspiracy theories in general, some belief in the existence of conspiracies is warranted not just because we know conspiracies occur but also because some conspiracy theories – odd though they might have seemed to some at the time – turned out to be perfectly good explanations of events caused by conspiratorial activity. Räikkä and Mandik, in particular, bring in the condition that conspiracies must be kept perfectly secret without much argument; in the end they are seeking to defend the *prima facie* suspicion that conspiracy theories are a class of suspicious beliefs by defining them as such. What makes it even worse for the views of Räikkä and Mandik here is that it is not clear that conspirators could ever rationally believe in the existence of their *own* conspiracies. After all, the fact someone knows about a conspiracy means that it is not being kept *perfectly* secret. Think of a whistleblower who decides to testify to her government that she was involved in a conspiracy to destabilise the state: as soon as she testifies, the conspiracy is no longer secret, so is the conspiracy no longer genuine? Is her belief in the attendant conspiracy theory to the conspiratorial activity she was involved with now irrational?

Second, if we were to buy into such a view it would be very easy indeed for people to get away with conspiratorial activity. By keeping the term 'conspiracy' as a pejorative, those who engage in the kind of conspiracy-like activity these philosophers are concerned with may well be all the more likely to get away with it. After all, under this kind of view, conspirators will be able to charge those who are suspicious of their activity as being *mere* conspiracy theorists whose conspiracy theories are obviously false because they are not referring to genuine conspiracies that have been kept perfectly secret.

When it comes to the secrecy condition of conspiratorial activity, all we need to say is that some agents will be more successful than others at keeping both themselves and their activities secret. Some conspirators will remain secretive for a period of time before proceeding to reveal all, while some agents will be found out through no fault of their own. We also do not need to say that any work was undertaken to achieve some given end, just that the conspirators *sought to achieve it*. The assassins could have been caught mere moments before they assassinated Julius Caesar and we would still think of them as conspirators. Conspirators can also still be considered to be conspiring even if they fail to achieve much of note. Consider, for example, the following analogy. A group of friends desire to organise a surprise party for a friend. They decide to get together a few days before the party but end up getting distracted. In the end they fail to organise the party. In some sense they were *planning* a surprise party, since they got together because they desired some end. They simply failed to have a party. In the same way, conspirators might plot together without even achieving their desired end. This would still be a conspiracy and the attendant conspiracy theory would, presumably, be a story about why they never achieved much of note.

If we restrict talk of what counts as a conspiracy to cases in which the conspirators manage to keep their conspiratorial activity perfectly secret, then not only are we using a restrictive (and possibly strange) definition of what counts as secrecy, but it follows that belief in conspiracy theories will be irrational *because it will not be based upon the evidence*. Indeed, as both David Coady and Lee Basham have argued, arguing for some notion of perfect secrecy seems strange. After all, not only do we only know about those conspiracies that have been exposed, but also:

a) we do not know about those that have not been found out about, and
b) just because some conspiracies are exposed, that does not mean they were not successful in obtaining some intended end (Basham, 2001; Coady, 2012).

Even a conspiracy that fails to achieve what the conspirators intended may still end up being a good explanation for some event. Take, for example, in the case of the Gunpowder Plot of 1605; the Catholic conspirators failed to blow up the English Houses of Parliament, but the activity of the conspirators still explains the events of that day, and the explanation is clearly conspiratorial in nature. This is a case of a conspiracy that was uncovered, yet can still be considered to be a good explanation of the event.

There is more to say about secrecy, but we must wait until the next chapter. For now, let us look at conspiracy theories and what counts as a 'conspiracy theory'.

What is a conspiracy theory?

If we take it that the most minimal definition of what counts as a conspiracy – simply the activity of agents working together in secret towards some end – then surely the most minimal definition of a conspiracy theory will be any explanation of an event that cites the existence of a conspiracy as a salient cause.

After all, a conspiracy is an activity that has an intended result, so a theory about a conspiracy is going to be some explanatory hypothesis that says an event was, in some way, causally related to a conspiracy.

This is, according to the taxonomy presented at the end of the last chapter, a type 1 definition, and, as such, is very general – since it allows that any explanation of conspiratorial activity, even minor conspiratorial activity, could be a conspiracy theory – and does not match the pejorative usage of a conspiracy theory being some kind of suspicious kind of belief. However, if we really are interested in answering the question of whether belief in conspiracy theories can ever be irrational, this is the definition we should be using.

The pejorative implication

A perfectly general, non-pejorative definition of what counts as a 'conspiracy theory' is not exactly the norm in the academic literature. Indeed, it is fair to say that the terms 'conspiracy theory' and 'conspiracy theorist' are often used as pejorative labels. For example, Gordon B. Arnold, in *Conspiracy Theory in Film, Television and Politics*, has argued that, as conspiracy theories have become mainstream, they have come to be seen neither as pathological beliefs nor even as alleging the existence of conspiracies, but, rather, as symptomatic of a worldview in which individuals have little power against 'enormous external forces, sometimes seen, sometimes not' (Arnold, 2008, p. 4). In this case, the term 'conspiracy theory' does not refer to an explanation but, rather, a mode of political expression. Victoria Emma Págan, as discussed in the previous chapter, argues that conspiracy theories are essentially political myths: the reason why belief in such theories turns out to be unwarranted is because of problems to do with conspiracy theorists and their crippled epistemology (to use Cass Sunstein's and Adrian Vermeule's terminology). Jeffrey M. Bale even goes so far as to blame conspiracy theorists – whom he characterises in the paranoid style – for the pejorative label of 'conspiracy theory', a term that, he argues, should be a perfectly general and neutral term (Bale, 2007, p. 56). Martha F. Lee has argued in a similar way: the term 'conspiracy theory' has taken on a pejorative meaning *because of its association with the beliefs of contemporary conspiracy theorists* (Lee, 2011, p. 2).

Peter Knight presents a version of this view, writing:

> [T]he label 'conspiracy theory' usually suggests that the interpretation offered is wrong. In effect the phrase is often not a neutral description of a form of historical analysis[.] ... Instead it usually carries an implicit accusation: there are undoubtedly conspiracy facts (the suggestion is), but in this case your view is just a conspiracy theory, a misleading speculation, and even wooly-headed thinking that verges on the mentally disturbed. (Knight, 2003, p. 16)

However, Knight – in an earlier work – had already questioned this kind of analysis, arguing that

> [L]abelling a view paranoid has now become an empty circular description with a gloss of scientific rigor: the paranoid is someone who (amongst other things) believes in conspiracy theories, and, conversely, the reason that people believe in conspiracy theories is that they are paranoid. (Knight, 2000, p. 15)

Joel Buenting and Jason Taylor argue along similar lines:

> [T]he terms 'conspiracy theory' and 'conspiracy theorist' are powerful labels with deeply pejorative implications. Their use is an effective way to dismiss the theory itself, or the thinker who proposes such a theory. One might wonder – as we do – whether such a priori dismissal is justified. (Buenting & Taylor, 2010, p. 568)

David Coady has expressed this sentiment in even stronger terms, describing the treatment of contemporary conspiracy theorists as being akin to an 'intellectual witch hunt'. Coady points out that, while some conspiracy theorists might deserve to be criticised, or even ignored, we should not criticise or ignore people *just because they are conspiracy theorists* (Coady, 2012, p. 111).

Like Knight, Buenting, Taylor and Coady, we should also worry about the way the pejorative labelling of 'That's *just* a conspiracy theory!' clouds the debate on whether the said conspiracy theory is worth taking seriously. It may well turn out that the intuition some conspiracy theory theorists and skeptics have – that the labels 'conspiracy theory' and 'conspiracy theorist' should be understood as pejoratives – is mistaken. Let us examine, then, some of the reasons why that might be.

Generalist vs. particularist views

Joel Buenting and Jason Taylor argue that when we look at the field of views about the rationality of belief in conspiracy theories there are, in effect, two opposing camps, the generalists and the particularists:

> According to the generalist view, the rationality of conspiracy theories can be assessed without considering particular conspiracy theories. On this view, conspiratorial thinking qua conspiracy thinking is itself irrational. The particularist view about conspiratorial thinking denies that the rationality of conspiracy theories can be assessed without considering particular conspiracy theories. (Buenting & Taylor, 2010, pp. 568–569)

The pejorative definition of conspiracy theory falls under the rubric of the generalist view. It should also be obvious from our perfectly general definition of what counts as a 'conspiracy theory' that we should be particularists, since our interest should be in assessing particular conspiracy theories to see whether they are warranted.

So, why is the notion that conspiracy theories are *prima facie* suspicious so deeply embedded into the generalist view? It is, in part, explicable by reference to the views generalists have, *not about conspiracy theories in general* but, rather, about conspiracy theorists in particular. There are a variety of reasons why people might use pejorative definitions of the terms 'conspiracy theory' and 'conspiracy theorist'. For one thing, the person using the term pejoratively might be acting disingenuously. For example, Tony Blair and George W. Bush attacked the critics of the invasion of Iraq by claiming such critics were conspiracy theorists. This seemed then, and certainly seems now – given the evidence – to have been a deliberate tactic designed to shut down debate. No one likes being called a conspiracy theorist, after all, and few of us ever admit to believing conspiracy theories. Indeed, we often point towards conspiracy theorists like David Icke and claim that his particular set of conspiracy theories – claims about inter-dimensional, shape-shifting alien reptiles – are both implausible and representative of the kind of things conspiracy theorists in general believe.

We can respect the notion that sometimes we are able to recognise pathological belief in conspiracy theories without tarring the class of conspiracy theorists who engage in conspiracy theorising as being *prima facie* irrational. The problem is that the existing literature is insensitive to the distinction between claims about the psychology of some conspiracy theorists and belief in conspiracy theories in general. To show why, we need to talk a little about the thesis of conspiracism, which is a kind of psychological thesis about conspiracy theorists *in general.*

Conspiracism

The thesis of conspiracism describes a particular problem with belief in conspiracy theories on the part of *certain* conspiracy theorists, 'conspiracists'. A conspiracist is someone who believes in the existence of conspiracies *without good reason*. The terms 'conspiracism' and 'conspiracist', then, are pejorative labels which reflect a pathological belief in conspiracies *sans* evidence.

Talk of conspiracism is rife in the conspiracy theory theorist literature. Daniel Pipes, for example, writes:

> Conspiracy theories have a way of growing on a person, to the point that they become a way of seeing life itself. This is *conspiracism*, the *paranoid style*, or the *hidden-hand mentality*. (Pipes, 1997, p. 22)

Michael Barkun, in *A Culture of Conspiracy: Apocalyptic Visions in Contemporary America*, claims conspiracy theorists have 'severed important ties with a realistic and accurate view of the world' and are, thus, conspiracists (Barkun, 2003, pp. 8–9).

Michael J. Wood, Karen M. Douglas and Robbie M. Sutton use the term 'conspiracist' to refer to conspiracy theorists and their associated conspiracy theories (Wood, Douglas, & Sutton, 2012, p. 768), a point which is reiterated in a paper by Wood and Douglas alone:

> [T]hose who generally believe conspiracy theories (whom we call 'conspiracists') and those who prefer conventional explanations (whom we call 'conventionalists'). (Wood & Douglas, 2013, p. 1)

They present conspiracism as a problematic form of belief in conspiracy theories, arguing that 'for people who hold a conspiracist worldview, the specifics of a conspiracy theory are less important than its identity as a conspiracy and its opposition to the official explanation'. Wood and Douglas construe this conspiracist worldview as 'a generalized opposition to official or received narratives. In this view, conspiracy belief is not about believing in particular alternative theories, but in disbelieving in whatever the official story is' (Wood & Douglas, 2013, p. 2).

All these conspiracy theory skeptics admit that conspiracies occur, but they take a generalist position when it comes to assessing belief in conspiracy theories because the processes that lead to the *formation* of conspiracy theories by conspiracy theorists are pathological.

Sometimes it is not clear that conspiracy theory theorists are operating with the thesis of conspiracism (and are thus conspiracy theory skeptics), since sometimes conspiracism is labelled as 'conspiracy thinking' or some other close term. For example, Viren Swami, Tomas Chamorro-Premuzic and Adrian Furnham, in 'Unanswered Questions: A Preliminary Investigation of Personality and Individual Difference Predictors of 9/11 Conspiracist Beliefs', offer what looks like a relatively neutral construal of what a 'conspiracy theory' is, writing that they are

> [L]lay beliefs that attribute the ultimate cause of an event, or the concealment of an event from public knowledge, to a secret, unlawful, and malevolent plot by multiple actors working together. (Swami, Chamorro-Premuzic, & Furnham, 2010, p. 749)

But Swami, Chamorro-Premuzic and Furnham base their definition on the work of Marvin Zonis and Craig M. Joseph, who, in 'Conspiracy Thinking in the Middle East', analyse belief in conspiracy theories in the mould of conspiracism. They write:

> [C]onspiracies are frequently invoked to explain events or states of affairs when, by any reasonable set of criteria, no conspiracy exists.

> Moreover, one often gets the sense that such a misidentification is not a mere mistake but rather the expression of a tendency to interpret the world in a particular way.
>
> This tendency is what we call 'conspiracy thinking[.]' (Zonis & Joseph, 1994, p. 444)

This looks like the thesis of conspiracism: Zonis and Joseph are defining conspiracy thinking (or conspiracy theorising) as a process whereby conspiracy theorists believe in the existence of conspiracies *sans* evidence.

Similarly, Jeffrey M. Bale distinguishes between what he calls 'conspirational politics' and belief in conspiracy theories. He takes it that belief in conspiracy theories is due to a paranoid mode of thinking, while belief in the existence of a conspirational politics refers to the kind of conspiratorial activity that, we take it, really occurs (Bale, 2007, p. 54). For Bale, conspiracy theories are implausible claims of conspiracy expressed by irrational agents, which indicates that he, too, is operating with the notion of conspiracism when referring to conspiracy theorists and their theories.

The reply to conspiracism

Robin Ramsay, a UK-based journalist, is concerned that we often confuse the psychological troubles of some conspiracy theorists with the warrant of particular conspiracy theories. He worries that one kind of conspiracy theory – those in which we think belief is *prima facie* unwarranted – are used by conspiracy theory skeptics to smear the beliefs of conspiracy theorists *in general* as being irrational. As such, skeptics downplay the incidence and importance of cases of warranted belief in conspiracy theories (Ramsay, 2006, pp. 143–147).

This seems right. While we can single out a subset of conspiracy theorists who believe that 'nothing happens by accident', the existence of such conspiracy theorists – the class of conspiracists – tells us nothing particularly interesting about conspiracy theories in general, since it is not obvious that *all* conspiracy theorists follow a conspiracist mode of thinking.

Coady expresses a version of this worry by pointing out that, although it is a standard tactic to deride specific conspiracy theorists and, thus, conspiracy theories in general, this line of argument is clearly fallacious. He writes:

> What needs to be shown is not that there are conspiracy theories and theorists with certain undesirable characteristics, but that there is a

> connection between being a conspiracy theory or theorist and these undesirable characteristics. What needs to be shown, in other words, is that the theories or theorists have the undesirable characteristics *because* they are conspiracy theories or theorists. (Coady, 2012, p. 131)

When we take a generalist view on the warrant of conspiracy theories and take them to be *prima facie* irrational because of the attitudes of *some* conspiracy theorists, we are performing our analysis in a back-to-front manner. While conspiracists – defined as conspiracy theorists who see conspiracies without good reason – certainly do exist, they are a *subset* of conspiracy theorists in general. We should not associate belief in conspiracy theories with just a subset of conspiracy theorists, since this runs the risk of defining out of court the interesting cases in which certain conspiracy theorists *get it right*.

Conspiracism is a folk-psychological thesis, in that when we tar someone with a label like 'They're *just* a conspiracy theorist' what we are, in effect, doing is saying: 'Look, this person believes some conspiracy theory because of some defect of reasoning.' Conspiracists – people who suffer from conspiracism – are not *merely* wrong to assume some event was caused by a conspiracy – that is, they have not just made a faulty inference; they have, rather, jumped to the conclusion that a conspiracy is the best explanation of some event because of some psychological defect.

While there is room for discussion about the psychology of conspiracy theorists and arguments as to whether such theorists are more or less likely to be paranoid, we should not let psychological theses about the rationality of certain types of conspiracy theorists intrude on a discussion of the epistemic warrant of *particular* conspiracy theories. People like David Icke and Glenn Beck might be what we call 'signature conspiracy theorists', given that they are the kind of people we often think of when we hear the term 'conspiracy theorist', but this does not make them typical. Rather, they are significant. Nothing about that significance, however, tells us about how typical they are with respect to the wider group of conspiracy theorists.

This is an empirical issue, of course, but, without data as to how typical people like Icke and Beck are with respect to the group of conspiracy theorists in general, we should be charitable and talk about conspiracy theorists in a non-pejorative manner. After all, it would be silly to tar the thesis of atheism with the facile arguments of atheists who became atheists merely because they have been socially conditioned to be atheists, or have a certain psychological attitude towards disbelief in the existence of God or the gods. In the same way, we should not tar conspiracy theories with the attitudes of a certain class of conspiracy theorist, the conspiracist. After all, the truth or falsity of the thesis of atheism is a fact *independent of what we believe about the world*. Either there are gods or there are not. However, what makes atheism a rational or reasonable belief for individuals to hold depends on the available evidence. In the same way, what will make a conspiracy theory a rational or reasonable belief also depends on the evidence; we should not just dismiss such a conspiracy theory *merely* because some conspiracist believes it. If someone alleges a conspiracy has occurred, we should examine the evidence for that conspiracy theory rather than simply dismissing it out of hand because we suspect them of being a conspiracist. We cannot analyse whether belief in conspiracy theories can ever be rational through the lens of conspiracism, because conspiracism is based upon the assumption that belief in conspiracy theories is *prima facie* irrational.

This gets us to the nub of the problem, because there are two problems we need to keep in mind: when is belief in a particular conspiracy theory irrational, and when is belief in conspiracy theories in general pathological? Answering the former does not necessarily tell us much about the latter. Whatever we believe about the potentially pathological psychology of some conspiracy theorists, this does not tell us anything particularly useful about the merits – or lack thereof – of individual conspiracy theories. We cannot use our skepticism of the beliefs of particular individuals to justify a suspicion of an entire kind of theories. If that were the case, Republicans of a certain stripe would be justified in thinking anthropogenic climate change was not occurring *merely* because some Democrats believe it is for less than rigorous reasons. That is obviously a fallacious move, and yet when conspiracy theory skeptics use conspiracism – a thesis about a certain kind of conspiracy theorist – to justify taking a dim view of conspiracy theories *in general*, this is exactly what they are doing.

There is a use for a term like 'conspiracism' in the psychological literature about belief in conspiracy theories, given that it describes a particular pathological belief in conspiracy theories which might well be explicable via a psychological account as to how people sometimes form false beliefs. However, we need to be aware that conspiracists are simply one kind of conspiracy theorist, and it is a mistake to treat conspiracists as representative of conspiracy theorists *in general*.

Conclusion

Pejorative definitions of what counts as a conspiracy theory either focus the debate on what, if anything, is wrong with belief in conspiracy theories on the wrong kinds of issues, or side-track us with misleading and sometimes confusing terminology. If we define 'conspiracy theories' as 'conspiracy theories that are (in some sense) irrational to believe', then the debate on whether a theory that posits a conspiracy is true, or reasonable, becomes a debate about whether it is really a *conspiracy* theory.

We should, then, favour the non-pejorative definition being defended here – any explanation that cites a conspiracy as a salient cause – because our interest in whether such theories can ever be rational to believe is best focused on an analysis of the *wider class of conspiratorial explanations*, which includes both warranted *and* unwarranted conspiracy theories. That way, we can analyse whether the alleged problems with belief in conspiracy theories – expressed in the various pejorative senses favoured by some conspiracy theory skeptics – are really issues specific to conspiracy theories, or whether they are really just part of a set of more general epistemic problems. As such, throughout this book the term 'conspiracy theory' will be used to cover the wider set of conspiratorial explanations *in order to emphasise* the similarities between the ones that people are interested in (which typically maps onto the pejorative sense of conspiracy theory) and all the other explanations that happen to invoke conspiratorial activity.

Still, some might have some lingering worries about this definition. They might agree that we should use a non-pejorative definition of 'conspiracy theory' *with respect to whether they can ever be warranted*. However, they might also believe that there is another pejorative sense this definition does not capture, which is that conspiracy theories are beliefs about sinister political agents who are up to no good. The definition advanced here, as it stands, seems so general as to include *conspiracies of goodness* and to allow theories, say, about *surprise parties* to be considered in some cases as examples of conspiracy theories. Let us now turn to this second set of issues to do with this general, non-pejorative definition of what counts as a conspiracy theory.

4
Some Problems with a General Definition

In the previous chapter we looked at one reason for adopting a general and non-pejorative definition of conspiracy theory: it helps us avoid a particular trap, which is confusing the pathological psychology of *some* conspiracy theorists with the question of whether it is rational to believe *certain* conspiracy theories. However, even if we divorce talk about the psychology of belief in conspiracy theories from talk of the epistemic issues of whether conspiracy theories can ever be rational, the common usage of the terms 'conspiracy theory' and 'conspiracy theorist' suggests the existence of another, different pejorative sense, which our definition of a conspiracy theory – any explanation of an event that cites a conspiracy as a salient cause – does not capture.

When people talk about conspiracy theories, the kinds of things that come to mind are stories about sinister, world-changing activities. So, for example, David Icke's conspiracy theories about alien, shape-shifting reptiles are theories about the *sinister* intentions of these reptiles. His conspiracy theories are not neutral descriptions of states of affairs but a call to arms. According to Icke, we should be disturbed to find out that our supposedly democratic societies are, in fact, illusions foisted upon us by shape-shifting reptiles. In the same respect, when people talk about the various 9/11 conspiracy theories that claim the terrorist attacks on New York and Washington, DC were orchestrated by the US government, they are talking about *sinister* plots and capers that have been falsely attributed to foreign nationals.

The common usage, it seems, of conspiracy and conspiracy theory are pejorative in the sense that we are not referring to conspiracies of goodness or the organisation of things like surprise parties. Rather, conspiracy theories are typically examples of beliefs about sinister conspiratorial activity with big goals.

It is hard to argue against common usage, but it is worthwhile to test the assumptions behind such usage. After all, people may well be mistaken to restrict talk of conspiracies and conspiracy theories to accounts of world-shaking, sinister activities being organised in secret by bands of conspirators. The minimal conception of what counts as a 'conspiracy' and a 'conspiracy theory' that was defended in the previous chapter does not mean that the pejorative sense of those terms is not useful philosophically in determining whether belief in conspiracy theories can ever be considered rational. So, let us look more closely at the claims that restrict talk of conspiracies to this other, pejorative sense of conspiracy theory.

The first feature: surprise parties as conspiracies

If we accept the definition of a conspiracy theory as *merely* any explanation of an event that cites a conspiracy as a salient cause, then it looks as if we are all conspiracy theorists. After all, surely each of us is committed to *at least one* explanation that features a claim of conspiracy as a salient cause of an event? For example, the activity of organising a surprise birthday party for a child qualifies as conspiratorial, and any explanation that cites this activity as the cause of an event – say, a group of children having fun on a Sunday afternoon – will turn out to be a conspiracy theory.

Now, some might find this surprising, even alarming, but on closer inspection surprise parties do turn out to be examples of conspiracies. This is because:

1. like conspiracies, they are hatched in secret;
2. like conspiracies, they have, as their organisers, a set of agents who work together in secret; and
3. like conspiracies, the organisers seek to achieve some end.

However, some might argue that, while surprise parties do look conspiratorial, or even are examples of conspiracies, *they are the wrong kind of conspiracy* because surprise parties are example of trivial conspiratorial activity. What we should really be interested in, when it comes to talk of conspiracy theories, are examples of non-trivial conspiratorial activity, such as political conspiracies.

Central to this intuition is some claim that the kind of conspiratorial activity we should be concerned with are claims about *institutional* conspiracies, of which political conspiracies are the most distressing/

interesting. The existence of institutional conspiracies might very well undermine our trust, say, in the relevant institutions. If we find out that a certain political group is acting conspiratorially, and that group has power over us, then our trust in that group and other similar groups will likely diminish. Given that we would like to trust the people who have power over us, this seems like a bad thing, and so we fear political conspiracies because they are an affront to our political values. As such, while surprise parties *might look conspiratorial*, they are not the kind of conspiratorial activity holders of such an intuition think we should be concerned about when analysing talk about conspiracy theories. When people worry about whether there is some conspiracy going on, they are, typically, not thinking about what the parents next door are planning for their five-year-old's surprise birthday party.

Institutional conspiracies

What do we mean by 'institutional conspiracy'? After all, it looks as if the term 'institutional conspiracy' is doing a lot of work, since it is being used to dismiss our interest in political conspiracies as really being part of our interest in the larger set of *institutional* conspiracies.

An institutional conspiracy is simply a conspiracy that is organised or run by some institution. Thus, an institutional conspiracy theory is simply any explanation of an event that cites an institutional conspiracy as a salient cause of some event. As such, political conspiracies are examples of conspiracies run by public institutions, which are part of the group of institutions *in general*.

So, what counts as an institution? Well, private organisations can be institutions, so we can talk about conspiracies like the Ford Motor Company's cover-up, in the 1970s, of the safety issues to do with the Ford Pinto's gas tank design. Charitable organisations can similarly be considered as institutions: the Roman Catholic Church and the Freemasons are institutions that are neither truly private nor fully public. Both can (and have) acted conspiratorially *and have been the subjects of conspiracy theories*. Thus, what defines an institution is its structure and, to a lesser extent, its size: structure, in that an institution is some organisation that centralises its power over its members in a subset of its membership, and size, insofar as it has sway over some membership. So, for example, a parish council can be an institution and conspire with respect to the set of parishioners it governs, as can a Department of Philosophy.

It is understandable that our interest in conspiracy theories tends to centre around claims of institutional conspiracies. However, this focus on such institutional – especially political – conspiracies and conspiracy theories does not rule out the utility of talking about surprise parties. As Lee Basham argues,

> Few greatly fear surprise birthday parties. But we often fear ambitious political and economic conspiracies. This returns us to the concern we are conflating *salience* with meaning. (Basham, 2011, p. 54)

If we restrict our focus solely to institutional conspiracies, we run the risk of ignoring other kinds of interesting conspiratorial activity – and associated explanations – and may thus miss some important similarities that weigh upon how we appraise and consider conspiratorial explanations *in general*. If we want to appraise whether belief in conspiracy theories can ever be warranted, it is useful to look at the wider class of conspiratorial activity and appraise all explanations of that activity. If we are to rule out surprise parties as the kind of conspiratorial activity we are interested in, we need to have some kind of criterion that allows us to distinguish interesting from uninteresting conspiratorial activity. It is hard to know where we should draw such a line, and making such a demarcation is akin to arbitrarily drawing a line in the sand, something many commentators on conspiracy theories seem to do.

Largeness

One line that could be drawn is this: the kind of conspiracies we are interested in when considering conspiracy theories are those that refer to large, involved affairs. This is to say, the kind of conspiracies we should be concerned with are those of a *large* institutional character, rather than surprise parties.

Daniel Pipes, for example, divides conspiracies into two sorts, the 'petty' and the 'world'. *Petty* conspiracies concern minor, largely non-political events, while *world* conspiracies tend to be states of affairs involving political institutions (Pipes, 1997, p. 21). Petty conspiracies – which refer to minor infractions like the organisation of surprise parties – should not be considered as the right kind of thing to be interested in *when thinking about conspiracy theories*. Rather, it is *world* conspiracies that we should be interested in, at least according to Pipes.

Michael Barkun also has a size criterion with respect to talk of conspiracies, ranging from 'event conspiracies' to 'systemic conspiracies' to 'superconspiracies'. It is rational, according to Barkun, to believe in event conspiracies, since they concern a 'limited, discrete event or set of events... [where] the conspiratorial forces are alleged to have focused their energies on a limited, well-defined objective' (Barkun, 2003,

p. 6). Belief in an event conspiracy might be rational, depending on the evidence. As such, surprise parties will qualify as event conspiracies, but they are not the kind of activity we associate with *conspiracy theories*. Barkun argues that belief in conspiracy theories is representative of a worldview, on the part of the conspiracy theorist, in which nothing happens by accident, nothing can be taken at face value and everything is connected. Like Hofstadter, Barkun associates belief in conspiracies with a kind of paranoia style (Barkun, 2003, p. 8).

Where event conspiracies may have some evidential support, systemic and superconspiracies, like Pipes' world conspiracies, refer to large-scale, institutional claims of conspiratorial activity. They are the kind of conspiracy talk we are meant to be properly concerned with when analysing whether belief in conspiracy theories can be rational. Systemic conspiracies refer to plots in which the conspirators have a broad goal, such as taking control of a nation state or subverting existing institutions. Superconspiracies are complexes of both event *and* systemic conspiracies: they are all-embracing conspiracies in which powerful and malevolent forces seek to control the world through multiple conspiracies. According to Barkun, conspiracy theories typically end up being irrational because, while such theories appear to be based upon evidence, that evidence becomes increasingly irrelevant the broader the scope of the conspiracy. Systemic and superconspiracies, citing as they do ever larger conspiracies that have infiltrated and subverted the institutions around us, cast into doubt any supporting evidence for the conspiracy, since *the conspirators may well have planted the said evidence to deceive.*

The notion that we can characterise the warrant of conspiracy theories by the size of the alleged conspiracy is an interesting idea, and it has seen traction in the works of other theorists. For example, Martha Lee talks about superconspiracies, *à la* Barkun, in her work (Lee, 2011, p. 7). Volker Heins also makes a similar distinction between types of conspiracies. There are 'real conspiracies', which are typically orchestrated by the rich and powerful and do not threaten the core values of our society – which map onto Barkun's event conspiracies – and conspiracies that are represented as polluting the core of our society. Heins contrasts belief in real conspiracies with belief in 'alleged but unproven conspiracies' – which roughly map onto Barkun's systemic and superconspiracies. These 'alleged but unproven conspiracies' range from conspiracy theories that are believed by only a few individuals to those that are believed by the masses, and it is these last two categories of conspiracy theory that are examples of irrational beliefs, according to Heins (Heins, 2007, p. 791).

Peter Knight has this to say about Pipe's 'petty' vs. 'world' distinction, which applies equally as a response to Barkun, Räikkä and Heins:

> Because petty conspiracy theories (and even some world conspiracy theories) do not lead to measurable political atrocities, Pipes and other commentators rule out in advance the very kinds of conspiracy theory that might challenge their model of what a conspiracy theory is. (Knight, 2000, p. 11)

Simon Locke offers another response to this same issue, one that focuses squarely on the size of world or superconspiracies. Locke argues against the notion that we should distinguish conspiracy theories by their size or breadth, arguing 'that larger conspiracies are often constructed out of smaller-scale materials'. He also argues against distinguishing conspiracy theories by subject matter, given that what one theorist thinks is worthy of serious investigation another theorist will downplay (Locke, 2009, p. 571).

We are rightly interested in talk of institutional, particularly political, conspiracy theories, because, as already mentioned, if such conspiracies are occurring, that might challenge our trust in the institutions that make up the kind of societies in which we live. However, this does not mean we should be uninterested in small conspiracies, institutional or not. It simply tells us that we might be more interested in bigger ones. As such, we should not need to rule out talk of, say, explanations of surprise parties as being examples of conspiracy theories, especially if it also turns out that the analysis of such surprise parties could end up being useful in analysing the warrant of the more general class of things we consider to be conspiratorial explanations.

Second, our interest in biggish claims of conspiracy is at loggerheads with the intuition that many of these 'world' or 'total' conspiracies are hogwash. We have all heard David Icke's thesis that shape-shifting reptiles control the bloodlines of the political elite, and many of us might well think these claims are vapid. Sometimes, though, big conspiracy theories turn out to be warranted, like the explanation of what really happened during the Great Terror of late 1930s Russia. Defining these biggish claims of conspiracy as *prima facie* unwarranted simply begs the question.

The second feature: conspiracies are not necessarily sinister

Let us agree, then, that any explanation of the organisation and execution of a surprise party counts as being an example of a conspiracy theory. Surely, though, some will argue, there must be something wrong with our definition, because conspiracies – by their very nature – are sinister states of affairs. Surprise parties might be many things, but they are rarely, if ever, sinister.[1]

The notion that we should treat claims of conspiracy as claims about sinister behaviour is common in the literature and matches common usage. For example, Marvin Zonis and Craig M. Joseph express this view when they define what counts as a conspiracy as activity that is 'unlawful or malevolent' (Zonis & Joseph, 1994, p. 448) and Volker Heins defines conspiracies in terms of criminal activity (Heins, 2007, p. 791).

However, just because something is unlawful, that does not make it *automatically* malevolent. For example, you might believe that drug possession is not inherently malevolent, even though it might be illegal. It might even be the case that you are a data collector for the NSA who decides to leak classified information for the public good, even though leaking such information is illegal. Compare this view with that of Michael J. Wood, Karen M. Douglas and Robbie M. Sutton, who claim that a conspiracy theory is 'defined as a proposed plot by powerful people or organizations working together in secret to accomplish some (usually sinister) goal' (Wood, Douglas & Sutton, 2012, p. 767). In this case it is the sinisterness of the activity that is a problem, rather than the suspicious legality. Wood and Douglas, in another piece, define conspiracy theories as 'allegations that powerful people or organizations are plotting together in secret to achieve sinister ends through deception of the public' (Wood & Douglas, 2013, p. 1).

Stephan Lewandowsky, John Cook, Klaus Oberauer and Michael Marriott make a similar claim, writing:

> [T]he presumed intentions behind any conspiracy are invariably nefarious: conspiracist ideation never involves groups of people whose intent is to do good, as for example when planning a surprise birthday party. Instead, conspiracist ideation relies on the presumed deceptive intentions of the people or institutions responsible for the 'official' account that is being questioned. (Lewandowsky, Cook, Oberauer, & Marriott, 2013, p. 4)

Lewandowsky et al. take it that conspiracy theories are inherently explanations of sinister, institutional activity because they are discussing conspiracy theories in *conspiracist* terms: they are talking about a particular kind of *pathological* belief in conspiracy theories. Conspiracists are unlikely to be the kind of people who think of surprise parties as conspiracies, let alone explanations of such parties as conspiracy theories, but this is merely because conspiracists are the kind of people who have *prima facie* irrational beliefs in the existence of conspiracies anyway. What conspiracists believe about the nature of conspiratorial activity is certainly interesting – particularly from a psychological standpoint – but that does not tell us that conspiracy theories *in general* are necessarily concerned with accounts of sinister activity.

However, not everyone takes it that we should treat conspiratorial activity as sinister or morally suspicious. Susan Feldman has argued that we should not add into any definition of conspiracy theory that the aims of the conspirators are necessarily nefarious or malign (Feldman, 2011, p. 15). This is somewhat odd, given that Feldman uses and extends Barkun's definition of a conspiracy theory and he claims:

> The essence of conspiracy beliefs lies in attempts to delineate and explain evil. (Barkun, 2003, p. 3)

For Barkun, it is the role of secrecy associated with claims of conspiracy that entails an associated belief in a sinister state of affairs. Contrast this with the views of Jeffrey M. Bale, who argues that conspiratorial activity is not inherently sinister. He writes:

> The Latin word *conspire* literally means 'to breathe together', and need not suggest anything more sinister than people getting together to hold a private meeting. Thus, every time officers of a company participate in a board meeting to plan a marketing strategy they are 'conspiring', and in this sense there are thousands of conspiracies occurring every single day. (Bale, 2007, p. 54)

Bale, like Daniel Pipes, considers belief in conspiracy theories to be the result of elaborate fantasies on the part of the conspiracy theorist. Still, given that conspiratorial activity is not inherently sinister for Bale, if we accept that a conspiracy theory is *merely* a theory about a conspiracy, then conspiracy theories, fantastical as they might be, are not necessarily about malevolent or sinister activities. It might be the case that they all accidentally turn out to be sinister, but that is a problem of representation rather than a problem with the class of things called 'conspiracy theories' (Bale, 2007, pp. 54–55).

David Coady also argues that we need not treat conspiratorial activity as necessarily sinister. He writes:

> Conspiracies are usually thought of as sinister. This characteristic does not seem, however, to be essential...It may be that we only think of

conspiracies as sinister if and to the extent that we think of secrecy itself in this way. (Coady, 2006b, p. 1)

The notion of 'secretive activity' is doing a lot of work here: we are suspicious of actions that occur in secret, and, if our interest is squarely in the institutional, particularly political, conspiracies, then the notion that members of the political establishment might be operating in secret has the result that the public will be suspicious as to what the said members are allegedly up to. The intuition as to why we might think that conspiracies are a kind of sinister activity is understandable: to conspire requires that conspirators act in a secretive manner, and we often have good reason to be suspicious of people acting secretly. As such, we understand why someone might claim that conspiracies are 'morally suspect if not morally wrong', as Brian L. Keeley has (Keeley, 2007, p. 141), or that conspiratorial activity need only be considered morally suspect, and only to some people, as Charles Pigden has (Pigden, 2006, p. 157), or even that *secretive* political activity is a kind of morally suspect behaviour, as Jonathan Vanakin claims in *Conspiracies, Cover-ups and Crimes* (Vanakin, 1991).

If you act secretively, then people who are aware you are up to something are going to treat whatever you are doing with suspicion. However, while secrecy is an important part of any conspiracy, the fact that someone is acting secretly *even in the case of a conspiracy* does not tell us that their activity is sinister or malevolent. There are various reasons why you might keep some organisational activity secret – that is, not report details about it:

1. The organisation of some event might only be successful *if the resulting event or phenomenon is a surprise*. (For example, some theatre events, game plans by sports coaches and, of course, surprise parties).
2. Certain activities are private. (For example, certain domestic situations, personal discussions between friends, or arrangements between a client and a professional).
3. If certain people found out about some activity before it was completed, they might (re)act inappropriately. (For example, this might be one reason why talks between governments might be kept secret).
4. The activities might be regarded as dubious by somebody, though perhaps not everybody. (For example, this is no doubt why some people hide their musical preferences or their political affiliations).

Reasons 1–3 show that secrecy might just be necessary for the obtaining of some end. It is, after all, hard to organise a surprise party if the 'victim' knows what you are up to, or to meaningfully discuss your personal problems if everyone is commenting on them. Now, in these kinds of cases, while it is true that acting in secret might suggest that something sinister is going on, this is by no means a strong inference. At best, in these kinds of cases, we might say that acting in secret is suspicious. It is the fourth reason – secrecy about dubious activities – that we might consider to be sinister in nature.

For example, let us suppose that our government is having secret meetings with a foreign power to ensure that we will no longer require visas when entering their country. Both governments decide to keep the negotiations secret, so that citizens do not get their hopes up and start booking extravagant holidays. However, interested members of the public begin to notice that the Foreign Minister is constantly away and that deputations from both countries are meeting with unusual frequency. Journalists chase the story, but the government refuses to comment on it, thus raising suspicion as to what is really going on.

We could (and probably should) call the government's secretive activity here suspicious, but does this mean that we should treat it as also being sinister? We could take a hard line and argue that, no matter what the eventual benefits of such negotiations, the activity of governments keeping secrets from its citizens is sinister, or we might take a less extreme, but still principled, position that the duplicitous relevant activity in the political case is inherently sinister *because acting duplicitously is something our elected representatives should never engage in*. Politicians, such an argument would go, have a duty to be honest with their constituents – no matter what the cost – and, thus, merely acting suspiciously is acting in a sinister way *for a politician*. However, the act of being duplicitous in a political setting cannot reasonably be regarded as sinister, until we know more about why the politicians are being duplicitous. Vanakin uses secret societies, like the Freemasons, as an example of organisations whose actions we treat as being morally suspicious because they are undertaken in secret (Vanakin, 1991). This is interesting, because such organisations are often suspected of acting immorally *purely because they keep their activities secret*. As such, secrecy here leads to a suspicion that the actions being undertaken are morally suspect, but such secrecy need not be construed as being necessarily sinister. The activity of organising a surprise birthday party for a five-year-old *and assiduously denying the impending occurrence of it to the said child* is suspicious and we should agree that, in this case, the activity is not sinister. We should deny, then, that conspiracies, as a class of activity, are inherently sinister. Some might be, but it is not necessary that they *all* are.

Indeed, there are numerous examples of clearly conspiratorial activities that were suspicious but not sinister. Take, for example, the work by the women and men at Bletchley Park in breaking the ENIGMA cipher. This was – from the perspective of the Allied Forces, at least – a praiseworthy and non-sinister activity, despite the secrecy involved in keeping their work hidden from both the Nazi Command and the general British populace. It has all the hallmarks of a conspiracy, but the activity itself was not sinister, merely suspicious.

It is the role of secrecy here that creates this tension between an activity being suspicious and an activity being thought of as sinister. Secretive activity is inherently suspicious precisely because when we do not know what is happening, why it is happening or who is behind the activity we are justifiably suspicious. If there is anything that is suspicious about acting conspiratorially, it does not automatically make it *morally* suspect, however. One can act suspiciously without acting in a morally transgressive way. It would be a mistake to conflate suspiciousness with *moral suspiciousness*. Indeed, a surprise party, no matter how virtuous the intention of the organisers, might be construed as being sinister or suspect *to the person for whom it is organised*. However, it would be a mistake to think that, just because you are suspicious about the why, how or who of some event, this means the event was brought about in a sinister fashion: to make that claim we have to say something about the intent of the agents.

Lee Basham has even considered the possibility that there could be conspiracies of goodness (Basham, 2011, p. 55). He uses as an example the practice of hiding your religious affiliation in times of oppression as an example of conspiratorial activity that is not inherently sinister. While hiding your religious affiliation in a time of oppression is a suspicious thing, it only qualifies as sinister with respect to the people who are oppressing you. Indeed, the people who are oppressing you are probably oppressing you precisely because they take it that your religious affiliation is of a sinister kind. However, hiding your religious affiliation is, for you, a sensible thing to do. While it might make you act suspiciously, it does not mean you are necessarily acting sinisterly. This shows just how easy it is to conflate suspiciousness with being sinister. We should not make the same mistake when it comes to talk of suspicious conspiratorial activity – which is undertaken in secret – and the subset of such activity, sinister conspiracies.

Conclusion

To recapitulate, the definition of what counts as a conspiracy theory being defended here is any explanation of an event that cites the existence of a conspiracy as a salient cause.

This is a very general definition that does not adhere to the pejorative notion that such theories are *prima facie* suspicious. In part, this is because it relies on a very general definition of what counts as a conspiracy, which is:

1. there exists (or existed) some set of agents with a plan;
2. steps have been taken by the agents to minimise public awareness of what they are up to; and
3. some end is or was desired by the agents.

Under this definition, surprise parties can count as conspiracies, given that they are typically arranged in secret by persons seeking to hide the existence of the party from the intended victim, and there is no problem with the notion of 'conspiracies of goodness'. It is not essential to think of conspiratorial activity as sinister. It is true that we are suspicious of such activity, but that is a function of the said activity being secretive, rather than because it is morally suspect.

We can understand why conspiracy theories are often thought of as sinister and non-trivial explanations of conspiratorial activity because we are, rightfully, concerned with the class of political conspiracy theories (those claims of conspiracy about our public institutions that, if they were true, would threaten our understanding of and trust in the political realm). However, if we are interested in examining whether our suspicion of such conspiracy theories is really warranted, we should focus the debate about the warrant of conspiracy theories on what is wrong – if anything – with *specific* conspiracy theories, rather than summarily dealing with conspiracy theories in general. The best way to do this is to focus on the epistemic issues of the wider class of conspiratorial explanations, of which institutional and political conspiracy theories are a subset.

This is why we should be interested in working with a perfectly general definition of 'conspiracy theory', one that subsumes under it not just the pejoratively labelled 'conspiracy theories' but also those historical explanations of pith and moment that happen to cite conspiracies as salient causes. Now, while many of us can rattle off a list of historically verified theories about conspiracies – such as the Moscow Trials or some piece of Elizabethan treachery – we cannot, and indeed should not, expect our interlocutors to share the same interest in conspiratorial history. However, if we use examples like surprise parties they will – with a little bit of imagination – also be able to come up with similar examples and say: 'Hang on, these things are more common than one might think!'

After all, for most kinds of explanation (e.g. psychological explanations, historical explanations) we tend to assume that some will be warranted, and some will not. We should, then, regard conspiratorial explanations in the same manner. There are a number of well-accepted, warranted explanations of events in history, politics and the like that cite conspiracies as a salient cause. If we accept that conspiracies, like the organisation of surprise parties, occur outside the political realm and are not inherently sinister activities, then suggesting that there is a conspiracy in existence here and now and that it can be used to explain the occurrence of some event becomes a much less startling claim than it would be if we restricted our talk of conspiracies to a specific class of, say, institutional and sinister activity.

The focus, then, on surprise parties as an example of a kind of conspiratorial activity sets the bar low precisely because it allows us to analyse all kinds of conspiratorial activity and theories thereof. Our analysis should be on the question: 'When, if ever, is it rational to believe a conspiracy theory?' Although the focus on institutional conspiracy theories is understandable – because we should be worried about claims of institutional conspiratorial activity – it risks skewing the debate towards claims we are intuitively suspicious of (institutional conspiracies) rather than asking whether our suspicions about conspiracy theories generally are justified.

So, although it is true that the definition of a conspiracy theory defended here – any explanation of an event that cites a conspiracy as a salient cause – does not conform to ordinary (and pejorative) usage, it is going to be easier to address the question of when it is rational, or irrational, to believe such an explanation, *if we take an interest in the broad class of explanations covered by this definition* rather than operating with a pejorative reading of 'conspiracy theory'. After all, anyone with even a smidgen of imagination should be able to point to some conspiratorial explanation that they consider to be a warranted explanation of an event, whether it is a historical explanation of some Elizabethan treachery, the recent actions of a government hiding trade deals with a foreign nation, or an academic department trying to bamboozle their dean. If people want to continue using the term 'conspiracy theory' as a pejorative, so be it, but we should not use that as a reason to dismiss belief in particular conspiratorial explanations out of hand.

5 Conspirators, and What They Want

Conspiracy theories explain the occurrence of some event or state of affairs with the claim that some set of conspirators intended it.[1] Take, for example, the cluster of New World Order conspiracy theories that are behind some – but by no means all – of the rhetoric of the 'Occupy' movement. Members of Occupy are concerned with increasing wealth inequality, and some of the protesters place the blame squarely upon Western governments, which, they claim, are deliberately funnelling money from ordinary workers to the already wealthy top 1 per cent of the population. For some members of the Occupy movement, the fact that the rich were getting richer and the poor were getting poorer was evidence of a conspiracy by political elites, who are themselves members of the aforementioned 1 per cent, to bring about a New World Order based upon debt-slavery: the poor would effectively be forever in debt to the rich and thus subservient towards them.

This particular kind of conspiracy theory is routinely dismissed by the said political elites as vapid and unwarranted because it ignores the complexity of modern economic policies. Skeptics of this particular conspiracy theory claim that such conspiracy theorists mistake the *unintended consequences* of economic activity – massive wealth inequalities – for a sinister plot.

There is something to be said for this kind of reply. Working out what a group of actors intended can be difficult. Sometimes this is rightfully used as a reason to dismiss explanations that rely on saying that someone desired or intended some event. After all, just because someone or some group desires some end, this does not mean they will get what they want. History is littered with plots that went awry, where the outcome of some caper turned out to be quite different from what the conspirators originally desired.

Sometimes our suspicion of explanations that rely on claims of 'they desired it' are based upon knowing that there is some alternative, not overtly intentional, account to hand that turns out to be the better explanation.

Intentions are often taken to be mysterious things. Conspiracy theories might even be the most problematic kind of intentional explanation, given that conspirators *work in secret* to minimise public knowledge of what they are up to. Working out what conspirators secretly intend may look like an insurmountable task, if the conspirators have even some success in keeping their activity private. However, as this chapter will show, the fact that conspiracy theories often make reference to the intentions of conspirators is no real problem.

For some, the issue this chapter is addressing is an issue that they feel does not need attending to. Either they will be perfectly *au fait* with some kind of Belief/Desire psychology – some account that allows you to say something about how beliefs or desires can be detected, even in the case of conspiracies – or they will think that we do not need to talk about the intentions of conspirators when talking about whether it is rational to come to the belief that a conspiracy exists (because, in the end, the evidence for a conspiracy will be documentary rather than based upon an inference to mysterious 'mental states'). Perhaps you might want to skip ahead to the next chapter, where we will examine whether our belief in the openness of our contemporary Western-style democracies gives us reason to treat claims of conspiracy dismissively. Then again, you might decide you want to know what the fuss might be about.

Conspiracy theories and historical explanations

Historical explanations account for the occurrence of some event in terms of a sequence of prior events that led to it. Historical explanations do not need to be about distant historical events. We can give a historical explanation about the building of the military complex or the death of a notable figure like Julius Caesar. Historical explanations do not even need to be explanations about events in history – conceived broadly as the study of development of human society – since we can also give historical explanations for the developmental evolution of the flagellum or why some organisation ended up endorsing some sale stratagem or grading mechanism.

It is obvious that this is a broad – but not overly so – definition of what counts as a historical explanation. Conspiracy theories are a kind of historical explanation that posit a conspiracy as a salient cause of the event we want to explain. So, for example, the conspiracy theory that claims that the recent increase in the prevalence of autism in the West is due to the early childhood vaccination schedule – particularly the MMR (Measles, Mumps and Rubella) vaccine – explains the increased prevalence of autism in the population by reference to a conspiracy to encourage vaccinating children *despite the adverse side-effects of said vaccines*. We can explain the increase in autism diagnoses, according to vaccine conspiracy theorists, by looking at the history of the early childhood vaccination schedule.

The thesis that conspiracy theories are explanations – let alone *historical explanations* – is not one shared by all conspiracy theory theorists or skeptics. Some have argued that conspiracy theories only *resemble* explanations. For example, Victoria Emma Págan argues that, while conspiracy theories look like explanations, they are really theories that reflect the concerns of the day and age. Págan, like Cass Sunstein (as we saw in Chapter 2), believes that conspiracy theorists suffer from a kind of 'crippled epistemology'. As such, conspiracy theorists' particular conspiracy theories are not based upon the evidence but are, as Págan puts it, 'a particular kind of political myth in which authority is mutated by the absence of positive evidence' (Pagán, 2012, p. 7). Belief in conspiracy theories, then, is a reaction to a lack of knowledge about why some event came to pass, coloured by what the conspiracy theorist is most concerned about.

Joseph Roisman runs a similar line. He associates belief in conspiracy theories with conspiracist ideation and then argues that the *rhetoric* of conspiracy arises as a reaction to a crisis (Roisman, 2006, pp. 156–160). While this suggests that Roisman considers conspiracy talk to be *prima facie* suspicious, he does think that the evidence for a given conspiracy theory will sometimes show that there really is a conspiracy in existence. It is just that claims of conspiracy are often attempts to place blame for the ills in society upon the usual scapegoats or shadowy cabals (Roisman, 2006, pp. 156–160).

There is something slightly odd about this kind of position, which is a chicken-and-the-egg-style problem: what is it that concerns conspiracy theorists such that they start blaming conspiracies for their worries? What comes first? The suspicion that there exists a conspiracy *or* the paranoid style of the conspiracy theorist? If it is the latter, then conspiracy theorists could be regarded as acting irrationally. If it is the former, then maybe some conspiracy talk is misguided, but it might also point towards very real issues in the society in which the conspiracy theorist lives.

Susan Feldman argues that a subset of conspiracy theories – 'counterfact theories' – are 'claims of fact which run contrary to accepted factual claims and their evidence' (Feldman, 2011, p. 15) and are not really explanations but, rather, expressions of the worries of certain conspiracy theorists. Feldman's worry about counterfact theories is similar to the kinds of worries both Págan and Roisman express about conspiracy talk: some conspiracy theories seem to exist not as *the* explanation of an event but, rather, as challenges or opposition to some well-accepted explanation.

The notion that conspiracy theories are theories that exist in opposition to what we might call an 'official theory' (or 'official story') is a commonly held intuition, one that arguably comes from understanding belief in conspiracy theories in conspiracist terms (conspiracy theorists are in some way suffering from a psychological defect, which makes them see conspiracies where there are none). In this respect, however, the kind of worry expressed by Págan, and to a lesser extent Roisman and Feldman, is a worry about conspiracy theorists, rather than a worry about conspiracy theories. As we saw in Chapter 3, it is a mistake to conflate worries about certain conspiracy theorists with worries about conspiracy theories, because we risk confusing the psychology of certain conspiracy theorists with the epistemic considerations about whether belief in particular conspiracy theories can be rational. It may well be the case that conspiracy theorists of some stripe have an acute fear of certain parts of the population – arguably many of the vaccine conspiracy theories stem from the worry that the medical establishment claims to know more about the health of your children than you do – but this tells us more about the beliefs and desires of the people who posit conspiracy theories than it does about whether the said conspiracy theories are warranted.

Intentions and conspirators

Some historical explanations are examples of intentional explanations. Intentional explanations explain events by citing the intentions – the desires and beliefs of agents – as causes (via the causing of actions) of the event in question. Conspiracy theories are examples of intentional explanations because they cite the existence of a conspiracy, an activity that is undertaken in secret by conspirators who *intend, or at least desire, to achieve some end*.

In order to satisfy some claim of conspiracy, we need to say that the following three conditions must be met:

1. *The Conspirators Condition* – There exists (or existed) some set of agents with a plan,

2. *The Secrecy Condition* – Steps have been taken by the agents to minimise public awareness of what they are up to, and
3. *The Goal Condition* – Some end is or was desired by the agents.

The *Goal Condition* – the claim about some end being desired by the conspirators – is doing a lot of work here, given that, in order to satisfy some claim that a conspiracy exists, we need to say something about agents *desiring or intending some end.* This requirement might give us reason to be suspicious of conspiracy theories *in general,* because inferring to the intentions – the causative beliefs and desires – of mysterious conspirators seems as though it should be a problem.

Steve Clarke has expressed a form of this worry. Clarke takes conspiracy theories to be 'dispositional explanations', which is another way to gloss conspiracy theories as intentional explanations. He writes:

> As explanations, conspiracy theories are highly dispositional. When conspiracies occur it is because conspirators intend them to occur and act on their intentions. The conspiratorial dispositions of the conspirators play the role of the cause in a typical explanation that involves a conspiracy. (Clarke, 2002, p. 145)

For example, Marcus Brutus, Cassius Longinus, Servilius Casca and their fellow senators had the *disposition* to kill the Roman dictator, Julius Caesar. This disposition was a cause in the chain of events that led to the conspiracy that saw Caesar assassinated. Clarke contrasts such dispositional explanations with what he calls 'situational explanations'. Situational explanations cite a situation, such as the historical context under which an event occurred. The situational explanation for the assassination of Julius Caesar, for example, would place Caesar's assassination *in the context of the series of popular uprisings and social disarray during the era of the Late Roman Republic.* It was this situation – a barely functioning Roman government and the rise of a new kind of demagogue popular with the people but not the traditional ruling class – which was the ultimate cause of Caesar's death.

Clarke argues that we should prefer situational explanations over dispositional ones. Understanding the situation in which an event occurred, he claims, produces a more unified explanation than claiming that someone *intended* the event to happen. Clarke uses this move to argue that, since most of the rivals to conspiracy theories are situational in character, this entitles us to a *prima facie* suspicion of conspiracy theories *in general* (S. Clarke, 2002, p. 145).

There is, however, no obvious contrast between a dispositional and a situational explanation. Any explanation might well be an example of both. For example, the orthodox history of the assassination of Julius Caesar phrases the intentions of the conspirators with respect to the historical situation. Marcus Brutus, Servilius Casca and Cassius Longinus desired to assassinate the Roman dictator not just because they wanted Caesar dead but also because of the political situation Rome was in at the time. So, while conspiracy theories almost certainly do invoke intentions (or dispositions, qua Clarke), this does not bar them from also invoking situational factors.

It is not even clear that conspiracy theories are any more dispositional than their rivals, or that the said rivals are any more situational. David Coady writes:

> [I]t is not clear that there really is a tendency for conspiracy theories to be more dispositional than rival theories. Although Clarke cites examples in support of his position, other examples seem to cast doubt on it. The official explanation of John F. Kennedy's murder, for example, seems just as dispositional as its conspiratorial rivals. All explanations agree that someone or some group of people intended the murder to occur and acted on their intentions. A disposition to murder the president seems to play an equally fundamental explanatory role in all accounts of that event, whether they are conspiratorial or not. (Coady, 2006b, p. 8)

Coady is right: Clarke's thesis about the overly dispositional nature of conspiracy theories is not borne out by investigation of actual conspiracy theories and their rivals. Clarke has since retracted his thesis about the dispositional nature of conspiracy theories, albeit only slightly (S. Clarke, 2006). He now argues that the dispositionality of conspiracy theories is really a problem to do with the *psychology of belief in conspiracy theories*, rather than a problem with conspiracy theories *as explanations*. Once again, what has been taken to be a problem with belief in the class of things we call 'conspiracy theories' actually ends up being a potential problem with the psychology of certain conspiracy theorists.

Desires and ends

While we should not reject conspiracy theories *merely* because they are examples of intentional explanations, there is another, related worry that might concern us. Conspiracy theories are examples of explanations that refer to secretive activity, and so we should ask: 'How do we infer to the specific ends or goals that drive the *secretive activities* of conspirators?'

Let us regard an end – at least, for our purposes here – as a desire that a certain state of affairs be realised or come about. Our question, then, is not just about the methods we might employ to uncover desires of conspirators, but also about who the people are who are qualified to make claims about them.

One way to approach this might be to ask what would be rational for an agent to do, given the desires (and other mental states) that they might have. For example, the conspirators who killed Julius Caesar probably believed that their action was the most rational course of action available to them, if we think of believing that killing Caesar would fulfil their desire to return Rome to senatorial rule. However, while the assassins might have thought that killing Caesar would lead to the return of senatorial control of the Roman Republic, we now know that the conspirators' plan failed because what they desired and what they achieved were two different things. When Caesar was killed, control of the Republic ended up being cemented in Caesar's chosen successor. This obtaining of an inadvertent end, however, should not be considered a problem for the claim of conspiracy, because, suitably filled out, we can still say that Brutus and his associates acted rationally. This is because:

1. They believed that the plebeians and the patrician classes opposed the now-permanent dictator status Caesar had awarded himself, and
2. They did not appreciate:
   a) just how much support Caesar had with respect to the plebeian class, and
   b) just how politically disenfranchised the plebeian class felt under the old, senatorial regime, and
3. They did not know that Marcus Antonius (Mark Antony) would use the sentiment of the plebeian class against the (patrician-class) conspirators.

So, we can say that the conspirators *thought* they were taking the most rational course of action *and* claim that the conspirators were mistaken in their rational deliberations about what they would achieve by killing Julius Caesar. This is because we *now* have access to information suggesting that the conspirators had certain beliefs about the political climate of Rome, which – with the benefit of hindsight and the surviving documentary evidence – turned out to be faulty.

When it comes to the well-accepted explanation about the death of Julius Caesar (which happens to be a conspiracy under the definition we are operating with), we have a lot of evidence we can refer to when judging claims about the conspirators and what they wanted. Some of the evidence includes reports and excerpts of letters written by the conspirators while in exile to their supporters in Rome. If we trust the correspondence to be accurate, it is not hard to gauge some of the intentions of the conspirators both before and after the assassination. They did, after all, write about both their plans and the aftermath of the said plans.

Sometimes, however, we must infer what some historical actor thought or believed with little, if any, personal documentary evidence. Some might think that in such a case there is a danger that an inference to the intentions of some historical actor will smack of *post facto* reasoning. Such an inference might assume that the agent or agents chose to act in a rational manner, relative to their objectives and the beliefs they held at the time, and the story we then tell about those intentions might *merely* fit the facts. If we are to avoid such claims of *post facto* reasoning – which is a charge levelled at many a conspiracy theorist – we need to come out with an account of how we can infer the desires or beliefs of agents who are keeping their activities and desires secret.

Conspiring together

To understand how we might infer to the secretive desires of conspirators, let us consider the following issue: conspiratorial activity is a kind of group activity. So, when we are appraising talk about some claim of conspiracy, we are not typically dealing with the intentions and desires of a single conspirator but, rather, a group of agents working together.

Imagine that an academic department is discussing how to standardise grades across papers of a certain level. The department has a meeting, and a model for grade standardisation is put forward. It is rigorously debated: while certain members of the department are for it, some are against it and a few are on the fence. Towards the end of the meeting a vote is held, and the model is narrowly voted in. Six months later, the dean of the faculty asks the head of the department how the model was arrived at, and the head of department simply says that the department agreed to the new model.

When the head of department says 'The department agreed to the new model', she is not, in any real way, guilty of a sin of omission. A more fleshed out story would have the head of department explain that the vote was narrow, but, assuming that the department and its members agree that a democratic vote mechanism, with associated discussion, is an acceptable decision procedure for matters such as these, saying 'The department agreed to the new model' adequately describes what went on at the meeting.

Yet, it is also true that the claim 'The department agreed to the new model' might suggest to someone outside the department a degree of consistency that we would not find if we were to poll each member of the department separately. Some of the members might well have strenuously opposed the new model and think it abhorrent. Others may have voted for it merely because it was better than the previous model, but not as good as the other options on the table, and so forth.

The point of the example is this: the individual members of the department, through joint activity, could be made to look as though they had adopted the model due to a common cause, despite their professed differences. Given that situations like the above state of affairs are fairly common, we should be very wary indeed of assuming that members of groups who work together all share the same wants, desires, dispositions. This adds a further wrinkle to providing an account of what it is the agents intended. While the members of the group might jointly perform an action, their individual motivations for performing that action may not just be different but, in some cases, wildly so. Indeed, some individuals in the group may not be motivated to perform it at all. Inferring what an individual conspirator desired will be difficult where there is no record of that individual's desires. For example, we still have references and quotes from the letters that Marcus Brutus sent to his disciples following his exile from Rome after the assassination of Julius Caesar. From these references we can infer a lot about what Brutus desired from the conspiracy. Servilius Casca, however, left behind no diaries or letters, so we cannot – outside of his complicity in the plot to kill Caesar – say much about what he intended from the conspiracy.

Problems to do with inferring to the individual desires of the members of group are not just issues to do with inferring to the desires of conspirators. Rather, they are problems common to intentional explanations *of any kind of collective activity*. Given that this is a general problem, it is not at all clear that conspiracy theories suffer from it especially. It is, simply, an issue to do with just how well the explainer, whether a *mere* conspiracy theorist or a qualified historian or political scientist, is able to infer to the desires, either individually or collectively, of the agents in question.

Doublethinking

Here is a further complication. Imagine a situation in which the members of some conspiracy are not fully aware of the intended goal of the conspiracy. It is not hard to find examples of this in the literature. Indeed, the full story of the assassination of Julius Caesar appears to rely on some of the conspirators having different desires from the others. The claim that Brutus, Casca and Longinus were simply seeking to restore the Roman Republic is not necessarily the whole story. How do we know this? Well, amongst the correspondence Marcus Brutus sent to his supporters in Rome we can find evidence that suggests he sought the death of Caesar because he thought that, following Caesar's death, the people of Rome would make him dictator.

Was Brutus's desire to become dictator the actual intention behind the conspiracy to kill Caesar? We will probably never know. However, it is not hard to imagine a situation in which two of the other conspirators, Servilius Casca and Cassius Longinus, talked long and hard about the need to free Rome from the thrall of dictatorship and knew that Brutus was acting merely for personal gain. Perhaps they downplayed Brutus's talk of personal glory. Maybe they ignored it, hoping that in the aftermath Brutus would see sense.

Now, this issue of 'doublethinking it', as we might call it,[2] is of real historical and political significance. For example, it seems possible (which is not to say it is likely) that the members of the respective Bush and Blair administrations – who spiced up or doctored the dossier about the alleged weapons of mass destruction in Iraq back in 2002 – were not consciously lying about the purported existence of the said weapons of mass destruction, even though some of the members of those administrations knew that some of the things they were claiming were false.

This, then, is an interesting case that throws some of what we have been talking about into sharp relief, as this is a good example of how conspiracies are made up of multiple conspirators who may well have slightly different agendas. Brutus was just one member of the conspiracy, and he may very well have intended a different end from the collective work than Casca and Longinus, even though they shared a common purpose, the death of the dictator, Julius Caesar. In the same manner, certain members of the respective Bush and Blair administrations may have realised that the intelligence they were receiving about the weapons of mass destruction was not entirely credible, but, as they believed they had other reasons for supporting the invasion – be they moral, monetary or something else entirely – they doublethunk[3] (or doublethought) it and endorsed the 'evidence' despite its lack of merit.

It might be considered controversial to say that the justification for the invasion of Iraq – based upon a dodgy dossier – was a clear-cut example of a conspiracy. If you do think that the rationale for the invasion of Iraq was due to a conspiracy by members of the political establishment of both the USA and the UK, then you might even argue that the notion of doublethinking here excuses what happened. However, we can accept that doublethinking happens – because explanations of collective activity are messy – without endorsing doublethinking as an excuse.

For one thing, there is always an onus on people making decisions to act responsibly. If Casca and Longinus knew Brutus had goals that were at loggerheads to their own, then we can ask what they would have done had the conspiracy resulted in both Caesar's death and the Senate once again taking up the reins of government in Rome. How would they have handled Brutus and his desire for personal power? Would they have turned against him?

For another thing, just because an organisation has structural issues, this does not in any way excuse the attendant problems such issues present. One (very) charitable story about the way the doctored dossier was received in Washington, DC was that, while the field operatives in Iraq knew it could not be true, the members of both the board of the CIA and the Office of the President assumed the intel within it was sound. After all, it had come from what seemed like appropriate sources and had been endorsed by who they considered to be the right people. According to this version of the story, the problem with the dossier was not just that it had been doctored but that the structure of the US intelligence community was such that they took certain endorsements as trumping what their very own field operatives were telling them. However, while this would explain why the dossier was well received in Washington, DC, it does not provide any moral justification for the resulting action. We will examine this issue in more depth in Chapter 7, when we discuss the role that endorsements play in conspiracy and non-conspiracy theories.

Qualified conspiracy theorists

Inferring what some agent or set of agents desire is tricky, whether or not we are talking about some conspiracy theory. So, what can we do? Well, we could consider what it is historians do when they offer explanations for historical events. Many explanations in history rest upon claims that an event occurred *because some agent, or set of agents, intended it.* If we can give an account of why it is that historians can make reliable inferences to the intentions of historical agents, then perhaps we can use that analysis to explain how we (or some suitably qualified expert) could do the same when it comes to conspiracy theories. Such a story might also tell us why it is that we are sometimes wary of such inferences when they are made by conspiracy theorists of a certain stripe.

Historians, typically, immerse themselves in the era they study, reading the extant literature of the time, the histories written by the then-contemporary historians, the commentaries on those histories, and so forth. While historians cannot know exactly what some historical agent believed at a particular time, they are, typically, better placed than a layperson to infer things about the past. This includes being better qualified to infer the kinds of beliefs, desires and intentions historical agents might have had. We can extend this argument by saying the same kind of thing about political scientists, sociologists and even journalists: with the aid of the right kind of training, these kinds of specialists can make plausible inferences to the intentions, beliefs and desires of the kinds of agents they routinely study or work with.

Many historians will be conspiracy theorists in their professional role. Historians who are interested in the various treacheries of the Elizabethan Age will turn out to be conspiracy theorists, because a great many of the explanatory hypotheses that account for those treacheries will be explanations of events that cite the existence of a conspiracy as a salient cause. So, to be a historian is to be a suitably qualified authority in an area of history that may well touch on conspiracy theories.

The common usage of conspiracy theorist – someone who believes or advocates belief in some conspiracy theory – suggests, if not relevant expertise, a particular interest in some conspiracy theory. A conspiracy theorist is the kind of person who, presumably, knows sufficient about some alleged conspiracy such that they believe they are justified in believing in it. However, unlike, say, history or sociology, there are no accredited courses or qualifications in conspiracy theorising. Being interested in a conspiracy theory does not automatically make you an expert. You might be interested in the history of Ancient Rome, and can tell many an exciting story of political intrigue at the end of the Roman Republic, but this does not make you a qualified historian with respect to Roman history. At best, you might be an interested amateur, and must refer back to qualified experts if you want to know whether the 'Lives of the Latter Caesars' accurately relates details about the history of the Roman Empire or whether it is an elaborate forgery.

So, while we can say that people like Glenn Beck and Alex Jones may know a lot about certain kinds of contemporary conspiracy theories about the nature of and intent of the US government – and they might even consider themselves experts in their field – the fact that they are interested in conspiracy theories does not make them qualified experts in conspiracy theories.

This is not an immediately obvious point. Arguably, ordinary people are good at inferring to the beliefs and desires of others from their behaviour. I know, for example, when the retail assistant I have just met is bored, based upon their body language. One plausible account of why we are good at inferring such things is that we develop a folk psychology from our daily interactions in the public realm. However, working out what a sales assistant thinks of you or their job is a different affair from inferring the collective desires of secretive actors. Conspiracies, like a lot of secretive activity, are private: they are a subversion or pathology of normal public interaction. Without some further qualification as to how a lay member of the public can infer what some secret group of agents desires (which might be as easy as saying: 'I found this document stating their intentions' or as hard as: 'Knowing the historical/sociological/political circumstances and some key facts about the figures involved, it seems they might well have intended to conspire at this time...'), we should be *cautious* but not *dismissive* of the claims of *unqualified* conspiracy theorists.

Ordinary people like ourselves can detect cases of secretive activity. The target of a surprise party need not be a trained journalist to think her suspicions about her friends' weird activity prior to her birthday indicate that something is being planned. As such, the caution being advocated for here simply recognises that ordinary reasoners, when it comes to complex social or historical phenomena, may be insensitive to alternative hypotheses, or lack sufficient background knowledge to be able to tell whether some event was the result of secret plans or just a coincidence (or some other alternative explanation).

This is not an arduous burden. If there is a conspiracy about my family, then being a member of my family may well be enough to warrant some claim about what my ancestors desired to achieve (as long as I have made some study of my family and its history). Of course, if a conspiracy theory is about some close friends of yours, whose behaviour together has often been successfully predicted by you in the past, then you may be a suitably qualified expert to rule on the credibility of that conspiracy theory. Not all qualifications are of the sort that can be framed or entered into a *curriculum vitae*. Sometimes being an appropriately qualified agent will be easy. In some cases it may not be. Conspiracy theories concerning the machinations of the Stasi in East Germany, with the elaborate conspiracies, double bluffs and disinformation campaigns, will likely require the conspiracy theorist to be conversant with the history and sociology of Germany in the 1960s and 1970s. This might be as 'easy' (so to speak) as having grown up in Germany at the time or as hard as studying the subject at school. Given the claim iterated throughout this book that we are all conspiracy theorists of some stripe, and that some of us will have warranted beliefs in particular conspiracy theories, some of us will either have discharged the burden of proof and shown that our inference to the existence of a conspiracy is warranted or have acquired our warranted belief from someone else who has discharged the burden of proof.

The worry, it seems, when we talk about conspiracy theorists – and when we are concerned as to whether someone has a warranted inference to the existence of some conspiracy, we are concerned with their inferential practices – is that we have a tendency to associate conspiracy theorists with conspiracists. We worry that people like Alex Jones and Glenn Beck see conspiracies everywhere not because there really are conspiracies everywhere but because they are suffering from conspiracism.

It may well be the case that Jones and Beck are conspiracists, despite their wealth of knowledge on matters to do with government cover-ups, financial irregularities and the like. However, their arguments must be assessed nonetheless, so we can test the strength of the inferences they make towards particular claims of conspiracy. If there is one criticism we can easily level at both Jones and Beck, it is that they implicitly claim to be specialists on a whole raft of matters: history, political studies, journalism, sociology and the like (given the kinds of conspiracy theories they typically advocate). If our skepticism of Jones and Beck is not merely based upon thinking they are conspiracists, it might, charitably, be based upon thinking they claim to be specialists in a dazzling array of subjects, such that their knowledge of the said subjects cannot be that deep.

Beck and Jones also dismiss the views of other experts who disagree with their claims of conspiracy, and maybe this is yet another reason why we think so poorly of two of the USA's leading conspiracy theorists. However, there is a problem with this response: hardly any historians admit to believing that some of their conspiratorial explanations are conspiracy theories. As such, if, say, historians are sometimes qualified conspiracy theorists, then we should expect the historical literature to be littered with books like *Conspiracy Theories of the Roman Republic* and *The Conspiracy Theories Which Gave Birth to the First Glorious French Revolution*. Yet many historians seem loath to identify as conspiracy theorists. Victoria Emma Págan, as we have already seen, argues against conspiracy theories as being in any way examples of good historical explanations. Joseph Roisman, similarly, views conspiracy talk *generally* as suspicious.

Now, historians might fail to admit they are conspiracy theorists because they take a dim view of conspiracy theories. They might, as we will see in Chapter 8, believe that their conspiratorial explanations are, in some sense, 'official' and thus not the kind of thing we would typically call a 'conspiracy theory'. The fact that many qualified historians do not identify as conspiracy theorists is not a problem for the warrant of conspiracy theories but, rather, a problem that centres around few academics wanting to be thought of a conspiracy theorists. Perhaps prominent historians do not characterise their explanations of the D-Day landings as examples of conspiracy theories, despite the fact that the said landings were the result of an elaborate conspiracy to mislead the Axis Forces in World War II. If *we* recognise that these theories are conspiracy theories *and* our reason for accepting that they are conspiratorial is due to the qualified inferences of specially trained historians, then we have grounds for thinking the said conspiracy theories are warranted.

Conclusion

Conspiracy theories, as putative explanations for some event, cite the existence of conspiracies as the salient cause, where part of the 'salient cause' is the collective desires of the conspirators to achieve some end. Talk of desires and intentions with respect to explanations is a fraught business, and there is an understandable suspicion about explanations that rely upon them. Given that conspiracy theories refer to the intentions not just of an individual desiring some end but of a collection of conspirators who are working together to achieve some goal, it is quite understandable that people might very well throw up their hands and think that the intentionality of such explanations is a reason to be suspicious of the class of conspiratorial explanations. When conspiracy theorists of a certain stripe blame the massive economic inequalities in the West upon a conspiracy by the rich 1 per cent, certain skeptics worry that the conspiracy theory:

a) downplays the messy nature of modern economic policies and

b) overstates (or mistakes) the desire of the rich to get richer with a plot by the rich to make the poor poorer.

These are interesting concerns. Any conspiracy theory about the real reason behind the massive wealth inequalities in our societies will need to take into account the nature of economic policy, the process that generates such policy and the fact that policies sometimes have unforeseen consequences. However, this does not mean that we cannot also ask: 'Is our current economic situation the result of purposeful design?' In the same respect, it is not unreasonable for those who are skeptical of claims of conspiracy to say: 'How could you know that?' After all, working out what some agent or set of agents intended is tricky.

It should be obvious from the preceding discussion that the intentional aspect of conspiracy theories is not a real problem for conspiracy theories. There are two reasons to think this. First, this is a problem that affects explanations of complex social phenomena in general. As such, this is not a problem specific to conspiracy theories. Second, it is a problem that seems soluble with respect to a class of well-regarded explanations, historical explanations. As such, if we can advance an argument as to how historians can talk about and work with the beliefs and desires of historical agents with respect to historical explanations, then we should be able to tell a story as to how we can talk about and work with the beliefs and desires of conspirators with respect to conspiracy theories.

Analysing the kind of expertise historians have with respect to appraising the intentions of historical actors is useful when thinking about the relevant expertise we should expect from conspiracy theorists when advocating some conspiracy theory. We should expect conspiracy theorists *who advocate belief in a particular conspiracy theory* to have the right kind of expertise (or to be able to point towards someone with the right kind of expertise) to show that their particular inference to a conspiracy is warranted. Many historians will be qualified conspiracy theorists, for example, as will some sociologists, political theorists and the like.

Now, some are going to argue that we are requiring too much of the qualified conspiracy theorist. It is true that most of us are good at folk psychology, but to be a suitably qualified conspiracy theorist you need to be able to make claims about the beliefs, intentions and desires of a *set* of secretive agents who are avoiding public scrutiny. This is a much harder task than working out whether your co-worker is being entirely honest with you, or whether your friends are organising a party behind your back. However, working out the intentions of conspirators is not an insurmountable task. We just need to recognise that explanations of collective activity can be messy and that we might need to refer to the expertise of others. Just how we recognise such expertise will be the topic of Chapter 7.

At the beginning of this chapter it was suggested that, for some, this talk of inferring the desires and beliefs of mysterious conspirators is unnecessary for the analysis of whether belief in conspiracy theories can ever be warranted. We can, in most cases, infer that a conspiracy exists based upon the documentary evidence. There is something to this argument: inferring that person x or group y desire some end might tell us that they want to conspire, but this does not tell us that they are conspiring (or that their conspiracy was successful). The wealthy 1 per cent may well want to get ever richer. Perhaps they also desire to make the poor ever poorer. Even if we can show that this is what they want, this does not tell us that the economic circumstances we find ourselves in are the result of the design of the 1 per cent.

Working out what some set of conspirators desired is simply one kind of evidence we might use to show that some conspiracy theory is warranted. In some cases we might not be able to say anything about the beliefs and desires of the conspirators we think are behind some conspiracy. In other cases we might be able to talk about their beliefs and desires only after we have shown that they were involved in some conspiracy. As such, there are other kinds of evidence we might bring to bear on the question: 'Is this particular conspiracy theory warranted?' Some of that evidence consists of our beliefs about what kind of society we think we live in, and whether our trust in the public influential institutions that govern us is warranted; this will be the topic of our next chapter.

6
The Public Trust

No matter what your personal view on whether belief conspiracy theories can ever be rational, the fact that conspiracies can and do occur *here and now* – in both the private and public spheres – is challenging for some. For example, if it turns out that pharmaceutical companies are suppressing new and cheaper treatments – in order to increase their profit margins – then that will undermine our trust in the medical establishment. Similarly, if it turns out our government engages in false flag operations – in order to make it easier to pass more draconian laws – then we are going to be suspicious of our lawmakers.

Gordon S. Wood, whom we looked at in Chapter 2, argues that there have been periods of time when it was rational to suspect conspiracies being behind momentous political events. In an era when political power was held by a few, and the systems of power were secretive, it made sense to think that acting conspiratorially was part and parcel of political activity. Wood argues, however, that in the here and now belief in conspiracy theories is suspicious. We now know, so Wood argues, that politics is not so much conspiratorial but, rather, a complex – and sometimes hard to fathom – process in which what is intended very rarely occurs.

Mark Fenster, in *Conspiracy Theories: Secrecy and Power in American Culture*, argues along similar lines: belief in conspiracy theories is symptomatic of the simplistic belief that conspiracies are a powerful factor in politics, which shows that conspiracy theorists do not fully understand the complexity of power in contemporary societies (Fenster, 2008, pp. 89–90).

Fenster, along with conspiracy theory skeptics like Hofstadter and Wood, argues that conspiracy theories are an understandable *but mistaken* reaction to a world where it *seems* that all political and social power is out of our reach. Gordon B. Arnold claims that the public see conspiracy theories as metaphors, which express how individuals have little power in a world filled with external forces beyond their control (Arnold, 2008, p. 4).

All these theorists are expressing the same kind of worry: they believe that conspiracy theorists, when they present a conspiracy theory, are expressing *genuine concerns* about whether we can really trust the powerful institutions that make up our society. However, these concerns are expressed *pathologically* when it comes to the associated belief in conspiracy theories about the said institutions. These conspiracy theory theorists see belief in conspiracy theories through the lens of conspiracism (which we looked at back in Chapter 3). As such, all belief in conspiracies is considered *prima facie* irrational. While Wood, Fenster and Gordon recognise that the worries of conspiracy theorists do have some basis in reality, these fears do not translate to warranted belief in conspiracy theories. However, if we accept the analysis of the earlier chapters, this skepticism of trust in powerful institutions looks as though it might be justifiable with reference to belief in *some* conspiracy theories after all.

Public Trust Skepticism

Not every conspiracy theory alleges the existence of some massive cover-up in the corridors of power. Still, as we have discussed, we often think of conspiracy theories in the terms of *big political conspiracies*. David Icke, for example, argues that we cannot trust our governments because they are institutions designed to trap us into believing our political power is limited. However, critics of Icke have challenged the entire basis for his thesis by arguing that he should doubt his own theory. Given that his evidence for an all-embracing conspiracy theory comes – in part – from his analysis of how the political world operates, he should doubt his theory about the nature of politics. In essence, his critics sometimes think that he should extend his skepticism of the political to his own theory about the political. Icke should be a radical skeptic, doubting everything.

'Why aren't conspiracy theorists skeptical of their own theories?' and 'Why aren't conspiracy theories radical skeptics?' are common complaints levelled against such theorists and belief in conspiracy theories in general. The philosopher Brian L. Keeley is sympathetic to some version of this argument. He identifies what he takes to be a particular problem for belief in conspiracy theories like those proposed by Icke: the increasing skepticism required to believe them. For Keeley, such skepticism is inappropriate because it leads to a loss of trust, not just in the institutions we suspect of being in on the conspiracy, but also of other, related institutions.

This, then, might be a reason for *prima facie* suspicion of conspiracy theories *in general*. As Keeley notes, there is no 'mark of the incredible' that allows us, at first glance, to tell the difference between warranted and unwarranted conspiracy theories (Keeley, 2007, pp. 121, 137). As such, the skepticism generated by belief in unwarranted conspiracy theories translates to the conspiracy theories that are rational to believe.

Keeley's analysis follows in the footsteps of Popper. Popper argues that, as we live in a relatively open society, it would be irrational to believe in conspiracy theories because it would be difficult-cum-impossible for the conspirators to act in secret and consummate their plans (a view that was disputed in Chapter 3). Keeley further develops Popper's analysis of the open society and how it shows that belief in conspiracy theories generally is irrational by introducing what we will label the 'Public Trust Skepticism' thesis (belief in conspiracy theories leads to an increasing distrust in our sources of public data), which we can identify with this argument by Keeley:

> [One] lesson of conspiracy theories is that we ought to recognize such theories as embodying an almost nihilistic degree of skepticism about the behavior and motivations of other people and the social institutions they constitute. To the extent that a conspiracy theory relies on a global and far-reaching doubt of the motives and good will of others, it is akin to global philosophical skepticism. (Keeley, 1999, p. 126)

Keeley's worry about the adverse consequences of belief in conspiracy theories centres upon our relationship and trust in public data: information that originates from, or is transmitted by, powerful public institutions. While most of us accept that businesses and private consortiums engage – perhaps quite frequently – in conspiratorial behaviour, we typically like there to be compelling evidence before we conclude that this happens with any great frequency in the public sphere. To some extent, Keeley (like Popper before him) is not so much concerned about the conspiratorial activity of non-political organisations and individuals, which is why this is a thesis about *public* trust. That being said, there is nothing to stop Keeley from extending his analysis to large corporations and lobby groups – to wit, powerful institutions that are not necessarily public in nature – especially those groups that have some kind of political leverage.

Keeley describes the problem thus:

> [T]he challenge of conspiracy theory is that it forces us to choose between an almost nihilistic degree of skepticism and absurdism: the conspiracy theorist chooses to embrace the hyperskepticism inherent in supposing dissimulation on a truly massive scale (by distrusting the claims of our institutions) over the absurdism of an irrational and essentially meaningless world. (Keeley, 1999, p. 125)

Keeley takes it that this skepticism is an inappropriate attitude for agents like ourselves to hold, not just because it amounts to a global skepticism but because it leads to a kind of conspiratorial thinking – which will be some version of the thesis of conspiracism – which attributes the complexity of the world we live in as being primarily the results of successful conspiracies (Keeley, 1999, p. 124).

The Public Trust Skepticism thesis is supported by a slippery slope argument. The first premise is plausible: 'If you believe certain political conspiracy theories then you will likely doubt some piece of public data that emanates from a public institution.' However, the next premise is doubtful: 'If you doubt some piece of public data, then you will probably come to doubt some other, related piece of public data, or you will come to doubt the utterances of other public institutions which make similar claims, which should, in turn, lead to an ever-increasing skepticism of public data *in general*.'

It is easy to point to examples of conspiracy theorists – like David Icke and Alex Jones – who appear to suspect large swaths of public data as a direct result of belief in their particular conspiracy theories. It is also easy to find examples of conspiracy theorists – like Glenn Beck or New Zealand journalist Ian Wishart – who are suspicious of any public data that emanates from, or is touched by, left-wing institutions, and who are sometimes overly credulous about any information that comes from the right.

It is true that *some* conspiracy theorists are highly skeptical about all sources of public data. However, Keeley's argument that belief in conspiracy theories leads to a radical skepticism of public data *and that this is a reason for taking a dim view of conspiracy theories* is not particularly good.

For one thing, as Charles Pigden argues, our knowledge of history and politics rather undermines Keeley's argument. History is rife with examples of verified conspiracies, and yet we do not seem to have developed the kind of radical skepticism that Keeley is worried about.

> [W]e can employ a variant of Keeley's chief argument against the superstition [that belief in conspiracy theories leads to a radical skepticism of public data] that he indirectly supports. If conspiracy theories are systematically suspect, then what we think we know about the past is systematically suspect.... But if we adopted that attitude, our knowledge of the past would dissolve into conjecture. We would, in effect, be committing epistemic suicide, at least with respect to large chunks of the past. If, as Keeley suggests, this would be a Bad Thing To Do, then we cannot afford to suppose that conspiracy theories are systematically suspect. (Pigden, 1995, p. 160)

This is to say that, as we know, conspiracies have occurred and we have not yet succumbed to a radical skepticism of history. Keeley, in other words, ought not to accept his own argument for the Public Trust Skepticism thesis. Unlike Wood, who argues that conspiracy theorists adhere to a paranoid-style kind of reasoning, Keeley's suspicion of conspiracy theories is based upon an argument as to why belief in them, even if some of them are warranted, entails a radical skepticism. Wood assumes that contemporary conspiracy theorists are conspiracists, while Keeley argues that belief in conspiracy theories has the unfortunate consequence of leading to conspiracism. Yet, if radical skepticism is not entailed by belief in conspiracy theories, then the argument in support of the Public Trust Skepticism thesis is surely going to be questionable?

Take, for example, journalists Bob Woodward and Carl Bernstein's investigation of the Watergate Hotel break-in. The story they told was that it seemed very likely indeed not only that senior Republicans were aware of the break-in to the Democratic Party's headquarters, but that elements in the White House were behind the plot. They were vilified for their pursuit of the story because, their opponents claimed, running with the claim that the Republicans had conspired to hide their dubious activity from the American people would lead to serious political and social repercussions, to wit, a loss of trust in the political system. However, not only did the evidence support Woodward and Bernstein's conspiracy theory; the terrible consequences of that revelation did not result in a radical skepticism by citizens of the USA about their political system.

Belief in a conspiracy theory may very well cause some agent to doubt a rival theory (or some evidence for the rival theory), but this does not entail a general skepticism of – and lack of trust with respect to – the entirety of our public institutions and their data. As David Coady argues, conspiracy theories are put forward as *the* explanation of an event, and so they are not the same kind of thing as a skeptical hypothesis about the origin and dissemination of public data (Coady, 2006a, p. 122). Steve Clarke has argued along similar lines: no matter how much doubt a particular conspiracy theory might cast on some public institutions, it is unlikely to lead to a radical skepticism about all public data (Clarke, 2002, p. 141).

While belief in conspiracy theories might well engender some skepticism about public data, it does not engender the kind of *extreme* skepticism that Keeley believes it does. We can accept a version of the first premise of the Public Trust Skepticism argument without needing to buy into the subsequent premises of his slippery slope argument. We should not be suspicious of conspiracy theories *merely* because believing some of them might lead to skepticism about some public data. Belief in a claim should not be based on what would happen if we believed it, but, rather, on the evidence. We should go where the evidence leads us, rather than worry about what might happen if we believe some particular theory.

An ethical objection

The preceding discussion indicates that, if conspiracy theories do engender skepticism about our trust in public institutions, that skepticism is neither total nor global. We can be conspiracy theorists who suspect our public institutions of negligence or outright duplicity *without becoming radical skeptics of public data.* As such, the Public Trust Skepticism thesis does not appear to be a good reason for us to take a dim view of conspiracy theories generally. This does not mean that we should embrace conspiracy theories with open arms, however. Juha Räikkä, for example, argues that political conspiracy theories – conspiracy theories about public institutions – are epistemically suspect. It is just that the problem with belief in them, according to Räikkä, is nowhere near as bad as Keeley's argument makes out.

Räikkä's interest is in political conspiracy theories. While he admits that non-public, private conspiracies occur and are even relatively common, he also claims that explanations of such conspiratorial behaviour are not typically considered conspiracy theories. Räikkä divides political conspiracy theories into three types: local, global and total (Räikkä, 2009b, p. 186). 'Local conspiracy theories' concern activities like attempts by councillors to pervert the vote in a local body election while 'global conspiracy theories' refer to major political events, like the various alleged conspiracies concerning the death of US President John F. Kennedy (aka JFK; Räikkä's chosen example). 'Total conspiracy theories' explain the occurrence of a particular event, and (almost) everything else connected to it, via the kind of claims of conspiracy we find in the various 'New World Order' theories. These particular conspiracy theories do not just explain, say, the election of a presidential candidate, but also how the general geopolitical climate – which led to that candidate's election – is the result of a vast and elaborate conspiracy.

It is not clear in Räikkä's analysis exactly what makes a conspiracy theory global rather than total (or even local). He claims that the conspiracy theories surrounding the death of JFK are examples of global conspiracy theories, but what makes this particular set of conspiracy theories global? One argument might be that JFK was the leader of a superpower, so his death was important on the world political scene. Conversely, as the leader of the USA, the various conspiracy theories about his death might be considered local, unless they cited some global rationale for the conspiracy (such as the assassins not being Americans). The point here is that *globalness* in Räikkä's analysis is vague. While there may well be utility in distinguishing between total and non-total conspiracies, it is not clear what use there is in demarcation between a global and a local conspiracy, in part because it is not clear that a hard and fast distinction can be made.

Whatever the case, Räikkä's argument against Keeley's Public Trust Skepticism thesis is that the degree of skepticism Keeley thinks is engendered by belief in conspiracy theories does not follow. Belief in political conspiracy theories – here construed as local political conspiracy theories – does not entail believing in explanations that are epistemically worse than their non-conspiratorial rivals (Räikkä, 2009b, p. 198). This is because he takes it that local *political* conspiracy theories simply describe what we might call 'standard operating practices' in both private affairs and local government. Thus, belief in such conspiracy theories is not extraordinary (Räikkä, 2009b, p. 188). What Räikkä fails to note, though, is that Keeley's worries are centred around belief in what Räikkä terms 'total conspiracy theories'. Keeley wants to claim that belief in this particular kind of conspiracy theory engenders too much skepticism of public data; total conspiracy theories entail such skepticism because they call into question everything you think you know about the political world in which we live. Räikkä might well be right that belief in local political conspiracy theories does not lead to a radical and all-embracing skepticism, but that is not the kind of conspiracy theory that Keeley is worried about. Keeley is worried about the consequences of belief in unwarranted *total* conspiracy theories. Since, according to Keeley, we cannot distinguish between them and the warranted kind, our belief in such conspiracy theories leads towards a radical skepticism of all public data.

In a different work, Räikkä argues for another version of the Public Trust Skepticism thesis by considering whether it is ethical to theorise about conspiracies. He starts by conditionally defending conspiracy theorising, writing:

> Political conspiracy theorizing may be a valuable cultural phenomenon, even if most or all political conspiracy theories have moral costs. (Räikkä, 2009a, p. 458)

Räikkä's analysis, however, is skewed from the start, since he also claims:

> For our purposes, it is more important to pay attention to the fact that every now and then people have negative attitudes toward single conspiracy theories. If we assume that they are justified in having their negative attitudes, we can ask what justifies them. (Räikkä, 2009a, p. 462)

This gets things back to front: we should not assume that the negative attitudes of some with respect to particular conspiracy theories are necessarily justified. Rather, we should ask whether such negative attitudes are justified.

Räikkä claims that a negative attitude towards belief in conspiracy theories *generally* is justified because the moral cost of conspiracy theorising is too high. He writes:

> When it comes to political conspiracy theorizing, publishing suspicions can be morally problematic, because harsh claims are made in too early a stage of the investigations. (Räikkä, 2009a, p. 466)

If this is the cost of conspiracy theorising, then it is the cost of accusing someone of being part of a conspiracy, rather a reason to dismiss conspiracy theorising. We should not reject conspiracy theorising or belief in conspiracy theories generally just because they might present people or organisations in a bad light. For one thing, that may very well allow conspiracies to flourish. If we have a reluctance to talk about conspiracy theories because people are afraid of harsh claims being made, then we are potentially chilling debate about the existence of conspiracies in our societies. Indeed, by ruling out common conspiratorial practices – as he does with talk of local conspiracy theories simply being 'standard operating procedure' and thus not properly conspiratorial – he sets the bar so high for claims of conspiratorial impropriety that, of course, such claims will be necessarily 'harsh' because they, by definition, have to be bold claims. For another thing, given the way we already treat conspiracy theorising in our society, it is not likely that such harsh claims will be taken very seriously anyway.

Finally, Räikkä characterises belief in conspiracy theories as 'sensible' only if it is in a particular kind of conspiracy theory, the local political conspiracy theory. Even then, such belief can be rejected on ethical grounds, because belief in political conspiracy theories is problematic for ethical reasons. Räikkä's approach to reserving a pejorative analysis of conspiracy theories generally ends up respecting a 'commonplace intuition' – that conspiracy theories are bunk – but the argument he puts forward in support of this intuition skews the debate on whether belief in conspiracy theories can be rational, rather than elucidating it.

The Openness Objection

We know, from the history books, that private and public institutions have conspired in the past. We should also be aware that there is a possibility that they might well conspire again, if they are not doing so already. Peter Knight argues that, while conspiracy theories, traditionally, functioned as a way of blaming others, they have come to 'express doubt about the legitimacy of authority in an age when less than a quarter of Americans trust the government (in comparison with fifty years ago when three-quarters trusted the authorities)' (Knight, 2000, p. 3). Knight provides a litany of conspiracies spanning the 'undeniably plausible to the wildly speculative' and argues that 'the few cases of actually proven conspiratorial misdealings (e.g. COINTELPRO, the FBI's much abused program of domestic spying on and infiltration of black activist groups, amongst others) warrant at least an initial skepticism about official denials in all subsequent cases' (Knight, 2000, p. 25). Knight contrasts this justified, if limited, skepticism of authority with Hofstadter's notion of the paranoid style and argues that, while Hofstadter saw conspiracy theorists as fundamentally misunderstanding history or politics, contemporary conspiracy theorising is

> [F]requently in tune with an institutional analysis of a political system whose self-vaunted commitment to democratic openness is

> undermined by the repeated revelation of conspiracy-minded wrongdoing. At the end of the day such conspiracy theories might well turn out to be unfounded, but, given all that we have learned about the less than democratic operation of government in the United States, it is a not unreasonable working hypothesis that there exists a clandestine or tacit collusion of vested interests that verges on a conspiracy. (Knight, 2000, p. 31)

Knight goes on to argue that, while it is quite possible that contemporary conspiracy theorists are paranoid – presumably in the Hofstadterian sense – their worries about the secretive nature of the political world are concerns that cannot be easily dismissed. Volker Heins argues in a similar manner when he writes:

> When sections of the population believe that there is nothing to be gained from political engagement because 'things don't change' anyway; when at the same time more and more can be known, while less and less knowledge seems to be reliable and indisputable, then we have a situation that is conducive to, among other things, conspiracy thinking. (Heins, 2007, p. 797)

while David Coady argues:

> First, openness is a matter of degree. There is no such thing as a completely, or even highly, open society. Second, openness, such as it is, is not the exclusive province of the United States and other Western societies. Some non-Western societies seem to be more open than some Western societies. Third, even in the most open of actually existing societies, conspiracy (including conspiracy by government) is common, important, and often successful. (Coady, 2012, p. 120)

We should agree with Knight, Heins and Coady: we have grounds for suspecting that some of our political institutions, at the very least, are either conspiring somewhat or have conspired recently. Thus, we have some grounds for a skepticism of public data, without necessarily having to endorse Keeley's radical and global skepticism.

The clearest rejection of Keeley's thesis of Public Trust Skepticism is found in the work of Lee Basham. Basham turns Keeley's argument on its head and asks whether we live in the kind of open society Keeley thinks underpins our trust in public data.

> The real issue haunting us is what a relatively conspiracy-free society that we would be *well justified in believing is relatively conspiracy-free* would look like. One thing is clear: it would not look like ours, *whatever* the truth about our society is. (Basham, 2001, p. 273)

He expresses the worry certain conspiracy theorists have as

> [N]ot driven by simple 'paranoia' – the irrational fear of others. It is instead a complex epistemic dispute, one that goes to the heart of how we make reasonable judgments about the motives and methods at work in our hierarchical, increasingly centralized system of economic, political and cultural power. (Basham, 2011, p. 51)

According to Basham, the worries conspiracy theorists express need to be taken seriously. Because we live in a world that features hierarchical institutions, many of which are powerful and political, our belief in the openness of our political world is conditional on just how open (and non-conspiring) we think the said institutions are. As such, some skepticism about public data might well be justified, depending on our conditional trust in public institutions. After all, we only have limited grounds to be confident in the utterances of public institutions, and we have abundant evidence that these institutions have deceived us in pursuit of their own interests.

The question Basham ponders is: 'How can we work out just how much trust we should have in our public institutions?' He is concerned that we do not have good enough reasons for complete trust in public institutions at this time because – although our society is open – it is not open enough that we can rest easy about conspiracies going on within such institutions. Basham's concern is – given that we know fairly large political conspiracies have occurred in the political realm (and some quite recently) – that we should *at least suspect* that there could be a fairly large political conspiracy in existence now (Basham, 2001, p. 272).

In a more recent work (Basham, 2011), Basham considers the problem of ambitious conspiracies, such as those about momentous events, like the assassination of JFK or the Gulf of Tonkin incident.

On 2 August and 4 August 1964, the US navy claimed it was involved in confrontations with North Vietnamese naval ships while on an intelligence patrol in the Gulf of Tonkin. These incidents led to the passing of the 'Gulf of Tonkin Resolution' by the US Congress. This granted then President Lyndon B. Johnson the authority to assist South-East Asian countries that were being threatened by Communist aggression, which led to the commencement of open war with North Vietnam.

The problem with this story is that, while the US navy was involved in a confrontation with North Vietnamese forces on 2 August, the incident on 4 August was caused by the USA.[1] Yet this information was not made public at the time, and so it looks suspiciously as though the incident on 2 August and the distorted report of what happened on 4 August were used as a pretext to grant the USA a legal reason to go to war with North Vietnam. In short, it looks as if there was a conspiracy by some members of the US political establishment to escalate a crisis so that it could be used politically.

Basham uses examples of ambitious conspiracies like the Gulf of Tonkin incident and the assassination of JFK to illustrate just how much trust we have to place in public institutions when we use such trust to dismiss belief in conspiracies about them. He writes:

> [The] objection [that ambitious conspiracies will almost inevitably be revealed to the public by government investigations or agents of the free press] assumes the trustworthiness of the very organizations that are often accused of being the sources or accomplices of the conspiracy. It ignores the many ways they might be manipulated, the manner in which hierarchy can intervene in their workings, and the over-ridding [sic] interest these organizations have in societal stability, even in the face of fairly rare but extreme governmental wrong doing. (Basham, 2011, p. 62)

Conspiracies are likely, in Basham's view, to occur as part of the operation of public institutions *rather than to make up all the activities of the said institutions*. So, while the individual field agents of the CIA may well be honest and sincere law enforcement agents who are acting for the good of America internationally, the board of directors of the CIA, who supervise such agents, may have their own agenda and be answerable to no one. This might well be the right story to tell about what happened with respect to the doctored dossier and the invasion of Iraq, as discussed in Chapter 5.

Similarly, if some set of conspirators committed electoral fraud by artificially increasing the vote in some electorate, then they could – should someone come to check the registry – have it altered. If the minutes of a meeting are kept by a secretary, then the council need only pay off the secretary, etc. The process of disseminating public data is governed by a bureaucracy, and bureaucracies are, by and large, hierarchical. It may be true that we have no reason to think our public institutions are, in fact, fronts, but the fact that most of our public institutions are hierarchical means that it is quite possible for our public institutions to look a lot more open than they really are. In an earlier work, Basham provides three reasons for thinking this:

1. Not all the evidence for and against the claim for the existence of a conspiracy is socially-transmitted (since basic claims, such as being an eye-witness to an event, can warrant belief in the existence of a conspiracy);
2. Conspirators are more likely to work within the constraints of public institutions rather than to exercise direct control over them and their output (since rather than exerting the enormous effort required to create and maintain institutions as fronts for their activities, conspirators can maintain the same level of control more simply, by subverting existing public institutions);
3. The presence of real and open public institutions will attract those who are ambitious for power, thus providing the conspirators with recruits for their conspiracies. (Basham, 2003, pp. 98–99)

Basham's argument is what we might call the 'Openness Objection to Public Trust Skepticism' (or, more simply, the 'Openness Objection'). We need not succumb to a total distrust of public institutions just because we recognise that our trust in them is conditional. While we might share the worries of certain conspiracy theorists – that our public institutions are not acting as sincerely or as honestly as perhaps those institutions might like us to think – this does not mean we will end up becoming radical skeptics. The Openness Objection is simply the argument that, as long as we accept that we live in a relatively-but-not-completely open society, then we can both accept that conspiracies occur *and* not succumb to a radical skepticism about public data.

A pragmatic rejection

Basham rejects Keeley's thesis that belief in conspiracy theories is suspicious because it leads to global and radical skepticism; he rejects Keeley's epistemic argument for taking a dim view of conspiracy theories generally. However, Basham thinks we have *pragmatic* grounds to reject belief in ambitious conspiracy theories, which are the kind of conspiracy theories that Keeley is concerned lead to a radical and global skepticism of public data (Basham, 2011, p. 81).

One part of Keeley's worry about belief in ambitious conspiracy theories is to do with the investigation of them. Ambitious conspiracy theories are difficult to investigate because there is liable to be a lack of hard evidence for the existence of the conspiracy. Basham argues that this is not a problem *per se* with belief in such conspiracies, as long as conspiracy theorists bring to light new evidence – which is likely to be examples of other, related behaviour by the institutions in question or similar activity by related institutions – and they continue to identify credible explanatory hypotheses (Basham, 2011, p. 80). As such, the secrecy inherent in conspiratorial activity – a secrecy that sometimes challenges our trust in public institutions – does not present particularly strong grounds for an epistemic rejection of belief in conspiracy theories. Rather, according to Basham, if we are going to reject belief in conspiracy theories generally, we will do so for pragmatic reasons. He presents three reasons for such a pragmatic rejection of belief in conspiracy theories:

1. If an investigation into an ambitious conspiracy theory is going to be inevitably futile, then there is no significant epistemic reason to investigate it.
2. If there is no epistemic reason or pragmatic reason to investigate, and there are grounds not to investigate, then we should not investigate.
3. Therefore, we can reject an investigation of an ambitious conspiracy theory on pragmatic grounds. (Basham, 2011, pp. 81–82)

The second premise hinges upon the notion that we already have some grounds not to investigate conspiracy theories. What grounds are these? Well, it is because 'There's nothing we can do about them!' Now, obviously it is not universally true that there is nothing we can do about the existence of conspiracies around us. For example, if you are suspicious about a surprise party being organised behind your back, there is plenty you can do. However, in the case of an ambitious conspiracy, most of us:

a) are not well placed to do anything and
b) will likely be frustrated by the fact that we can do nothing.

It is these two claims taken together that ground Basham's argument as to why we might have pragmatic grounds to reject belief in conspiracy theories generally. Basham argues that such a pragmatic rejection would produce a kind of 'epistemic irony' because we will end up 'discovering something deeply disturbing about our epistemic relation to the basic processes of the political and economic structure we live in, a relationship in profound need of repair' (Basham, 2011, p. 84). So, even when we pragmatically reject such ambitious conspiracy theories, we can still question just how open our society is.

David Coady, on the other hand, argues against the usefulness of referring to ambitious conspiracy theories when grounding such a rejection. He writes:

> You can't foil conspiracies if you can't know they exist. Conspiracy theories of this [ambitious] kind are a form of radical skeptical hypothesis, like the evil demon and brain-in-a-vat hypotheses that philosophers have been grappling with for centuries. Whatever you think of these hypotheses, they are not conspiracy theories as we know them. The conspirators of actual conspiracy theories, justified and unjustified, true and false, are not omnipotent. Their conspiracies can be seen through (that is what the conspiracy theorists believe themselves to have done), and thwarted (that is often what the conspiracy theorists hope to do). Hence our impotence in the face of Basham's malevolent global conspiracies cannot be the reason many people reject conspiracy theories, because few people have heard of any such conspiracies. (Coady, 2012, p. 133)

There is something to Coady's criticism here. Non-ambitious conspiracy theories are not likely to be problematic in the sense Basham finds ambitious ones to be. As such, Coady is right to think that non-ambitious ones are the ones we should probably be more worried about when analysing belief in conspiracy theories. While Basham might be right to think that there is little we can do about ambitious conspiracies, there is much we can do about the non-ambitious ones. Coady is also right to think that our worry about the openness of our influential public institutions needs to be centred around talk of non-ambitious conspiracies. After all, these are the conspiracies we tend to have epistemic grounds to believe in, and the kind of examples conspiracy theorists use to bolster their case for the existence of the ambitious conspiracies they want to bring a stop to.

However, Coady misses the mark by not quite grasping what it is Basham means by 'ambitious'. Basham takes it that some of the conspiracy theories surrounding the death of JFK are ambitious conspiracy theories, and these are hardly the kind of conspiracy theories few people have heard of. A conspiracy theory is ambitious, at least according to Basham, when it concerns a momentous event. It is the kind of conspiracy that, if true, would promote some skepticism of public data.

Basham's argument in support of a pragmatic rejection of conspiracy theories is not entirely convincing, but not for the reasons Coady has expressed. Rather, the worry with Basham's argument is that the thesis 'There is nothing that can be done!' is self-defeating. In the face of ambitious conspiracies most of us can do nothing directly to stop the conspiracy (or ameliorate its consequences), but this does not mean there is nothing we can do. Basham's argument sounds like an argument for apathy. Then again, Basham is not required to advocate that we *must* reject ambitious conspiracy theories on pragmatic grounds. Rather, he is simply saying: 'Here's a story as to why some people might reject or take a dim view of such theories, but it isn't for epistemic reasons.'

Conclusion

Our trust in officialdom is often taken to be fundamental for the operation of our society: we need to be able to trust our governments and we need to trust the utterances of numerous experts if we want to live in a civil society. The problem with some conspiracy theories is that they suggest this trust is misplaced, and for some this questioning of trust in the various bodies that make up our public and powerful institutions is equivalent to expressing heretical thoughts about some civil religion.

Keeley's thesis that belief in political conspiracy theories engenders a radical and inappropriate skepticism of public data – the Public Trust Skepticism thesis – is an argument that we do have grounds for a warranted *prima facie* suspicion of conspiracy theories in general. Both David Coady and Lee Basham have shown, however, that, while belief in conspiracy theories may lead to some skepticism, it does not lead to the radical and global skepticism Keeley is concerned with.

We all know that conspiracies have occurred and we know that people still act conspiratorially here and now. Not only that, but 'sensible' people (read: 'non-conspiracy theorists') will happily admit to this without rushing out to buy a tinfoil hat.[2] Belief in the existence of conspiracies in influential institutions does not necessarily lead to a radical skepticism about public data and the institutions that disseminate it. Even belief in big, all-embracing conspiracy theories does not typically result in people giving up on claiming to know anything about the world in which they live. 9/11 Truthers – those who suspect the events of 11 September 2001 were a terrorist plot by powers within the USA – may very well suspect the George W. Bush administration of great evils, but that has not lead some of the prominent conspiracy theorists in the movement – like Richard Gage or David Ray Griffin – to become radical skeptics of all public data.

Many of the stereotypical fears that conspiracy theorists of a certain stripe have should be considered seriously. Some of these issues, as we have seen, are common to explanations of complex social phenomena in general. Some of their concerns, however, are to do with notions of authority and the tricky interplay between officialdom and claims that institutions are conspiring. Perhaps one place to start examining these issues in depth is by examining just exactly what we mean when we say we trust some expert, and what role this trust plays in grounding or dismissing conspiracy theories and their rivals.

7
The Trouble with Authority

In the 1930s Joseph Stalin, the then leader of the Communist Party of the Soviet Union, was convinced that his former ally (but now enemy-in-exile) Leon Trotsky was plotting to take control of Russia. So concerned was Stalin about this possibility that he ordered his agents to keep close tabs on not just Trotsky but also those who might still be sympathetic to his cause. When the said agents reported back, claiming that Trotsky did not appear to be involved in any conspiracy to depose Stalin, Stalin ordered the arrest of the 'sympathisers' anyway. The arrestees were subsequently tortured, both physically and psychologically, for a number of months. Over this time they were persuaded to give false testimony: 'Yes!' they said, 'we have been conspiring both to sabotage Stalin's regime and to install Trotsky as the new leader of the Soviet Union.' A series of mock trials, known now as the 'Moscow Trials', were held, and because of this false testimony a conspiracy by Trotsky to seize power and overthrow the Communist leadership of the Soviet Union was 'uncovered'. Trotsky's suspected sympathisers, the 'conspirators', were found guilty of conspiracy and executed, and a warrant for Trotsky's arrest was eventually issued.

Stalin and his cronies assured the governments of both the USA and the UK that the trials were free and fair, and those governments accepted that assurance. The USA and the UK believed in what turned out to be an unwarranted but *endorsed* theory that purported to explain the verdicts of the Moscow Trials. This seems understandable, given the context. The governments of the USA and the UK assumed that the government of the Soviet Union was the relevant authority to refer to when it came to matters of judicial investigations into treasonous acts by Soviet citizens. Arguably, the USA and the UK accepted the story told to them because of its official status, which had been conferred upon it by influential political institutions: the Russian government and judiciary.

You might be forgiven for asking 'What's the issue here?' The governments of the USA and the UK made a poor decision when they decided to trust the Soviets' assurance that the trials were free and fair. They should have looked at the evidence rather than just assuming that, if some influential institution had endorsed it, then it must have been warranted. After all, whatever we may think of a particular conspiracy theory – such as the claim that the Moscow Trials were a sham – if we know that a rival theory is not supported by the evidence, then we should not accept it. However, many people – including some conspiracy theory theorists – think we have grounds for preferring official theories over conspiracy theories precisely because of their attendant official status.

For example, Neil Levy, in 'Radically Socialized Knowledge and Conspiracy Theories', asserts that any conspiracy theory that conflicts with an official theory is *prima facie* unwarranted (Levy, 2007, p. 182). Brian L. Keeley has a more moderate position. While he does not argue that conspiracy theories must be contra some official theory, he certainly treats conspiracy theories as typically being in contrast to them. He argues that our suspicion of conspiracy theories – which he thinks is justified – is grounded *in part* in our preference for theories with official status (Keeley, 1999, pp. 116–117).

It is easy to understand why agents might *prefer* theories with official status – if we think the issue is about agents making judgements regarding what to believe under conditions of imperfect information – but this is a preference that has some unfortunate consequences.

For one thing, proponents of this kind of view will often claim that if some conspiracy theory is warranted by the evidence, then it is not really a conspiracy theory. For example, David Aaronovitch argues that belief in conspiracy theories is irrational (because conspiracy theories are bunk), but he then proceeds to spend considerable space seeking to show how his belief in several warranted examples of conspiratorial explanations does not make him a conspiracy theorist. Aaronovitch's sleight of hand here is to claim that official theories *that happen to cite conspiracies as a salient cause of an event* cannot be conspiracy theories, and thus he cannot be a conspiracy theorist (Aaronovitch, 2009).

This notion that conspiracy theories are somehow unofficial is pervasive and damaging. Pervasive, in that a lot of people believe it. Damaging, not just because it leads to a situation where conspiracy theories are typically treated as being *prima facie* suspicious, but also because it can have a chilling effect on political debates. While claims of conspiracy can be extraordinary – and we should demand evidence in support of such claims – if we end up treating claims of conspiracy derisively just because they are unofficial, then conspirators will likely find it easier to conspire.

To make sense, then, of the claim that the officialness of some theory might be some reason for thinking we should have a preference for such a theory, we need to be aware of the different endorsing or authorising practices that grant official status. It turns out that only in a limited range of cases does the officialness of some theory suggest it is supported by the evidence. So, to understand when an official theory might trump some conspiracy theory, it is going to be necessary to look at the role endorsements play in the warranting of theories, and how not all appeals to authority are equal.

Official status

Between the Moscow Show Trials of the 1930s and the events of September 11 2001, one of the most talked about conspiracy theories concerns just who killed American President John Fitzgerald Kennedy (aka JFK), and why? The dominant explanation, commonly known as 'The Lone Gunman hypothesis', is that the assassination was the act of a lone assassin, Lee Harvey Oswald, whose motivations remain a mystery to this day.

The Lone Gunman hypothesis has what we might call 'official status' since it has been endorsed by influential and powerful institutions in the USA. The said institutions have accredited the theory with official status because the hypothesis that Lee Harvey Oswald acted alone, it is claimed, is supported by the evidence. As such, the various rival conspiracy theories, which range from the minimal 'Oswald did not act alone' to the more fleshed-out 'Oswald was a patsy for a CIA hit squad', are often sneered at because they lack official status, and are thus assumed to be lacking good evidence to support them.

However, just because some theory has official status, this does not mean that it is actually supported by the evidence. All such an endorsement entails is that some influential institution approves of or has accredited it. Sometimes official status can be conferred by a signature or by being written down in a formal document. It can come from the results of an experiment being replicated (or at least not being falsified). Sometimes it is as easy (or as difficult) as having your work cited with approval by some major names in your field and not cited with disapproval by others. Because the structures of institutions are many and varied, official status can be conferred in a myriad of different ways.

The official or institutional status of a theory can also be independent of the evidence that supports the theory. A theory could have superb evidential credentials but be sneered at by some influential institution. The theory might have little to no evidence to support it, but might well be nonetheless endorsed by some influential institution. As such, there are two questions we should ask to help categorise the different kinds of theories we typically encounter:

1. What evidential support does the theory have?
2. What is the official status of the theory?

Sneering or endorsing

When it comes to evidential support, theories can be warranted or unwarranted. When it comes to official status, theories can be endorsed, unendorsed or even sneered at. So, for example, a theory that is endorsed by an influential institution will have official status *with respect to that institution*. A theory which has been *sneered* at does not just lack official status; it will have been rejected by the members of some influential institution.

We do not need to say much about unwarranted and unendorsed theories – given that they lack both evidence and official status – or warranted and endorsed theories, since they are theories that are supported by the evidence and are approved of by accrediting institutions. However, the range of possibilities between them is worth investigating.

Warranted and unendorsed theories:

> Some theories are supported by evidence but have no official status: they are neither endorsed nor sneered at by some influential institution. Many new scientific theories, before being submitted to peer review, may well be warranted by the evidence but lack official status with respect to the scientific establishment.

Warranted but sneered at theories:

> Some theories are supported by the evidence – and are thus warranted – yet have been sneered at by some influential institution. Historically, tectonic plate theory and the thesis that *H. pylori* causes peptic ulcers were examples of warranted but sneered at theories, since the theories went against the 'received wisdom' of the day.

Unwarranted and sneered at theories:

> Some theories are lacking in evidence and also have negative official status. The conspiracy theory that claims the Twin Towers were

> destroyed by ultrasonic weaponry, and the two Boeing 747s that were seen to impact the Towers were, in reality, holograms, has no evidential support and has been sneered at by various influential institutions.

Unwarranted but endorsed theories:

> Some theories – despite a lack of evidence – still end up having some official status. One theory that was advanced as to why it was necessary to invade Iraq in 2002 was the claim that the Saddam Hussein-led regime was creating weapons of mass destruction (WMD). This, it turned out, was an unwarranted but endorsed theory: there was no evidence for the WMD programme, but the theory was nonetheless endorsed by influential political institutions like the governments and intelligence agencies of both the USA and the UK.

In an ideal world, a warranted and endorsed explanation will be one for which the evidence will be readily available, should we want to look at it. However, there are going to be cases in which we will prefer unwarranted but endorsed theories over warranted yet sneered at theories. This preference, if left unexamined, is problematic.

For example, some conspiracy theorists are worried that warranted theories are being sneered at *just because they are conspiracy theories*. On the other hand, conspiracy theory skeptics worry that occasionally people fail to recognise that some conspiracy theories are endorsed by experts or institutions *who have no relevant expertise with respect to that theory*. Herein lies the issue: both the conspiracy theorist and the conspiracy theory skeptic are right to be concerned. Although theories may come tagged with institutional credentials, they do not usually come pre-identified as being either warranted or unwarranted. It might seem reasonable – when we do not know the details of the evidence – to take the endorsement of an influential institution or an expert as evidence the theory is warranted. After all, why would some institution endorse a theory if it was not warranted? However, we need to understand what 'endorsing a theory' means. Not all institutions are on a par, nor do they necessarily accredit theories equally. Indeed, the general lesson need not be about conspiracy theories at all, but, rather, about how endorsements can trump epistemic credentials in some cases.

Appealing to authority

We should all be able to point to cases in which experts in one field endorse an explanation in some other area. We should also be aware that sometimes ordinary agents – like ourselves – can fail to recognise that specific expertise in one area is not necessarily transferable to another. Although the following example is trite, it is also revealing.

After the election of Barack Obama as president of the USA in 2008, the members of the 9/11 Truth Movement – who doubt that Al-Qaeda was responsible for the destruction of the Twin Towers – tried to persuade President Obama to meet with one of their members, the actor Charlie Sheen. Opinion pieces were placed in the national media to create a groundswell of support for such a meeting, and one of the op-eds proclaimed:

> [W]hen someone with the gravitas of a **Charlie Sheen** issues a statement, anyone is forced to listen. (Malcolm, 2009; emphasis in original)

If Charlie Sheen were speaking on matters theatrical, where, arguably, he has some expertise, then maybe that might be a reason to listen to him. However, whatever gravitas Charlie Sheen has, it is not clear that he has the right training or background to endorse theories about 9/11. He has endorsed a theory – the claim that the events of 11 September 2001 were committed by forces within the USA – but it is not clear that he has the necessary expertise to say a theory is warranted.

The problem with endorsed theories – which agents might prefer due to an appeal to official status – is that they can be confused with, or taken for being, theories that we should prefer because of an endorsement made by someone or some organisation with the *relevant expertise*.

If a relevant authority has endorsed a theory that explains why some event occurred, then we should probably prefer it to a rival theory with no such endorsement *if we are in no position to inspect the evidence*. However, if a theory for an event has been endorsed, this tells us very little about what the experts believe: a theory can be said to be endorsed by people even if the endorsers lack the right epistemic credentials. Charlie Sheen endorses conspiracy theories about 9/11 without the relevant kind of expertise that might make us think we should take the theories he propounds seriously. *Relevant* expertise is important, then, when it comes to assessing whether an endorsement weighs upon the question: 'Is this endorsed theory warranted?'

Mistaking a theory having some attendant official status – with respect to having been endorsed by some influential institution – for being a theory that is supported by the evidence is a problem. However, it is an understandable mistake to make, because, in a situation where agents might be required to express a preference for a theory in circumstances in which they do not have access to the evidence, they might very well want to go with one that has been endorsed. This is why such a preference is understandable. However, it also means that sometimes we will choose to accept theories that have been endorsed, even though they are not warranted by the evidence.

Recall the earlier example of the Moscow Trials: most epistemic agents at the time either did not have access to the pool of evidence cited in the trials, or lacked the time to pore over the evidence to check whether it supported the official theory. It was understandable – in those circumstances – that people had a preference for the theory that had been endorsed by the judiciary. However, for conspiracy theorists of a certain stripe, this move is controversial. If a preference for endorsed explanations is understandable, then agents could be excused for preferring the official theory for the Moscow Show Trials, despite its being, at the time, an unwarranted but endorsed theory.

This is important because, when the trial verdicts were announced, a rival conspiracy theory was formulated, claiming that the verdicts were a sham precisely because the theory was unwarranted: the evidence cited in the trial did not indicate that the verdicts were sound. Concerned citizens of both the UK and the USA, led by John Dewey, went through the trial transcripts and analysed the evidence. They came up with a rival explanation to the official theory: Trotsky had been set up and innocent women and men had been executed in order to legitimise Stalin's continued attempts to get rid of his political rival. This rival theory was sneered at by the Soviet, US and UK governments as being a *mere* conspiracy theory despite the evidence presented to them by the members of the Commission. The Dewey Commission's report was warranted *yet* sneered at. However, in 1956, Nikita Khrushchev – who became the leader of the Soviet Union after Stalin's death – admitted the trials were a sham and, by extension, that the Dewey Commission had been right all along. After nearly 20 years, the Dewey Commission's theory was no longer something to be sneered at and was, finally, recognised as warranted.

What's a Muscovite to do?

If, in the 1930s Russia, you had been an office worker in the Kremlin, or a senior aide to a minister of state, then you might have known that the Moscow Trials were a sham. But what if you were a peasant, or an ordinary factory worker? What would have been reasonable for you, as a humble Muscovite, to believe? If you had been a humble Muscovite, then it would have been understandable – both epistemically and also pragmatically, given the political circumstances – for you to accept the official theory about the Moscow Trials.

It is fair to say that, typically, most agents – certainly the average Muscovite of the 1930s – will appeal to a theory that has been endorsed by some influential institution as suggesting that it is supported by the evidence. They will assume that if a theory has official status it is because:

a) it appeals to an authority, or a set of authorities who are in substantial agreement with one another that the explanation that has been endorsed is well evidenced, and
b) the authority or authorities are testifying honestly.

The worry some conspiracy theorists have – and we should share this worry with them – is that many official theories are not simply *unwarranted* yet *endorsed* theories; rather, they are theories that have been endorsed by inappropriate authorities or experts in irrelevant fields. Conspiracy theory skeptics will reply in kind, of course, and argue that many conspiracy theorists also mistake irrelevant experts for people with suitable qualifications, like Charlie Sheen.

For example, some claim that the general acceptance of the official theory about the events of 9/11 – that it was an act of terrorism committed by foreign nationals – is mistaken for one or the other of two reasons. Either people are mistaken in believing that the government of the USA was the right body to endorse such an explanation, or, if that is not a mistake, they are mistaken in believing that the US government reacted honestly to advice from the relevant experts. Opponents of the official theory will then point to their rival theory, such as the claim that the government of the USA – or a body that controls the said government – was responsible for the events of 9/11. They will go on to say: 'You can't trust the government because they're not just inappropriate authorities but they actually caused the event to happen!' These particular conspiracy theorists will then recommend that you should listen to people like Richard Gage and Dr David Ray Griffin, experts who have endorsed a rival, conspiracy theory about the events of 9/11.

However, skeptics of the 9/11 Truth theory will point out that these supposed 'experts' are not what they are made out to be. Richard Gage might be an architect with some training in structural engineering, but he is not suitably qualified to give opinions about the engineering of skyscrapers, given that this is a specialist subject. Dr David Ray Griffin, who writes extensively about conspiracies in the White House, is a philosopher of religion rather than a political theorist. So, while they might have both endorsed various versions of the 9/11 Truth theory, it is not clear that their endorsement tells us anything much about whether the theory (or the set of theories) is warranted.

Now, it may be the case that an expert's specific expertise may not be directly relevant to some discussion but we might think that their expertise is transferable because they have what we might call 'methodological expertise'. Their education makes them 'good enough' to be able to assess some theory. However, assessing some theory is not quite the same thing as endorsing it. You might not be a philosopher of religion, but as a philosopher you should be able to tell a good argument in the general field of philosophy when you see one. Relevant expertise is important when the said expert is endorsing a theory, because, presumably, such endorsements are offered as a reason for non-experts to think the theory is warranted. So, under what conditions is it reasonable to say that the endorsement of a theory provides a reason for assuming that it supported by evidence? What sorts of endorsers can forge such a relationship?

When theories are endorsed by the academic sector, then we should expect that the said theories are supported by the evidence, and are thus warranted. This is because of the rigorous research methodologies and the process of peer review in the academic realm, which works as a system of checks and balances to ensure that theories are, by and large, supported by the evidence. We should also like to think – and we probably have good grounds for believing this – that academic institutions do not endorse any old theory, just the theories that are supported by evidence. We should, if we are going to believe or even advocate for one of these endorsed theories, examine the evidence for them ourselves, but we still have an adequate justification for belief in them based upon the appeal to authority alone *in the academic case*.

So, for example, it seems reasonable to say, when a literate but not scientifically inclined layperson appeals to the cohort of climatologists and says: 'I accept the thesis of Anthropogenic Climate Change because I trust in the judgement and endorsement of that theory by the set of relevant authorities, the climatologists', that they are taking it on trust that, if the relevant experts agree, then the theory has evidence to support it. So, while they are not explicitly examining the evidence for the theory, they are relying on the processes in the discipline of climatology and appealing to the consensus of the scholars in that field.

What is meant here by 'consensus', of course, gets a little confusing. For some, consensus seems to be the notion that all (or just about all) experts must be in agreement with one another. Others take it that, if most experts agree (and a large, but not significant, set of experts disagree), then we have consensus. For people of the former view – let us call it a 'narrow' notion of consensus – the fact that there are a goodly number of experts who, say, disagree with the official theory of 9/11 indicates that this is evidence of dissent amongst researchers. This is then taken to be evidence that we should look more closely at the evidence on which these experts are basing their theories. For those who hold to the other view – the 'broader' consensus – the fact that there is disagreement between experts does not tell us much at all unless we know something about the nature of that disagreement or can say something about the number of dissenting voices in the expert community.

We do not have to take a stand as to whether we take a broad or narrow notion of consensus. We can say that it is always preferable – epistemically speaking – to look at the evidence whenever possible. If there is disagreement amongst experts, then presumably, if the theory being disagreed upon is of interest to us, we will want to find out why. It may turn out that there is no real disagreement going on: either the disagreement is between relevant experts and irrelevant third parties, the evidence is not yet in, or it might be the case that there are reasons for the disagreement in play other than the evidence.

Can we trust political sources?

The notion that in the academic case our authorities are testifying honestly or sincerely is doing a lot of work in our analysis here. Yet sometimes experts are insincere. However, if an academic is dishonest, then the result is often career termination. This can be a kind of formal termination, when the institution to which the academic belongs severs all ties with the academic and her work, or it can be informal, when the academic's work is no longer trusted or cited by her peers. In either case, dishonesty by an academic with respect to her research will, effectively, end her career. Insincerity need not be outright dishonesty, either. Academics who have less than rigorous research methodologies will normally find their results being called into question by other, more rigorous members of the academic community, which will then typically lead to questions being asked about the quality of the said academic's other research.

The story of peer review in the academic realm and how it works, when suitably finessed, does not guarantee that, when a theory is endorsed, it is supported by the evidence. All such a story tells us is that the process of auditing academic theories has a robust system of checks and balances and is, thus, a reliable one when it comes to assessing whether the theories that have been endorsed by the academic realm are well-evidenced.

There does not, however, seem to be a similar process that we can appeal to when it comes to endorsements from the political sector. The mere fact that the government, say, of New Zealand says it not only accepts but also endorses – as an explanation of the current state of geophysical affairs – the thesis of Anthropogenic Climate Change does not entail that the government's endorsement is based upon the evidence. It is quite possible that the endorsement is entirely pragmatic. For example, you could claim that, because voters believe Anthropogenic Climate Change is occurring, the government, in order to secure votes, decides to endorse that theory on vote-securing, pragmatic grounds. The appeal to authority in this particular kind of political case, then, is a problem because we do not know that:

a) The political institution is appealing to relevant authorities, who are in substantial agreement with one another that the theory that has been endorsed is correct;

and we might also be suspicious as to whether:

b) The political institution is acting sincerely.

So, are politicians worthy of trust? Well, what we can say is this: we know that they do not necessarily acquire their beliefs via rigorous research methodologies. We also know that they are sometimes prone to changing their beliefs for unfathomable reasons. Politicians are also sometimes deceitful, and, on occasion, they might even have good reasons for being so. For example, engaging in sensitive negotiations with foreign powers might require working behind closed doors, or even denying that such negotiations are going on. It is even possible that there might be good reasons for deceiving the public about a scandal that could bring down a government (although this is very arguable). Whatever the case, it seems that we have adequate grounds to be suspicious that at least some of the endorsements conferred by members of the political sector are pragmatic or insincere.

Is there, then, a story we can tell that allows us to say that we can reliably trust political endorsements? After all, in the case of the Moscow Trials members of a political institution *knowingly* and *insincerely* endorsed a theory that did not have the right kind of evidential support. So, how can *we* know whether a theory was endorsed *sincerely* by some influential institution? After all, conspiracy theorists of a certain stripe are sometimes worried theories that have been endorsed by influential institutions have had their official status bestowed upon them even though the endorsers *knew* that the theory was unwarranted. Sometimes the instrument of officialdom acts insincerely *in order to discredit some rival conspiracy theory* (like the Dewey Commission's theory about the verdicts in the Moscow Trials).

Sometimes, when we judge whether we should treat some claim seriously, we are in a position to appraise both the competence of the person who put forward the claim and their integrity. Someone who is competent but lacks integrity is the kind of person we might think we can trust but should not. While they have the ability to do the job – they are competent, after all – they lack integrity. Someone who is incompetent but has integrity is the kind of person we might also trust but should not, since, although they are trustworthy, you cannot guarantee that they can do their job properly.

Understanding this distinction between competency and integrity seems particularly important when it comes to appraising members of the political sector. While we can argue that peer review provides a check for competency *and* for integrity in the academic world (at least, to some degree; presumably the peer review of how someone got their fancy accreditation in the first place is the test for integrity), in the case of political endorsements we really need to know that someone is competent and also has integrity before we can treat what they say with any due seriousness.

Indeed, we should question whether members of influential political institutions even seek to enquire after the truth of the theories they propound. In some cases the answer looks to be 'Yes!', especially with claims about evidence-based policies. Yet, even in those cases, it is possible members of the political sector endorse theories not because of the evidence, but, rather, because the populace demands that they do.[1] We could think of members of the political sector as *merely* expressing beliefs without necessarily asserting them, which is the reverse of what we expect of members of the academic sector. If politicians and civil servants are just expressing theories, then they are, in essence, simply endorsing theories without necessarily being concerned about whether they are warranted.

While this is a very tempting way to think about the issue of political endorsements – especially given the way it sits with certain intuitions about the sincerity of political actors – it muddies the waters. Even if this thesis about members of the political sector were true, the worry we need to be concerned with here is about how *members of the public* interpret the endorsing activity of the political sector.

Insincerity

There is an interesting empirical debate to be had here as to how frequently explanations are insincerely endorsed by such institutions. Lee Basham's version of the Openness Objection is an argument to the extent that we do not live in a sufficiently open society to warrant any claim that such institutions are not involved in at least one major conspiracy occurring now. It is likely, he argues, that at least some influential political institutions are acting insincerely here and now. We should agree with Basham on this matter, but it is worthwhile noting that he is possibly downplaying just how bad the situation might really be. Although Basham does not underplay the possibility that conspiracies are occurring now, he does advance a very hesitant case for trust in future public institutions.

> [S]ocietal structures with much less emphasis on secretive hierarchical power are significantly less vulnerable to routine, overarching conspiracy. While there may be no absolute standards that can identify a society as free from conspiratorial control, relative progress is possible and extremely valuable.... Understanding the necessary limits to this heightened openness is as important as understanding how it might best be achieved. (Basham, 2003, p. 101)

Basham argues that we could do better: if we were to have truly open institutions, then we would be safer from conspiracies by members of influential institutions. The worry, then, is about appearance: increased openness is something that could be easily faked, especially if the grounds for believing our society is increasingly open are simply because we have been brought up to believe it. Recall the discussion in the previous chapter about the hierarchical nature of both our society and the majority of our influential public institutions. The story of how open our society is might be part of some official theory that is meant to explain how much better our current governance model is compared with those of old. However, it might also be a theory that has been *endorsed* despite its lack of warrant in order to hide malfeasance going on within the said institutions.

The argument that our society is open enough to warrant taking a dim view of conspiracy theories is what we might term a 'weak justification' for trust in official-qua-political sources and their explanations. It is a *weak* justification in that it is a psychological excuse, rather than epistemic justification, for preferring official theories. David Coady has argued that such a weak justification would be subject to manipulation. He writes:

> It may be that in an ideal society official stories would carry an epistemic authority such that it would almost always be rational to believe them. But that is not our society, nor I suspect, is it any society that has ever been or ever will be. What is more, if such a society were to come into existence, it seems likely that it would be unstable, since the complacency about officialdom that it would engender would be exploitable by officials hoping to manipulate public opinion to advance their interests. (Coady, 2007a, p. 199)

This is a live option, and this is why this kind of justification, when we talk about the political sense of 'official', must be considered weak. At best, this story works where we have no access to the evidence and we are being forced to choose between an *endorsed* and an *unendorsed* or *sneered* at explanation. Where we have that choice, we are justified in having a psychological preference for the explanation with official status, but that is all we can say. This preference can only be expressed when we have no access to the evidence, and is a problem even then. We should only trust officialdom to the extent that there is a good argument for the reliability of officialdom, and, if we have no good grounds to trust officials, then we should be agnostic on the matter rather than prefer the official theory.

As such, what grounds we have for trust in the political sector are shaky at best. Sometimes unwarranted but endorsed explanations are examples of unwarranted yet insincerely endorsed explanations, because the political sector can and does deceive and betray our trust in it. We might be able to argue that we have a case for a kind of naive trust in the political sector because most of us feel that we have a handle on what politicians do, which is to make decisions based upon the advice of their advisors. The decision-making members of the political sector are, in many cases, just like the rest of us. Contrast this with the case of academics, who seem to make issues seem more complex than the average Jane Doe or John Smith sees them. At the very least, politicians often portray themselves as applying the common sense of the masses to complex decision-making processes, which may lead to some thinking that we have a better case for trust in the endorsement of the political sector than we do for trust in the endorsement of the academic sector. Whether we express this via an analogy of politicians being just like us, or by arguing that we feel disempowered by the complexities and requirements of academic endorsements, it is an understandable sentiment. While this is not a good argument for trust in the endorsement of explanations by members of the political sector, it does explain why people might prefer a government official's explanation over a rival explanation from a member of the academic sector.

Individual vs. group trust

One possible response to the argument just presented is to say that we should distinguish between the trust we have in the individual members of political institutions and the trust we have in the political sector as a whole. The individual members of political institutions can be untrustworthy, say, in their private lives, but does this distrust necessarily extend to the political sector – the group of such members – as a whole? We might distrust Bill English the MP, but does his insincerity with regard to his own private fiscal responsibilities reflect badly on his trustworthiness in the role of Minister of Finance? We can go further and say that individual politicians could be untrustworthy even in their political dealings, and yet the endorsements of the political institutions they belong to might incorporate sufficient checks and balances to neutralise this individual untrustworthiness.[2] Indeed, the political sector has an auditing system of checks and balances, which is often called 'oversight' (or 'political oversight'), and it is this system, surely, that Keeley has in mind when he argues that we have a preference for official theories. After all, journalists and interested members of the public can check the public records, minutes, etc. of their elected representatives to ensure that everything they do is above board.

The same can be said for the trust we have in the academic sector: a proper understanding of the peer review system, for example, allows us to admit that some academics might act unscrupulously (and even fabricate their data) and yet still allows us to say that we have a case for a *prima facie* trust in the academic sector's output (their research) in general. Political oversight, the argument would go, similarly allows us to claim that there is, at least, a case for a naive trust in the political sector. This is not a strong analogy, however, because there is a good argument that political oversight is nowhere near as powerful a check-and-balance mechanism as the process of peer review. This is because the openness required for political oversight to function properly might:

a) not exist or
b) be overstated.

Our trust in political endorsements rides on our trust in political sources. There will be cases in which some theory is endorsed only for pragmatic reasons, not because it is supported by the evidence. There will also be cases in which a theory with superb evidential support is rejected or is treated skeptically for entirely pragmatic reasons. Politicians sometimes endorse explanations for purely pragmatic reasons, such as securing votes or paying their dues. Political oversight, then, only weakly suggests that the political endorsement of an explanation indicates that it is supported by the evidence.

Now, maybe we want to hold on to a naive trust in political sources. We could admit that bad things can and often do happen in the political world, but that the system *in general* only works if we assume that these things happen infrequently (despite evidence to the contrary). There are lots of similar examples where we hold beliefs for similar reasons, such as our assumption that our partner will not eventually cheat on us (even though, according to the statistics, they probably will). Perhaps the best case – and this is cold comfort – is to think of politicians as being agnostics as to the evidential merits of theories and simply wanting to please their constituents.

Conclusion

Recall the example of the Moscow Show Trials. The then Communist government of Russia was ostensibly a government for the people, driven by the people. While the average citizen of 1930s Russia might have harboured some suspicions as to how communist their government really was, they were constantly assured that tales about corruption in the ruling party were pieces of disinformation spread by outsiders. Indeed, there was evidence of this, by way of the occasional arrests of dissidents and political agitators. These arrests were said to be warranted by the evidence, but in reality the claims that these outsiders were responsible for crop and other failures were *endorsed* by politicians because that was the pragmatic thing to do. It was either that or admit that the various three or five-year plans – the unwarranted but nonetheless endorsed economic theories – were not working, which might have led to a new revolution. That is a charitable way to interpret what was happening in 1930s Russia. Less charitably, we could talk about how the ruling party used fear and conspiratorial tactics to control and subjugate the Russian populace. Whatever the case, numerous people and organisations – both in Russia and around the world – took the various political institutions at their word. Why? Because the said theories were *endorsed*, even though we now know (and many had justified suspicions at the time) that many of these theories were *unwarranted*.

Whether or not you think you are a conspiracy theorist, the arguments presented in this chapter should demonstrate that at least some of the concerns of the prototypical conspiracy theorist are ones we should all share. When it comes to appealing to authorities to back up why we think it is reasonable to believe some theory, we need to be aware of how different kinds of institutions accredit theories. We also need to be cognisant that just because some theory has been endorsed – which is to say it has some official status with respect to an influential institution – that does not mean it is warranted or backed up by the evidence.

So, while we can show there is a case for thinking that academic endorsement strongly suggests that academic theories are supported by the evidence, there is no similar argument in the case of political endorsements. It seems understandable that we have a preference for theories that have been endorsed, because it is easy to assume that the availability of an endorsement implies that the theory is supported by the evidence. But, as we have seen, that is not always the case, and so we should expect agents, if they want to say they are properly justified in believing some theory, to examine the evidence that supports it whenever possible.

Further to this, whether or not we make a distinction between academic and political theories, we know that a theory can be endorsed yet not have the right kind of evidence to support it. This could happen for a variety of reasons. For example, a theory might once have had the right kind of evidence to support it but, due to changes in relevant theories, remains endorsed despite its credentials having crumbled. A theory might be endorsed for pragmatic reasons, with its endorsers seemingly agnostic about the theory's evidential support. The issue the conspiracy theorist of a certain stripe is concerned with, however, is the worst case scenario: the theory has been endorsed insincerely when the relevant authorities know that it does not have the right epistemic credentials.

A theory that has been endorsed may well be one we prefer over some rival that has not been endorsed or has even been sneered at. Such a preference, however, could end up being a problem for the average agent who simply does not have the time or expertise to analyse the evidence for each and every theory she holds. This is a consequence of just how social our knowledge really is, given that we defer to one another all the time. Our trust, we would like to think, is well-founded, but, as the example of the Moscow Trials of the 1930s shows us, sometimes that trust is misplaced.

There is more to say on this. We have touched upon one worry about officialness: the distinction between theories that have been endorsed and those that have been sneered at. However, the elephant in the room is the troubling intuition that there is still some useful distinction between an official – which is to say endorsed – theory and a conspiracy – which is to say sneered at – theory. The analysis of this troubling intuition is the work of the next chapter.

8
Should We Prefer Official Theories?

There is a view found in the work of several conspiracy theory theorists that goes something like this: theories with official status – to wit, theories endorsed by some powerful institution – that happen to cite conspiratorial activity *cannot* be conspiracy theories.

Take, for example, the Moscow Show Trials of the 1930s (which were discussed in the previous chapter). We know the verdicts were the result of a conspiracy. The conspiratorial machinations of Stalin and his cronies are now part of the standard histories of Soviet Russia. For some, this means that this particular conspiratorial explanation is not a conspiracy theory. Why? Well, because the theory has been endorsed by influential institutions: academic, with respect to historians, sociologists and the like; and political, with respect to the Russian government. Thus, the story of the Moscow Show Trials is what we might call an 'official theory' *and such theories are not typically considered to be conspiracy theories*. The same can be said of the Shoah: the explanation of the Nazi programme to eradicate the Jewish people in Europe during the 1930s and 1940s features elements of conspiracy, but, as it is part of our orthodox history, we would not typically call it a 'conspiracy theory'.

The notion that conspiracy theories are never official theories is an interesting proposition. It respects an intuition shared by some that the term 'conspiracy theory' has pejorative implications – and thus cannot be a theory that is part of the orthodoxy – or that conspiracy theories are, in some sense, unofficial.

Michael J. Wood and Karen M. Douglas, for example, contrast conspiracy theories with what they call 'conventionalist explanations', which are both warranted by the evidence and, in some sense, official. Wood and Douglas claim that 'for people who hold a conspiracist world-view, the specifics of a conspiracy theory are less important than its identity as a conspiracy and its opposition to the official explanation' (Wood & Douglas, 2013, p. 2).

Susan Feldman argues that we should distinguish between conspiracy theories and conspiratorial explanations *that happen to be in some sense official*. She takes it that conspiracy theories are examples of counter-narratives. She writes:

> [A] conspiracy theory is a proposed explanation of events, contrary to an officially sanctioned alternative, involving the causal agency of a group of agents working together in secret, often or usually for a sinister purpose. (Feldman, 2011, pp. 15–16)

As we saw in the last chapter, there are several senses of 'official'. Surely, then, in a world where conspiracies occur, we cannot privilege some theory merely because it is official? This seems like a particular problem for Feldman, because some of the official theories which these conspiracy theories are counter-narratives to end up being theories about the conspiratorial activities of the bodies that officially sanction the said official theories. So, just because some theory has official status, this, on the face of it, tells us little about the epistemic merits of the theory *unless we can tell some story about why we might trust the accrediting institution*.

A naive trust

Neil Levy argues that, when conspiracy theories exist in contrast to some official theory, we should prefer the official theory. Levy takes it that official theories are theories that have been formed by appropriately qualified epistemic authorities and, as such, are preferable to any rival conspiracy theories (Levy, 2007, p. 182). However, Levy fails not only to distinguish between the different kinds of official theories, but also to explain how official status can be conferred upon a theory regardless of whether it is supported by the evidence. The officialness of a theory is conferred by influential institutions, and, as we saw in the last chapter, we can distinguish between the accreditation of theories by political institutions – which might sometimes bestow officialness upon some theory for pragmatic or insincere reasons – and what should be the more robust endorsements of academic institutions. Echoing the critiques of Lee Basham, David Coady and Charles Pigden, Axel Gelfert writes:

> While it may sometimes be rational to accept the 'official story', an official source will enjoy *epistemic* authority if and only if it is *in fact*

> sufficiently competent, sincere, and forthcoming with the relevant information. And, all things considered, it is *epistemic* authority (deriving from actual competence and reliability) which is what we are aiming for when assessing the merits of an informant as a source of knowledge. Whether, in any given setting, the distribution of social power is such that occupants of 'official' positions are, in fact, epistemically authoritative is a contingent matter – and is something that anyone wishing to rely on official sources had better be able to judge. (Gelfert, 2013a, p. 772)

Levy has what we might call a 'naive trust' in authority, given that he conflates political and epistemic authorities when talking about our reasons for preferring official theories. Such a naive trust is troubling, however. For example, whether or not we think there are conspiracies going on here and now, our trust in authority may well be subject to abuse. We do not need to be a conspiracist to think that sometimes people in positions of power trade on their ability to conflate endorsements of a political nature with academic accreditation. A prime minister of New Zealand, John Key, once famously claimed that the opinions of scientists are like those of lawyers, in that you can get them to endorse any view you please (Sackur, 2011). This is obviously a confused (or deliberately obtuse) take on what we mean by endorsement. As we have already seen, not all endorsements are created equally, and so Levy's confusion as to how official status works is dangerous: he fails to recognise that some endorsements do not entail that the theory is warranted by the evidence.

If we seriously consider the general worries of conspiracy theorists about whether influential institutions are worthy of our trust – worries we should at least entertain – then we should be concerned that a naive trust in authority might be abused by conspirators working within the said institutions. If you were, say, a member of the executive branch of the government of the USA who had conspired with her peers to commit a terrorist act on American soil, you might very well endorse some theory that placed the blame on foreign nationals. After all, you would know full well that some people will automatically believe such a theory if it comes from an influential institution. This is a problem that is not restricted to influential political institutions, either. Many people confuse astroturf groups – organisations designed to look like homegrown activism but which are really industry-funded lobby groups – with the views of concerned citizens, and the like.

Now, this is clearly a psychological point: people are sometimes impressed by authority. Sometimes being impressed by authority means that people will take an endorsement by the said authority as conferring laudable epistemic status on a theory. Thus, we need to be careful in distinguishing exactly what we mean when we say we prefer some official theory. If there really is a *prima facie* case for preferring official theories over conspiracy theories, it is going to be based upon understanding that only *some* official theories are preferable when considered epistemically. While we might be primed psychologically to treat official statements with reverence, this does not tell us that the said statements are worthwhile in an epistemic sense.[1] However, when conspiracy theory skeptics claim we have some preference for official theories, and this preference justifies our dim view on conspiracy theories in general, it looks as though some of them might be confusing or conflating *epistemic* authorities with *mere* authorities.

Genuine conspiracies

Juha Räikkä argues that we have grounds for preferring official theories over conspiracy theories. His argument for this preference comes out of his rejection of Lee Basham's contention that it would be surprising if there were not one fairly involved, all-embracing and disturbing conspiracy in operation now. Räikkä writes:

> In my view, however, history does *not* prove that 'the current existence of even one fairly involved, long term, widespread, and shocking conspiracy' is likely. Given that people's belief in God or children's belief in Santa Claus are not caused by genuine conspiracies, the history of mankind is probably not familiar with any conspiracy that have involved hundreds of people and dozens of institutions. (Räikkä, 2009b, p. 197)

Räikkä's concern is that things like surprise parties do not qualify as 'genuine conspiracies'. He is worried that theorists like Basham set the bar for what counts as a conspiracy at an arbitrarily low level. However, if things like surprise parties do not qualify as examples of conspiracies, then we cannot use the prevalence of such parties as the basis for the claim that it is reasonable to assume that similar activities in the political realm are also common. As we discussed in Chapter 6, Räikkä simply rules out a lot of conspiratorial activity in the political sphere as being the proper subject of conspiracy theories because it is simply standard operating practice. It looks as though, if we were to agree with him that Basham is setting the bar low, Räikkä is setting it far too high.

Räikkä has this to say about official theories and conspiracy theories:

> [O]fficial explanations can be theories and they can refer to conspiracies, but they cannot be conspiracy theories (unless they are official explanations of wrong authorities). (Räikkä, 2009b, p. 187)

In another work, published the same year, he elaborates on this point, writing:

> [W]hen conspiracy theories turn into official wisdom, people cease to call them conspiracy theories.... If all the explanations that include references to conspiracies and secret action were conspiracy theories, then the history of the world would be a massive conspiracy theory, which it is not. (Räikkä, 2009a, p. 460)

There are a number of points to be made here.

First, what constitutes a 'wrong authority'? It seems as if Räikkä is recognising that there are different kinds of authorities that endorse or accredit theories, some of which endorse pragmatically and some of which endorse epistemically. As such, we can challenge Räikkä as to what he means by the claim 'unless they are official explanations of wrong authorities'. Is an authority right when it is right and wrong when it is wrong? Surely this is just trite and obvious? If Räikkä really believes that conspiracy theories can never be official theories, then it looks as though Räikkä is defending institutional endorsements *while only paying lip service to the very worry – wrong authorities – he is arguing against.*

Second, Räikkä is clearly wrong when he claims that, if theories about surprise parties and secret actions were treated as conspiracy theories, then the history of the world would be one massive conspiracy theory. For one thing, not all secret action is conspiratorial. On a trivial level, I can, on my own, hide my passion for cheesy pop music from my peers. More importantly, lots of political activity is secretive and yet not necessarily conspiratorial. The negotiation of trade treaties between sovereign nations is often done behind closed doors and not publicly minuted. Räikkä must be aware that a lot of secretive political activity goes on *every day*, and yet he does not seem to have succumbed to the allure that is conspiracism.

Let us put it another way: just because there might be a lot more genuine conspiratorial activity in the world if we accept that activities like the organisation of surprise parties are examples of conspiracies, this does not necessitate us buying into some version of Popper's *conspiracy theory of society* (which we looked at back in Chapter 2). Belief in the existence of individual conspiracies – even lots of individual conspiracies – does not entail that we need to believe everything is due to the existence of conspiracies, or that all conspiratorial activity is somehow connected.

Third, Räikkä, like Popper before him, takes it that the official theory about what happened during the Holocaust fails to be a story about a genuine conspiracy because we *know* about the Holocaust. As such, the story of the Shoah is just part of our orthodox history. He writes:

> Large-scale secret actions, such as extensive military operations, should not be confused with genuine conspiracies. The Holocaust was planned and conducted with the connivance of many people and many organizations, as was the Great Terror of 1934–1939 in the Soviet Union, but it is contestable whether these should be called genuine conspiracies, as it was generally 'known' what was going on. What was not known was who was responsible, how extensive the action was, and so on. (Räikkä, 2009b, p. 197)

This view is untenable for several reasons. For one, as we discussed in Chapter 3, while secrecy is a necessary condition for an act to be considered conspiratorial, what we mean by secrecy is just that the conspirators desire to keep their plans and activity hidden. It is not that non-conspirators cannot know about the said plans or activities. To claim that a genuine conspiracy is one where the conspiracy is unknown rules out of court any belief in a conspiracy theory being rational.[2] Does this mean that corporate whistleblowers, who discover and publicise evidence of criminal conspiracies, are not, in fact, uncovering criminal conspiracies?[3] Yet Räikkä seems committed to this view. He is worried about claims of total political conspiracies – like the New World Order theories – but he is not concerned with smaller conspiratorial activity, which he considers to be standard operating practice in politics (and, presumably, business).

Räikkä's view is also untenable because it rules out *known* conspiracies as being interesting examples of conspiracy theories. This is because he takes it that known conspiracies cannot be *genuine* conspiracies. Take, for example, the commonly accepted, official theory of the D-Day landings at the end of the Second World War. The D-Day operation was an elaborate conspiracy organised by the Allied Forces. It was designed to fool the Axis Forces into thinking the invasion of Europe by Allied Forces would occur elsewhere than Normandy, and on a different day. The D-Day operation has all the features of being a conspiracy. However, because the plot was revealed after the successful landing at Normandy, this cannot be, according to Räikkä, a genuine conspiracy. After all, the explanation of the D-Day landings is now a part of our standard histories about the Second World War. This seems like an odd view, since it rules out any belief in a conspiracy theory being warranted, on the basis that, if you can show that a conspiracy occurred, then it is not really a conspiracy, and thus there can be no warranted attendant conspiracy theory. At best, the conspiracy theorist who believes in what turns out later to be a warranted conspiracy theory – which they may or may not have had adequate evidence to believe at the time – are retroactively official theorists, at least according to Räikkä. In either case, Räikkä defines away the possibility that belief in some conspiracy theory can be warranted by making it impossible for someone to have a warranted belief that there exists a conspiracy.

Consider this final example: no matter what you believe about the events of 11 September 2001 (aka 9/11), the various theories about the attack on New York City are theories about a conspiracy. Either the conspirators were members of the organisation known as 'Al-Qaeda' or they were agents working for the CIA or the executive branch of the government of the USA. All the various theories about 9/11 seem to be about conspiracies, of which the genuine article – the best explanation of that event – is a theory about a conspiracy that is no longer being kept secret. Now, perhaps talking about the official theory of 9/11 as a conspiracy theory goes against common usage, but, if our interest is in asking whether belief in conspiracy theories could ever be warranted, then we should be interested in the broader class of conspiratorial explanations rather than a restricted class that we already think to be examples of suspicious beliefs.

According to Räikkä, any proposed conspiracy theory that turns out to be warranted – like the explanation of how Stalin and his cronies conspired to rig the verdicts of the Moscow Trials of the 1930s – ends up retroactively being an official theory. This is like a weird metaphysical trap, one that he claims is in line with common usage (Räikkä, 2009a, p. 460). Räikkä wants to respect what he takes to be the common and pejorative usage of 'conspiracy theory' – a suspect theory, which is never official – and he does this by restricting the scope of what counts as a conspiracy. However, it would be easier for Räikkä to simply allow that conspiracy theories can be official theories. After all, he could still keep his suspicion of total conspiracy theories if it turned out that there are no warranted examples of such theories.

Merely unofficial conspiracy theories

David Coady also takes it that conspiracy theories are never official theories. However, unlike Levy and Räikkä, he does not think we have grounds for preferring official theories over conspiracy theories, because the officialness of some theory is separate from its epistemic credentials (Coady, 2012, p. 132).

David Coady argues that the terms 'conspiracy theory' and 'conspiracy theorist' are what he terms 'the respectable modern equivalents of "heresy" and "heretic" respectively' (Coady, 2012, p. 123). While Coady rejects the 'common sense intuition' that conspiracy theories are *prima facie* irrational, he does also argue that there is a difference *of some kind* between an official theory (or what he calls an 'official story') and a conspiracy theory, such that a conspiracy theory can never be official.

Coady's understanding of official status is close to the account presented in the previous chapter, recognising as it does the different ways in which a theory can be endorsed by influential institutions. As such, just because a theory has been endorsed – and is thus considered 'official' – this does not tell us it should necessarily be believed *unless we know something about the actual endorsing practices of the institution in question.* So, why does he think that conspiracy theories are never official theories? Well, it is because conspiracy theories are theories that contradict official theories. He writes:

> [T]he relationship between conspiracy theories and officialdom is like the relationship between rumors and officialdom, with the difference that rumors are defined as merely lacking official endorsement, whereas conspiracy theories, on this way of understanding them, must actually contradict some official version of events. (Coady, 2012, p. 122)

Coady is respecting common usage – the modern superstition that conspiracy theories are bunk – without necessarily defending the rationale behind it. However, Coady's gloss on the notion that conspiracy theories are somehow unofficial takes some weird turns.

For example, he takes it that people who are accused of being 'conspiracy theorists' are the kind of people who believe or are interested in theories that rival official theories. This paints the term 'conspiracy theorist' as a pejorative. Although Coady is not committed to the claim that conspiracy theorists are irrational, the fact that he preserves this distinction is unfortunate. This is particularly troubling because he also admits that the terms 'conspiracy theory' and 'conspiracy theorists' can be applied in cases *where the rival to some official theory is not a conspiracy theory.* In such cases, the claim 'That's a conspiracy theory!' is simply being used to call into question some rival theory. It ends up being a rhetorical move whereby some theory is sneered at, presumably so people will not judge it on the evidence.

Lee Basham points out that Coady's respect for the intuition that conspiracy theories are rivals to some official theory, and thus never official theories, conflates *salience* with *meaning*. Basham's argument is that conspiracy theories that exist in opposition to official theories might seem more salient or interesting to us – because such theories suggest nefarious activity on the part of influential institutions – but it would be a mistake to characterise conspiracy theories solely with respect to one particular type, since 'doing so unfairly portrays conspiracy theories as *necessarily deviant*' (Basham, 2011, pp. 53–54).

Coady's reply to this is presumably to reiterate that he is not buying into the view that official theories are epistemically superior to conspiracy theories. All he is doing is respecting a certain common usage. However, we should ask why we – particularly philosophers – would want to preserve common usage if it does not advance our analysis of these things called 'conspiracy theories'. We can add to this that Coady's defence of this particular common usage might also have the negative effect of enabling government conspiracies. If we preserve the notion that the terms 'conspiracy theories' and 'conspiracy theorists' are pejoratives, then this might shield conspirators from the accusation that they are conspiring.[4] After all, marking out conspiracy theories as essentially unofficial theories means that, even if we think official theories are not necessarily epistemically superior, it still gives us grounds for thinking we should be suspicious of conspiracy theories.

There is also the fact that official theories are often fluid. Today's official theory might not be tomorrow's. We have already seen that the *current* official theory about the Moscow Show Trials was the *then* conspiracy theory of the 1930s. As such, the notion that conspiracy theories are rivals to official theories seems confused, given that we have cases of official theories that used to be conspiracy theories and conspiracy theories that turned out to be the received, official wisdom after all.

Choosing not to believe

Joel Bunting and Jason Taylor, working from Coady's analysis of official stories, present belief in conspiracy theories as a choice *not to believe some official theory*. They write:

> Choosing to believe a conspiracy theory is the choice to believe in one theory (the conspiracy) over another theory (the official story). Though this may seem obvious, it is crucial to note because it draws to attention the idea that a rational choice to believe any theory depends on considerations of evidence. Judging any theory to be insufficient independently of considerations regarding the evidence is irrational. Thus, a rejection of conspiracy theories simpliciter seems irrational; rational rejection or acceptance of a theory must supervene on the quality of evidence for or against that theory. (Buenting & Taylor, 2010, pp. 569–570)

While the general sentiment expressed above seems sound – that we should inspect the arguments for a conspiracy theory rather than reject them outright because they belong to the class of things called 'conspiracy theories' – the notion that, when we choose to believe some conspiracy theory, we are choosing not to believe some other, official story (or theory) is a problem for two reasons:

1. Sometimes our choice of theories that explain some event might be restricted to different conspiracy theories. Any putative explanation of 9/11 seems to involve choosing between different conspiracies, for example.
2. It is not entirely clear what work 'official' is doing here with respect to these things called 'official stories'.

To make matters even more confusing, Buenting and Taylor introduce into their analysis what they call 'uncovered conspiracy theories'. Uncovered conspiracy theories are examples of endorsed and warranted theories that happen to cite conspiracies as a salient cause of some event (Buenting & Taylor, 2010, p. 570). One such uncovered conspiracy theory, according to Buenting and Taylor, is the Watergate Affair. The Watergate Affair is now part of the standard history of contemporary American politics: it is an official theory. So, if Watergate is an uncovered conspiracy theory, does that mean that official theories can be uncovered conspiracy theories? If so, how, exactly, do conspiracy theories and uncovered conspiracy theories differ?

As we discussed in Chapter 3, Buenting and Taylor argue for a particularist analysis of belief in conspiracy theories. They argue – and we should agree with them – that conspiracy theories should be analysed with respect to the evidence that is purported to support them, rather than dismissed as belonging to a class of theories of which we typically take a dim view. However, this talk of 'uncovered conspiracy theories' and our having a preference for official theories over conspiracy theories somewhat calls into question Buenting and Taylor's commitment to the particularist argument. It is not clear why a particularist approach needs to make mention of official theories *at all*. If our analysis of whether belief in some particular conspiracy theory is meant to be based solely on the evidential merit of the said theory, then adding in a proviso that belief in such theories means choosing not to believe some official theory adds an unnecessary (and contentious) complication.

The problem for Buenting and Taylor's gloss on particularism here is that they use the term 'conspiracy theorist' in a loosely pejorative way. They write:

> Uncovered conspiracy theories suggest that it is sometimes rational to believe conspiracy theories and that sometimes conspiracies occur. These cases strongly suggest that assessing the rationality of a conspiracy theory should be done on a case-by-case basis. Thus, these cases suggest that if we are to take conspiratorial thinking seriously, we ought to adopt the particularist approach.
>
> This is a victory of sorts for the conspiracy theorist, but a minor one. A conspiracy theorist wants something more than the (backhanded) compliment that her theory type is not unequivocally irrational; a conspiracy theorist wants recognition that her theory token reflects the true state of affairs, the actual explanation of the event in question. (Buenting & Taylor, 2010, p. 570)

While we should take it that anyone who believes a conspiracy theory is a conspiracy theorist, Buenting and Taylor are dangerously close to conflating conspiracy theorists with conspiracists because of their emphasis on both the type (conspiracy theories in general) and the token (the particular conspiracy theory). However, it would be a mistake to think that the people who hold to a particular token conspiracy theory are necessarily the kind of people who wish to vindicate the general type. After all, we can accept some conspiracy theories as being rational to believe in and yet be skeptical of others.

Coady, Buenting and Taylor want to respect what they take to be the common usage of both 'conspiracy theory' and 'conspiracy theorist', which is loosely pejorative. Conspiracy theories are theories that are in some sense unofficial. However, it is just not clear that we should respect the intuition behind common usage. Conspiracy theories are not necessarily the rivals of official theories, and even if they are – given what we know about the potential abuses of endorsements by powerful institutions – the fact that some theory is official does not tell us it is *rational* to believe it, as Coady, Buenting and Taylor admit.

It is also not clear that official theories are never conspiracy theories. Any explanation of the events of 9/11 is a theory about an event that cites a conspiracy as a salient cause. That is true whether we are talking about the official theory, which cites a terrorist action by Al-Qaeda, or the unofficial theory that claims it was the result of a false flag operation run by powerful individuals inside the USA. Thinking that this means the official theory is not also a conspiracy theory is an odd move to make, given that it robs us of an example of a conspiracy theory that is warranted.

The consequences of taking Coady, Buenting and Taylor's views here seriously also inadvertently undermine the credibility of warranted conspiracy theories, given that some people will continue to take it that there is something epistemically suspect about unofficial theories. Now, this might be an unfair accusation to put against Coady, who goes to great lengths to show that there is nothing epistemically superior about official stories. However, Buenting and Taylor claim that choosing to believe some conspiracy theory means choosing *not to believe* some official theory. This ends up privileging official theories, given their defence of the loosely pejorative connotations of the terms 'conspiracy theory' and 'conspiracy theorist'. Although Buenting and Taylor say we should analyse conspiracy theories on their merits and reject the intuition held by some that conspiracy theories *in general* are irrational to believe, they still set up conspiracy theories as essentially *oppositional* theories: a conspiracy theory is a theory that is not part of the received wisdom, and thus we have some reasons for being suspicious of them. It is all well and good to advance a particularist argument saying: 'Judge conspiracy theories on their merits', but defining what counts as a conspiracy theory in a pejorative way (even if we do not think this has any effect on the epistemic considerations about such theories) makes the case for particularism harder. Given that particularism about conspiracy theories is atypical, it seems odd for particularists to make defending their own theory a more difficult proposition.

Coincidence or cock-up theories

As we have seen, some conspiracy theory theorists explain their preference for non-conspiracy theories – which are sometimes, but not always, official theories – by positing that, when we have a choice between a conspiracy theory and some other non-conspiracy theory, we should prefer the non-conspiracy theory. Sometimes, though, this preference is explained not in terms of conspiracy theories and official theories or stories but as a choice between being a conspiracy theorist or a coincidence or cock-up – a charming English expression referring to an act that results in some unexpected and unfortunate result, or an inefficient undertaking – theorist.

A coincidence theory explains away some claim of conspiracy by positing that the event in question is most likely due to a series of coincidences or mistakes. It is the claim that, while some event might have come about because some conspirators intended it, the more likely explanation is that it was a chancy event or the accidental by-product of some other (presumably complex) process.

An example of rival coincidence and conspiracy theories can be seen in a number of the New World Order 'One World Bank' conspiracy theories. These particular conspiracy theories – some of which were expressed by members of the 'Occupy' movement (as were discussed in the last chapter) – allege that the massive wealth transfer to the ultra-rich 1 per cent of the populace is the result of a concerted, long-term conspiracy. The purpose of this conspiracy is not just to create a new meritocracy based on wealth, but also to enslave the poor by forcing them to take on massive and unpayable debt or keeping the working population barely above subsistence level. Skeptics of this type of financial conspiracy theory will often admit to the problem – that the 1 per cent are getting forever richer and the poor are increasingly worse off – but deny that this is an intended result brought about by political actions of the 1 per cent. Rather, they will argue, the problem is the result of failures, or unpredicted outcomes, in the free market. They might even admit to cock-ups in social policy, all of which contributed unintentionally to the mass wealth inequality we see today.

It is true that sometimes theories about coincidences turn out to be better explanations than some rival conspiracy theory. This does not tell us, though, that in *most* cases a cock-up or coincidence theory is more likely than a conspiracy theory; that is an empirical issue. It is not immediately obvious just how likely cock-ups are compared with conspiracies, especially if we admit that surprise parties and their ilk – as discussed in Chapter 4 – qualify as examples of commonplace conspiratorial activity. Yet this has not stopped certain conspiracy theory skeptics from making some version of this claim. Daniel Pipes, for example, claims that coincidence theories are just *prima facie* more likely than conspiracy theories (Pipes, 1997, p. 44), while Pete Mandik argues that, when we have a choice between a conspiracy theory and a cock-up theory, we are no worse off when choosing the coincidence theory (Mandik, 2007, p. 206).

Michael Barkun claims that conspiracy theorists are the kind of people who believe nothing ever happens by accident:

> In an odd way, the conspiracy theorist's view is both frightening and reassuring. It is frightening because it magnifies the power of evil, leading in some cases to an outright dualism in which light and darkness struggle for cosmic supremacy. At the same time, however, it is reassuring, for it promises a world that is meaningful rather than arbitrary. Not only are events nonrandom, but the clear identification of evil gives the conspiracist a definable enemy against which to struggle, endowing life with purpose. (Barkun, 2003, p. 4)

Barkun is working with a notion of what counts as a conspiracy that is couched in conspiracist terms, imputing that the reason why conspiracists see conspiracies where none exist is because they attribute intention to events that may have occurred by accident. This view is echoed by the journalist David Aaronovitch, who writes:

> I think a better definition of a conspiracy theory might be: the attribution of deliberate agency to something that is more likely to be accidental or unintended. And, as a sophistication of this definition, one might add: the attribution of secret action to one party that might far more reasonably be explained as the less covert and less complicated action of another. (Aaronovitch, 2009, p. 5)

Yet Aaronovitch is confused about conspiracy theories. He accepts that conspiracies occur, given that the first half of his book *Voodoo Histories* is a litany of examples of conspiratorial explanations in history. Many of the cases he discusses can be explained due to a conspiracy, *but a different one than was hypothesised by the original theory.*

Jeffrey Bale argues that conspiracy theorists downplay or ignore the role of coincidences in explanations, and that for them 'nothing that happens occurs by accident. Everything is the result of secret plotting in accordance with some sinister design' (Bale, 2007, p. 53). Martha Lee also argues for a preference for coincidence theories over conspiracy theories because belief in conspiracy theories suggests there is purpose to history, a claim Lee says historians know to be false (Lee, 2011, p. 9).

Yet preferring coincidence theories over conspiracy theories is problematic. For one thing, it is not clear that coincidence theories are typically better explanations than conspiracy theories; that will entirely depend on the evidence. It would be weird to think we have a case for preferring coincidence theories over conspiracy theories *in cases where there is clear evidence that there was a conspiracy*. We are only going to have a *prima facie* case for preferring coincidence theories if we are using some pejorative form of the term 'conspiracy theory' *that includes the claim that such theories are unwarranted.*

David Coady turns the table on coincidence theorists by showing how coincidence theories can be as troublesome as some conspiracy theories. He writes:

> A coincidence theorist fails to connect the dots, no matter how suggestive of an underlying pattern they are. A hardened coincidence theorist can watch a plane crash into the second tower of the World Trade Center without thinking that there is any connection between this event and the crashing of another plane into the other tower of the World Trade Center less than an hour earlier. Similarly, a coincidence theorist could be aware that all the editors of Rupert Murdoch's publications around the world endorsed the invasion of Iraq, without seeing any connection between their expressed views and those of their boss. (Coady, 2007a, pp. 196–197)

After all, no one thinks the events of 9/11 are explicable *solely* with reference to a coincidence theory in which two planes happened to hit the towers, the towers came crashing down and then Al-Qaeda just happened to take responsibility for a terrorist act.[5]

It is also not clear that coincidence theories and conspiracies are at loggerheads, given that they can be compatible with each other. The assassins of Julius Caesar, for example, intended not just to kill the dictator of Rome but also to return power back to the Senate, yet they did not bargain on Caesar's supporters turning the public against the assassins. The assassins successfully conspired on one hand and cocked up on the other. Some conspiracies can only be explained with reference to a cock-up; the Oklahoma City bomber, Timothy McVeigh, cocked up while conspiring, which revealed the existence of the conspiracy he was involved in.

State crimes against democracy

Mark Fenster points out that the 'coincidence theory' label is not just used by conspiracy theory skeptics as a way to call into question belief in conspiracy theories; some conspiracy theorists use it to call into question official theories. David Ray Griffith – who argues that the events of 9/11 were orchestrated by the government of the USA – refers to the official theory about 9/11 as a 'coincidence theory'. He argues that to deny the claim that the events were orchestrated by sinister forces within the USA requires buying into a series of increasingly unlikely coincidences (Fenster, 2008, p. 242). An interesting example of a conspiracy theorist using the coincidence theory label to call into question official theories can be found in the work of Lance deHaven-Smith in his book *Conspiracy Theory in America*.

deHaven-Smith argues that we should not treat claims of conspiracy dismissively. However, he worries that the terms 'conspiracy theory' and 'conspiracy theorist' are too closely associated with claims of paranoia and hare-brained speculation.[6] As such, conspiracy theories can never be accepted as official theories. deHaven-Smith also worries that, as the term 'conspiracy theory' can refer to both *warranted* and *unwarranted* explanations, we cannot tell, just from looking at the label, whether the conspiratorial account under consideration is worth considering seriously[7] (deHaven-Smith, 2010, pp. 797–798). Because of this, deHaven-Smith wants us to adopt a new term for warranted conspiracy theories. His argument is that we should jettison the terms 'conspiracy theory' and 'conspiracy theorist' and focus our attention on what he calls 'state crimes against democracy', or SCADS. He writes:

> SCADs are concerted actions or inactions by government insiders intended to manipulate democratic processes and undermine popular sovereignty. By definition, SCADs differ from other forms of political criminality in their potential to subvert political institutions and entire governments or branches of government. They are high crimes that attack democracy itself. (deHaven-Smith, 2010, p. 796)

SCADs are political conspiracies of an ambitious (to use Lee Basham's terminology) or total (to use Barkun's terminology) nature. SCADs are explanations of events of momentous importance that cite big conspiracies as salient causes. Since conspiracy theories will always be unofficial (at least according to deHaven-Smith), we should accept that the term 'conspiracy theory' will be used (sometimes wrongly) to mark out a theory as being irrational to believe. However, SCADs can be official theories, and thus we should adopt this as our label when investigating claims of conspiracy in our influential institutions.

deHaven-Smith also has another reason for wanting us to adopt the SCADs label. He is worried that the people behind such state crimes against democracy are using the coincidence theory label to counter legitimate claims of conspiracy. deHaven-Smith wants to change the nature of debate about whether belief in conspiracy theories can be rational by dropping the loaded terms 'conspiracy theory' and 'conspiracy theorist' and, instead, focus our attention on the sometimes conspiratorial activity of people in influential political institutions. He writes:

> In disparaging speculation about possible elite criminality, the conspiracy theory label posits as given what actually needs to be falsified empirically, namely, whether democratic processes are being improperly and systematically manipulated by strategically placed insiders. In the post-WWII era, official investigations have attributed assassinations, election fiascos, defense failures, and other suspicious events to such unpredictable, idiosyncratic forces as lone gunmen, antiquated voting equipment, bureaucratic bumbling, and innocent mistakes, all of which suspend numerous and accumulating *qui bono* questions. In effect, political elites have answered conspiracy theories with *coincidence* theories. (deHaven-Smith, 2010, p. 799)

deHaven-Smith asserts that the best way to investigate SCADs is to join the dots and analyse our suspicions of influential political institutions under the rubric that everything is connected. Surely, though, the claim that all our 'power elites' are conspiring against us is something we need an argument for, rather than being smuggled in by the definition of what a SCAD is. Indeed, the SCAD hypothesis is simply a conspiracy theory about the role of power elites in our society, one that requires us to assume the existence of some conspiracy before we even begin to analyse the evidence. deHaven-Smith writes:

> Although including the latter brings some risk of error, excluding them would mean accepting the judgment of individuals and institutions whose rectitude and culpability are at issue. Public officials are usually quite reluctant to allow independent investigations into questions about their own actions or those of their close associates. (deHaven-Smith, 2010, p. 799)

Indeed, the SCAD label ends up suffering from the same problem as conspiracy theories. This is evident from the way deHaven-Smith discusses officially corroborated SCADs, like Watergate and Iran-Contra, and what he calls 'suspected SCADS', which are 'corroborated by evidence that is credible but unofficial' (deHaven-Smith, 2010, p. 799). Suspected SCADs include the Gulf of Tonkin incident, the Inside Job hypothesis about 9/11 and the October Surprise thesis (deHaven-Smith, 2010, p. 796). These suspected SCADs are also commonly known by another name: conspiracy theories. Not only that, they are examples of conspiracy theories that have been sneered at by both political and academic institutions. To say that they rest upon credible but unofficial evidence is disingenuous, given that the very issue for these theories is just how credible the supposed evidence for them really is.

Now, if there is a conspiracy in operation, we might very well be able to tell that some evidence is credible, which is to say it is warranted, even though it is unofficial. However, the examples of suspected SCADS deHaven-Smith uses to support his notion of 'credible but unofficial' evidence – the October Surprise thesis and the Inside Job hypothesis about 9/11 – do not support this charitable interpretation. While deHaven-Smith asserts that the evidence for both of these putative explanations is credible, the evidence is credible *because it supports deHaven-Smith's notion that there is a widespread conspiracy already in operation in our influential political institutions*. deHaven-Smith has smuggled in as an assumption the very thing the SCAD analysis is meant to prove: the existence of an all-embracing, total conspiracy. It looks as though all he is doing, when arguing that we should use the SCADs nomenclature, is attempting to render his conspiracy theorising about the October Surprise thesis and the Inside Job hypothesis about 9/11 as perfectly normal. Not only that, but, because suspected SCADs rely on credible and unofficial evidence, most suspected SCADs are going to be unfalsifiable.

deHaven-Smith is interested in rehabilitating one particular kind of conspiracy theory – theories about conspiratorial behaviour which involve most, if not all, of our influential political institutions – so that we might take them seriously and investigate them. However, we do not need to introduce new terms into the debate and thus confuse the issues even further; if we stick with a perfectly neutral construal of both what counts as a 'conspiracy theory' (any explanation of an event that cites a conspiracy as a salient cause) and a 'conspiracy theorist' (anyone who believes some conspiracy theory), then we can talk about theories that are warranted or unwarranted and theorists who are sensible and those who are not. Perhaps we might have to sometimes explain to people that the terms can be (and should be) used non-pejoratively, but in the end this is better than introducing new terms into the debate, particularly terms that serve the purpose of making some conspiracy theories *prima facie* sensible in an unfalsifiable way.

Conclusion

The notion that officialness plays any role in deciding whether a theory is warranted or unwarranted is a curious one, as we have seen. It should be clear from the preceding discussion that there is no particular merit in distinguishing between conspiracy theories and official theories, or claiming that cock-ups and conspiracy theories are somehow mutually exclusive. Yet, some conspiracy theory theorists – who are not necessarily conspiracy theory skeptics – seem to think it is a distinction worth preserving. Perhaps part of the problem here is that some conspiracy theory theorists are perfectly willing to salvage the notion that belief in conspiracy theories can be rational, but at the same time they want to respect the intuition that there is something pathological about *being a conspiracy theorist*. Or perhaps it is simply a strange respect for common usage, given that most everyone else writing on the matter takes it that there is something suspicious about conspiracy theories; here is a story as to why that might be.

We do not need to make such distinctions. We can stipulate that a conspiracy theory is simply any explanation of an event that cites a conspiracy as a salient cause of the event. This may go against our common usage, but our interest should be in the analysis of the concept of conspiracy theories and whether belief in such theories can ever be rational. As such, we can say that conspiracy theories can be official or unofficial, and being one does not preclude the possibility of being the other. Some conspiracy theories will contain elements of cock-ups. Sometimes coincidences will play a role in the outcome of the conspiracy, which might be at odds with the intentions of the conspirators.

Perhaps we might be tempted to bypass all this talk of officialness and unofficialness, and the related notions of who are the right kinds of authorities to refer to when choosing to believe one theory over another, and simply focus on the evidence. However, as we are about to see, what counts as the 'evidence' is not all that clear cut.

9
Evidence and Conspiracy Theories

If we are to judge a particular conspiracy theory on its merits, this means examining the evidence put forward in support of the said theory. However, one worry *some* conspiracy theory theorists have about belief in conspiracy theories is that the kinds of evidence used to support them look suspicious.

Claims of conspiracy are extraordinary, if only because we should be concerned when someone alleges that a conspiracy is occurring. After all, even if we think conspiracies are relatively common, and not necessarily a sinister kind of activity, we are still justified in being suspicious as to what it is the alleged conspirators are up to.

The adage 'extraordinary claims require extraordinary evidence' is a useful lesson. However, it is not clear that conspiracy theories are extraordinary in the sense that many conspiracy theory skeptics would have them be, given that conspiratorial activity is not as rare as some might think, nor is it clear that convincing evidence for the existence of a conspiracy is extraordinary *in the sense of being hard to come by.*

However, there is one notion of 'extraordinary' that we have not looked at, which is the sense in which the evidence is said to be questionable. Evidence can be questionable when it is a carefully curated subsection of the sum total evidence. Evidence can also be called into question when it turns out to have been fabricated to make an explanation look warranted when it is not. Sometimes evidence turns out to be too good to be true. As such, there are a set of issues about the role of evidence with respect to any kind of explanation in the social world, which raise interesting questions as to:

a) how the evidence has been presented and
b) whether the propositions that have put forward even qualify as evidence.

Selectiveness

It is not hard to think of cases when someone tries to justify a claim with less than adequate evidence. People tinker and play with evidence all the time. For example, if I want to justify my poor choice of a high-sugar, low-fibre breakfast, then I am likely to only mention the evidence that is salient to the story I want to tell. The said story will feature a curated pool of evidence specifically selected to aid in the appreciation of why I had to eat a sucrose-laden cereal. I will probably also fail to mention how I had the means and the opportunity to fill my pantry with healthier breakfast foods. This is an example of 'selectiveness', which is an activity associated with the presentation of evidence in explanations.

> *Selectiveness:*
> The activity of presenting an explanation that uses evidence that has been specifically *selected* from a wider pool of evidence to make a candidate explanation look warranted when it otherwise might not be.

Take, for example, Peter Shaffer's play *Amadeus* (Shaffer, 1979), in which he proposes that the death of Wolfgang Amadeus Mozart was due to the machinations of Antonio Salieri.[1] Shaffer carefully selects evidence from the historical record to support the 'Salieri killed Mozart' hypothesis and leaves out any evidence that would count against the hypothesis.

Shaffer is not asserting that Salieri was responsible for Mozart's death. He is merely telling a story in the mould of speculative historical fiction. However, sometimes people take such fictions seriously. The central motif of Dan Brown's series of Robert Langdon novels – such as *The Da Vinci Code* (Brown, 2003) – is that there are secrets encoded into art and architecture, which tell us the true, hidden history of Western civilisation. Brown's work is treated by many as a plausible explanation of certain motifs and recurrent features of art worldwide.

It turns out that sometimes people mistake fiction for fact. This is because sometimes:

a) all they know about some subject – like the life of Mozart or art history – is informed by having heard about certain famous 'historical' narratives, and
b) these narratives are close enough retellings of the historical details that many people are unable to discern where the fabrications begin and the history ends.

The selective use of evidence to make some story look plausible is an acceptable mode of expression in fiction. Umberto Eco's *Foucault's Pendulum* (Eco, 1989) is possibly the best and most erudite piece of fiction about conspiracy theories.[2] It concerns the creation of an entirely fictitious conspiracy theory that is nonetheless plausible because its authors have deliberately selected pieces of the historical record to give it a sense of verisimilitude. Yet, while selectiveness is a useful device in fiction, the worry is that influential institutions are selective in their use of evidence when countering conspiracy theories.

Operation 8/The October Raids

In October 2008, a series of police raids – known formally as 'Operation 8' and informally as the 'October Raids' – took place throughout New Zealand (Aotearoa). The Threat Assessment Group, a branch of the New Zealand Police Force set up under the '2002 Terrorism Suppression Act' to investigate potential terrorist threats in New Zealand (Aotearoa), claimed the raids were justified because there was credible evidence of the existence of a network of homegrown terrorists.

The story of the October Raids is a tale of two competing conspiracy theories, each of which relies on the use of selective evidence. The first is the official theory, which was proposed by the New Zealand Police about the existence of terrorist training camps. The second is the theory put forward by the alleged terrorists, who claimed not only that nothing untoward was going on, but that the police hid the fact that the arrests were baseless by disseminating *disinformation* about the accused.

Selective evidence and the official theory

The police claimed the arrests were justified because of credible evidence – a dossier of intercepted phone calls, e-mails and SMS messages – that indicated the existence of terrorist training camps in New Zealand (Aotearoa). The accused, however, claimed the intercepted material was:

a) selective, in that it was comprised of the edited fragments of much longer, more mundane conversations, and
b) selective by virtue of placing the said edited fragments *out of context* in a single document, which in turn strongly suggested that the accused were terrorists.

There are, then, two kinds of alleged selectiveness in the official theory. The first is the reliance by the police on small snippets of the total evidence. The police intercepted a large volume of the accused's communications but only presented a subsection of it as justification for the raids. The accused claim that the *total evidence* does not suggest they were engaged in terrorist activity.

The second kind of selectiveness follows from the first. Bundling the said fragments into one document in such a way as to strongly suggest terrorist activity where the total evidence does not – if this is indeed what happened – is more than just suspicious. Rather, it is evidence that the police actively sought to mislead the public.

Now, it is possible that the police engaged in *unintended* or *unwitting* selectiveness. However, even if this were possible, that would not excuse it. For one thing, it would be an example of bad tradecraft by the police. For another, the public have a reasonable expectation that members of public institutions, like the police, should be rigorous in the presentation and defence of their theories. The unwitting selection and misrepresentation of the evidence would be a contravention of the duty of care the police have towards the public they serve.

The conspiracy theory and selective evidence

The conspiracy theory put forward to explain the deficiencies in the police case is also selective in its use of evidence. Proponents of this thesis frequently claim, for example, that the Solicitor-General stated the police evidence did not justify bringing in charges of terrorism against the accused. However, in this case they are selectively ignoring parts of what the Solicitor-General said, because he also claimed, on the basis of the evidence presented, that, nonetheless, serious and dangerous criminal activity had been uncovered by the police. The problem of charging the accused with terrorism was not a lack of evidence, he claimed. Rather, it was because terrorist activity was ill-defined by New Zealand law. Wittingly or otherwise, the accused:

a) relied on some unrepresentative, edited, fragments of evidence, and
b) wove these into a narrative that strongly suggested that the official theory was unwarranted.

There is, however, a salient difference between the police case and the arguments advanced by the accused and their defenders. The New Zealand public cannot legitimately see all of the intercepted communications collected by the police, because the said evidence has been suppressed. While parts of the intercepted communications were leaked to the media, most people had to take it on trust that the raids were justified with respect to the evidence. In contrast, the rival theory, no matter how selective its evidence might be, relies on information that is in the public record. We can judge the merit of their arguments on the evidence, rather than worrying about whether the police case relies upon an appeal to political or epistemic authority. This difference makes their theory seem like a more trustworthy account because we can judge the evidence for ourselves.

We might be tempted to think there is a sufficient check against selectiveness if we know we can go and inspect the evidence for ourselves. If the cited evidence is part of the public record, then people in positions of authority – so such an argument will go – will be less likely to be selective in their presentation of evidence because they could be found out. However, this is only going to be a check against selectiveness if the consequences of being found out have repercussions. If we live in a society where such bad behaviour is hushed up or ignored, then such public scrutiny might just lead to an increasing mistrust of certain kinds of authorities. This is part of what makes some version of the Openness Objection (as discussed in Chapter 6) seem to be a plausible view to hold about whether the presumed openness of our society tells us anything about whether belief in conspiracies here and now is irrational.

The selective citation of evidence is a potential problem when it comes to the presentation of any argument for or against some theory. However, how do we detect evidence for or against a theory that has been completely fabricated? What are we to make of claims of disinformation?

Disinformation

The worry that fabricated information exists in the public record is a challenge to our notion of how open our society is.

> *Disinformation:*
> The activity of presenting *fabricated* information in support of a candidate explanation in order to make a candidate explanation look warranted when it otherwise might not be.

Fictional examples of disinformation campaigns are easy to come by. For example, some have suggested that *The X Files*, a late-1990s TV show (Carter, 1993), was part of an elaborate government disinformation campaign to hide the existence of extraterrestrial activity on Earth. If someone alleges, say, that there is a government-level conspiracy to subdue the Earth's population in advance of an alien invasion, the suspected conspirators could simply respond with 'Wasn't that an episode of *The X Files*?' What is interesting about *The X Files* is just how much actual history was mixed in with the fabrications. Some of the plots cited by characters within the show were not the inventions of the show's writing staff but actual cases of disinformation that had come to light. *The X Files* was the cultural by-product of an age when revelations of government malfeasance were becoming increasingly common.

There are also historical examples of disinformation. The story of how Stalin and his cronies manufactured the evidence in the Moscow Trials (as discussed in Chapter 7) is a good example of a state-organised disinformation campaign.[3] Along with disinformation campaigns, we also have the related notion of 'false flags', operations run by members of the political establishment but which are designed to look like the actions of some foreign power or local set of dissidents. As such, they are termed 'false flag operations' because the 'flag' (or alleged identity) of the culprits is, in fact, a ruse.[4]

You do not need to believe in the existence of conspiracies to be worried about disinformation or false flag operations. You could trust officialdom and yet still suspect some piece of information disseminated by a public institution[5] of being fabricated. This is to say that disinformation is not solely the product of institutional corruption or conspiracy. However, the worry conspiracy theory skeptics have is that disinformation ends up being evidence used by conspiracy theorists of a certain stripe to prove the existence of conspiracies.

Errant and unaccounted-for data

One way to examine disinformation and why disinformation is something we need to be aware of is by looking at what Brian L. Keeley calls 'errant data': information that is not part of the pool of evidence for some explanatory hypothesis but can be construed as evidence for a rival hypothesis. Keeley characterises two kinds of errant data: 'unaccounted-for data' and 'contradictory data'.

> *Errant-unaccounted-for data:*
> Data that supports one candidate explanation but is unaccounted for (is not mentioned or explained) by some rival candidate explanation. (Keeley, 1999, p. 118)

Examples of errant-unaccounted-for data can be found in some of the conspiracy theories surrounding the assassination of American President

John F. Kennedy. Conspiracy theorists who claim Lee Harvey Oswald was a patsy, or worked with others, often rely on claims that witnesses heard more than the three gunshots Oswald is alleged to have fired. Sometimes they voice suspicions about what were the real reasons for the last-minute change to President Kennedy's schedule and motorcade route through Dallas. These pieces of evidence or suspicions are taken as data that is errant to the official theory but happens to support the conspiracy theory that Oswald had accomplices, or that he was a dupe for the real assassins.

Keeley argues that the existence of errant data is not a special problem for conspiracy theories *per se*. He writes:

> What conspiracy theories get wrong, however, is that the existence of errant data alone is not a significant problem with a theory. Given the imperfect nature of our human understanding of the world, we should expect that even the best possible theory would not explain all the available data. (Keeley, 1999, p. 120)

Indeed, errant data is not a special feature of conspiracy theories.[6] As David Coady has argued, while conspiracy theories will sometimes offer explanations of data that are explained by or contrary to some rival hypothesis, some official theories also seek to explain data that are in conflict with their rival conspiracy theories (Coady, 2006a, p. 119). For example, part of the evidence for the official theory of 9/11 is a videotaped message by Osama bin Laden, in which he admits to being behind the attack on New York and Washington, DC. Some of the Controlled Demolition theories about 9/11 either ignore, or do not take into account, this piece of evidence because it conflicts with these conspiracy theories. This, then, is a piece of data that is errant to a set of Inside Job conspiracy theories about 9/11 but is cited by the official theory as a reason to take a dim view of those conspiracy theories. The official theory also accounts for the errant data cited as supporting the Controlled Demolition hypothesis – that the Twin Towers look as if they were brought down by a controlled demolition – by claiming that the data has been misinterpreted by the said conspiracy theorists. The official theory for 9/11 rests upon the claim that we learnt a great deal about the collapse of skyscrapers – like the Twin Towers – because of the analysis of the events of that day, which the rival conspiracy theories have not taken into account.

Contradictory data

The existence of contradictory data in a theory presents a different, and possibly more interesting, concern.

> *Errant-contradictory data:*
> Data cited by one candidate explanation that contradicts another explanation. (Keeley, 1999, p. 118)

Going back to the story of the October Raids, the New Zealand Police claim they are unable to tell the full story of why the raids were justified *because the intercepted communications have been suppressed by the courts* and so the defendants have been able to put out data which *appears* not only to be errant to the police case, but to also contradict it. If this errant-contradictory data has been fabricated, then the accused are using disinformation to make the police case look unwarranted when it might otherwise not be.[7]

Disinformation – the activity of presenting *fabricated* information to make some explanation look warranted when it otherwise might not be – is a particular concern for conspiracy theorists of a certain stripe. If there really is a conspiracy, and the conspirators are actively seeking to hide evidence of their existence, then fabricating 'evidence' that points to the conspiracy theorist being crazy/paranoid/holding a grudge, or suggests a more mundane explanation than the conspiracy theory, is to be expected.

For example, the official theory of 9/11 is based upon the claim that the impact of two Boeing 747s, piloted by terrorists, caused the destruction of the Twin Towers. However, conspiracy theorists who claim the Twin Towers were brought down by a controlled demolition cite – as data contradictory to the official theory – the claim that the towers collapsed in a way that is only consistent with the use of explosive charges. This, they take it, is evidence contradictory to the official story and, as such, the claim that the towers fell in a way consistent with structural damage caused by the impact of two planes and fire damage is *disinformation* put out by the US government to hide what really happened.

Counterfacts

Susan Feldman presents an interesting gloss on disinformation in her discussion of 'counterfact theories', which are a kind of conspiracy theory that assert the existence and activities of powerful and secretive conspirators who are actively covering up their activities.

Feldman argues that there is, typically, a two-step schema to the positing of a counterfact theory:

1. Counterfacts are asserted, and
2. A cover-up is invoked (Feldman, 2011, p. 17).

A counterfact is some piece of information contrary to a received explanation of an event (Feldman, 2011, p. 16). For example, the controlled demolition conspiracy theory about 9/11 makes use of counterfacts, given that the official theory excludes the possibility the Twin Towers were demolished by explosives, despite appearances.

Feldman's analysis is tied explicitly to Michael Barkun's idea of systemic conspiracies – claims of conspiracy in which the conspirators have a broad goal that they achieve typically by subverting existing powerful institutions – which were discussed in depth back in Chapter 4. Given that Barkun asserts systemic conspiracies are irrational – because they are not based on evidence – belief in counterfact theories is irrational *by definition*. Counterfacts, then, despite what Feldman claims, are not just pieces of information counter to some received explanation that happen to be, when analysed, a good reason to doubt some counterfact conspiracy theory. Rather, they are examples of information put forward in support of a theory that is *prima facie* irrational to believe in the first place, and just happens to exist in opposition to some official theory.

Feldman can respond to this criticism of her view in two ways. The first is to claim that counterfact theories can never be official theories (which is in line with Barkun's view), but this move compounds the issue. If we have official theories with the characteristics of counterfact theories, which are not counterfact theories *merely because they happen to be official theories*, then what role are counterfacts playing in the analysis? Either they identify something wrong with an explanation – conspiracy or official theory – or they do not. Marking them out as problems *only for conspiracy theories* begs the question.

The second way Feldman can respond is to say she is only interested in analysing the faults of belief in systemic conspiracies. As such, counterfacts explain why belief in systemic conspiracies is irrational. This is a weird solution, though, given that it once again raises the question of what role counterfacts are playing in the analysis of systemic conspiracies. If counterfact theories are unwarranted *because alleging large-scale cover ups is irrational*, this gets the analysis back to front. Given that we know institutions and individuals do sometimes disseminate disinformation, and there are examples of what appear to be counterfact theories that turned out to be warranted – like the Moscow Show Trials – we should be asking: 'When is it rational to accept that counterfacts have been asserted?'

Feldman's analysis of counterfact theories also confuses the production of disinformation as being a core tenet of a particular kind of conspiracy theory, when we should really regard claims about disinformation as being associated with only *some* conspiracy theories. While there are historical examples of conspiracy theories linked to claims of disinformation – like the Moscow Trials – the claim that conspiracy theories *predict the existence of disinformation* is not an auxiliary hypothesis of all such theories.

Recall the list of conditions from Chapter 3 that must be satisfied to satisfy a claim of conspiracy:

1. There exists (or has existed) some set of agents who plan,
2. Some end is/was desired by the agents, and
3. Steps have been taken to minimise public awareness of what the agents are up to.

The final condition states that the conspirators will be seeking to keep their activity secret, but this does not entail that the conspirators will be disseminating disinformation. It is quite possible to hide the existence of a conspiracy without disseminating contradictory data. As such, claims about the dissemination of disinformation are not a prediction of the *core* conspiracy theory but of some *auxiliary hypothesis*. When such a hypothesis is cited in conjunction with a conspiracy theory, then the presence of contradictory data will not falsify the conspiracy theory because it is compatible, or even implied by, the conspiracy theory *plus* the auxiliary theory.

The auxiliary theory that predicts the existence of disinformation might itself be falsifiable. For example, it was suggested by some conspiracy theorists prior to the invasion of Iraq in 2003 that evidence of an Iraqi programme to produce weapons of mass destruction would be found once American troops were on the ground in Iraq. The fact that no such 'evidence' was found falsified an auxiliary theory associated with some of the conspiracy theories about the real reason for the invasion of Iraq.

This also tells us something interesting about disinformation, which is that, even if we can show that disinformation is not being produced by some public institution, this does not necessarily show that the related conspiracy theory is unwarranted. Claims of disinformation are claims about how the conspirators are engaging in a particular kind of activity designed to keep their conspiracy secret. Falsifying such a claim does not mean that there is no conspiracy but, rather, that this particular kind of evidence for the existence of the conspiracy does not apply. Perhaps this is the real worry conspiracy theory skeptics have when it comes to claims of disinformation: if we show that some piece of supposed disinformation is not fabricated, then a conspiracy theorist can easily shift their attention to some other piece of evidence they take to be suspicious. Such goalpost shifting is usually frowned upon, but this ignores the fact that, if a conspiracy really is in existence, some disinformation might well be in the pool of purported evidence.

For Feldman this does not seem to matter, however, because she does not think counterfact theorists are interested in getting to the truth of whether there is a conspiracy in existence. Rather, they are expressing a particular conspiratorial mode of thinking about the world in which they live (Feldman, 2011, p. 22). Now, aside from the fact that Feldman's thesis is unfalsifiable – because, even if someone who puts forward counterfacts to support her conspiracy theory claims to be evidence-based, Feldman can say: 'But she isn't, really' – Feldman's analysis suffers from the same kind of issue as conspiracist analyses of belief in conspiracy theories suffer from. It confuses a psychological fault on the part of some conspiracy theorists with talk about the merit of citing a theory about disinformation in support of some conspiracy theory.

Falsifiability

If disinformation is being put out by conspirators, then what do we do with evidence that indicates some conspiracy theory should not be believed? If there really is a conspiracy, then that evidence has surely been fabricated. It does not seem unreasonable to think that, if a conspiracy is in existence, then you might take evidence against the associated conspiracy theory as being evidence of the conspiracy.

Such a move would render the said conspiracy theory unfalsifiable. No matter what the evidence against the conspiracy, it could be interpreted as supporting the claim of conspiracy. As such, conspiracy theories that cite this kind of errant-contradictory data are unfalsifiable, and surely unfalsifiable theories are the kind of theories we are justified in taking a dim view of?

Interestingly, views on whether unfalsifiable conspiracy theories present a problem for belief in conspiracy theories vary widely in the literature. Volker Heins argues that the unfalsifiability of conspiracy theories is a problem (Heins, 2007, pp. 791–792). Although he admits conspiracies do occur, conspiracy theorists – defined here as conspiracists – are content to bamboozle us on matters of whether there is any 'official' truth. As such, conspiracy theories reinforce the suspicions of conspiracy theorists and make showing that some conspiracy theory is false an impossible task.

Michael J. Wood, Karen M. Douglas and Robbie M. Sutton argue that conspiracy theories are not, by definition, false, but belief in such conspiratorial explanations is 'notoriously resistant to falsification' (Wood, Douglas & Sutton, 2012, p. 767). Stephan Lewandowsky, Klaus Oberauer and Gilles E. Gignac (citing Jeffrey Bale, as well as Cass Sunstein and Adrian Vermeule) write:

> Conspiracist ideation is, by definition, difficult to correct because any evidence contrary to the conspiracy is itself considered evidence of its existence. (Lewandowsky, Oberauer, & Gignac, 2013, p. 630)

In a follow-up article, Stephan Lewandowsky, John Cook, Klaus Oberauer and Michael Marriott (referencing Keeley) also state that:

> A defining attribute of conspiracist ideation is its resistance to contrary evidence. (Lewandowsky, Cook, Oberauer, & Marriott, 2013, p. 13)

Michael Barkun also claims that conspiracy theories are unfalsifiable. He writes:

> But the obsessive quest for proof masks a deeper problem: the more sweeping a conspiracy theory's claims, the less relevant evidence becomes, notwithstanding the insistence that the theory is empirically sound. This paradox occurs because conspiracy theories are at their heart nonfalsifiable. No matter how much evidence their adherents accumulate, belief in a conspiracy theory ultimately becomes a matter of faith rather than proof. (Barkun, 2003, p. 7)

Barkun is talking about the unfalsifiability of conspiracy theories with reference to his belief that it is the *thesis of conspiracism* that best captures talk of conspiracy theories and their lack of warrant (Barkun, 2003, pp. 187–188). As we saw in Chapter 3, even if we accept there is a pathological kind of belief in conspiracy theories that we can mark out as conspiracism, then it is not belief in conspiracy theories *per se* that is problematic but, rather, *conspiracist belief* in conspiracy theories.

Keeley, unlike the aforementioned theorists, argues that, if disinformation is being put out by conspirators, then conspiracy theories would be unfalsifiable, *but this is not a problem per se for such theories.* He writes:

> Falsifiability is a perfectly fine criterion in the case of natural science when the target of investigation is neutral with respect to our queries, but it seems much less appropriate in the case of the phenomena covered by conspiracy theories. (Keeley, 1999, p. 121)

Think of it this way: imagine that the New Zealand Police acted hastily with regard to the information they had collected during Operation 8 and, once the dust had settled, realised that the intercepted evidence did not justify the raids. However, given that the raids had occurred and the public were asking searching questions about them, the police decided to both select some of the intercepted evidence – so as to bolster their case – and introduce some fabricated evidence, in the hope that it would not be noticed. If this were the case, then the police would be conspiring to hide the fact that the raids were not justified with respect to the evidence. However, if you were one of the accused and knew you were innocent of the charges levelled against you, you would know both that the evidence was really disinformation and that the disinformation was evidence of a conspiracy against you. In this respect, your conspiracy theory would be unfalsifiable, because the evidence that falsifies the claim a conspiracy exists can be taken as evidence of the said conspiracy. This does not seem like an irrational move as long as you could warrant the claim that the conspiracy actually exists.

This point is made by Steve Clarke (and Lee Basham (Basham, 2011, p. 63)), who writes:

> Once a conspiracy theorist has become committed to a conspiracy theory, she is able to account for almost any relevant evidence that is presented. It is either evidence of the cover-up, which the conspirers are attempting, or it is evidence of discrepancies in the received explanation. Strictly, none of this can be described as ad hoc. A theory that involves an attempt by some people to deceive other people is a theory that involves reasons both to expect a cover-up and flaws in the cover-up. (Clarke, 2002, pp. 135–136)

Normally, evidence that contradicts some explanation should be taken (in a naive sense) as falsifying that hypothesis. However, because conspiracy theorists of a certain stripe often predict the existence of errant-contradictory data – data that would ordinarily falsify the conspiracy theory – this makes it impossible for such errant data to falsify the conspiracy theory.

Toxic truths

Lee Basham, in 'Conspiracy Theory and the Accusation of Cover-up', introduces the notion of a 'toxic truth' or 'toxicity', which is

> [T]he likelihood that some conspiratorial scenarios, even if well-evidenced, are too 'toxic' for our usual institutions of public

> information to pursue and disseminate to the public. Neither law enforcement nor mainstream media will 'touch them'. Cover-up is the consequence. Our ordinary trust in these institutions—our *public trust*—is dramatically compromised. (Basham, forthcoming)

Such toxic truths are interesting because they suggest that in some cases individuals within influential institutions might fail to endorse some theory *despite knowing it is warranted* because the cost to the institution of endorsing the said theory is too high, or because admitting to wrongdoing by the institution is unthinkable.[8] The existence of toxic truths – which are not out of the question, given what we know about the leaked existence of rendition programmes, the revealed mass surveillance of the public by the NSA and the like – calls into question our trust in the utterances of political authorities, at the very least. Such toxic truths may also exist in the academic sphere: it has been suggested by certain conspiracy theorists that, while there might have been reason to think that the thesis of anthropogenic climate change was plausible several decades ago, recent evidence refutes it. As such, the continuing funding of climate science and its role in directing public policy would be a toxic truth in both the academic and political spheres.

The existence of toxic truths calls into question our trust in public data. Even when faced with what looks to be good evidence for a theory, authorities might dismiss it. We can imagine a situation in which the evidence for the Inside Job hypothesis is good enough to open a new investigation into who was behind the 11 September 2001 attacks. In this respect, an appeal to authority to decide the matter here would be problematic. However, an appeal to the evidence would be just as troubling: if there is a certain toxic truth about some event or influential institution, then we should expect disinformation about it, as well as the presentation of selective evidence in favour of the claim that no toxic truth exists. Sorting out the evidence from the non-evidence in such a situation would be non-trivial.

Disinformation, selectiveness, false flags and toxic truths are all claims about evidence that both assume the existence of duplicitous activity and are used to show that such activity is going on. Perhaps the question we need to ask is just how likely conspiracies are in the kind of societies in which we live.

Prior probabilities

The possibility that powerful institutions are engaging in disinformation campaigns is part and parcel of the claims of many conspiracy theorists.

The much-mentioned David Icke, Alex Jones and Glenn Beck back up their suspicion of information that emanates from anybody associated with officialdom by providing a litany of examples of people in power having lied to the public and actively engaged in the spread of disinformation. They will point to such examples as Iran-Contra, MK-ULTRA, the Moscow Trials, Operation Northwoods, the claim that Saddam Hussein was developing weapons of mass destruction – examples where the official story was suspicious at best – to call into question the official theories of 9/11, the capture of Saddam Hussein, the death of Osama bin Laden, anthropogenic climate change and the like. They claim that the official explanations for these events are based almost entirely on disinformation – or are examples of false flag campaigns. What is interesting about these cases is that it is not at all clear that these conspiracy theorists are acting irrationally, *even if you think they are mistaken in their beliefs*. After all, the American government was complicit in both the Iran-Contra affair and the development of the MK-ULTRA programme. So, if we know they did those things, why is it such a stretch to claim that 9/11 was an inside job?

As Peter Knight notes:

> [I]t is becoming increasingly hard to be certain of the difference between the plausible and the paranoid. With both a restricted access to real information (despite the Freedom of Information Act) and an overload of data (particularly on the Internet) it is proving more difficult to distinguish between false rumors and actual revelations. As far as the conspiracy theorist is concerned (and to some extent we are all conspiracy theorists now), the possibility of deliberately planted false clues – 'disinformation' – means that we can never rest in our interpretative endeavors. (Knight, 2000, p. 25)

This point is pressed by Lee Basham (Basham, 2011). Our notion of the prior probability of conspiratorial activity happening right here, right now depends on what kind of culture we believe we live in. When it comes to a subjective judgement as to whether an appeal to the existence of a conspiracy is plausible, people are very much affected by what they already believe or know. If you grow up in a criminal family where deceit and cover-stories are commonplace, then you will be much more inclined to believe conspiratorial activity is happening elsewhere. After all, surely all families are just like yours? What conspiracy theorists of a certain stripe do is point out that we live in a world where conspiracies really do occur, here and now. They then use these examples to justify their suspicion that events similar to those that were caused by actual conspiracies might also be explicable with respect to a conspiracy theory.

Fortitious data

Joel Buenting and Jason Taylor identify a special kind of disinformation: evidence that is too lucky to be true. For example, the official theory about the 9/11 attack on the Pentagon makes reference to a piece of very lucky evidence, the claim that American Airlines Flight 77 crashed into the only section of the Pentagon reinforced to withstand such an impact. Some conspiracy theorists about 9/11 wonder whether this evidence is 'too lucky to be true'. Joel Buenting and Jason Taylor call this kind of evidence 'fortuitous data'.

> *Fortuitous data:*
>
> i) data that supports the official theory but
> ii) fits the official story so well that it looks too lucky/too good to be true, and
> iii) the 'lucky' nature of the data is unexplained by the official theory (Buenting & Taylor, 2010, p. 572).

Fortuitous data is information that is so lucky in nature that its luckiness requires an explanation.

Buenting and Taylor do not need to restrict their talk of fortuitous data with respect to a contrast between conspiracy and official theories. Fortuitous data may well be found in non-conspiracy theories *and their rivals* or between competing conspiracy theories. However, for Buenting and Taylor, fortuitous data is a kind of disinformation cited in support of conspiracy theories. They argue that the citation of fortuitous data helps distinguish between warranted and unwarranted conspiracy theories. If a conspiracy theory relies on fortuitous data, then that is a good reason to dismiss it (Buenting & Taylor, 2010, p. 569). However, they also end up arguing that the citation of fortuitous data in conspiracy theories renders such theories rationally superior to non-conspiracy theory explanations of the same event (Buenting & Taylor, 2010, p. 578). This striking inconsistency in Buenting and Taylor's work comes out of failing to distinguish between fortuitous data and what we might call 'fortunate data'.

> *Fortunate data:*
>
> Information that:
> i) supports the official story;
> ii) is lucky; and
> iii) finally, the 'lucky' nature of the data is unexplained by the official story.

Fortunate data is data that is *merely* lucky. The problem with fortuitous data is that it is a subset of fortunate data. While fortuitous data has the *added* property of being 'too lucky to be true', fortunate data is *merely* data that is lucky, and the said luckiness is left unexplained by the official story. So, we could say it was very lucky that Flight 77 hit the recently reinforced wall of the Pentagon, but is the lucky nature of that piece of information too good to be true?

Fortunate data is a kind of errant-unaccounted-for data and is, as such, evidence – admittedly of a lucky kind – whereas fortuitous data is evidence for the existence of a conspiracy. However, we cannot tell whether data is merely fortunate or fortuitous at first glance. There is no 'mark of the incredible', harking back to Keeley once more. Sometimes what looks like fortuitous data will turn out to be merely fortunate data – genuine but lucky evidence – which only looks fortuitous either because we are insufficiently sensitive to just how chancy evidence can be or because we assume that someone is tinkering with the evidence. For example, many criminal prosecutions hinge upon fortunate data, like DNA evidence, someone just happening to walk past the house at the moment of the break-in, and the like. This data is clearly lucky, but is it lucky in the sense that it is merely fortunate or is it lucky in the sense that it is fortuitous?

One response is that the demarcating factor here will be claims about the luckiness of the evidence along with claims about how well we trust the source of the evidence. We might take it that the police are, all other things considered, trustworthy when it comes to presenting evidence of criminal wrongdoing *now*. However, if we were looking at a case from the context of the 1970s – when the fitting up of suspects was more commonplace – our suspicions of the police as a corrupt institution will affect our suspicion about just how lucky data that emanates from such a source appears to be.

Buenting and Taylor seem aware of these kinds of issues, given that they consider a weak and a strong reading of their view (Buenting & Taylor, 2010, pp. 575–576). The weak reading claims that fortuitous data occurs only in cases of *poorly concocted conspiracies*, where the conspirators fail to grasp that the fortuitous data they produce will be picked up upon by judicious conspiracy theorists. The stronger reading claims that the production of fortuitous data is the kind of thing clever conspirators should try to avoid. Buenting and Taylor argue that the stronger thesis ends up being too strong. In the terms of our analysis here, then, we should assume – according to the stronger reading – that the suspected fortuitous data is really just fortunate data. After all, clever conspirators would not leave evidence of their activity in the evidential record.

Buenting and Taylor cite what they take to be a clear example of fortuitous data that supports the weaker reading: the infamous eighteen-and-a-half-minute gap in the recordings of conversations Nixon had with officials about the Watergate Hotel break-in in 1972. Nixon denied knowing about or being involved in the break-in to the Democratic National Committee headquarters, but let slip that his conversations in the White House were routinely recorded. When the recordings were released, there was a gap in the conversation about the break-in that was too good to be true. This gap suggested Nixon was hiding something. Not only that, but the gap in the recording could not be explained, which suggested that the evidence had been tinkered with (Buenting & Taylor, 2010, p. 577).

Contrast this example with that of Flight 77. In the Watergate case, the eighteen-and-a-half-minute gap really was too good to be true, and thus counts as an example of fortuitous data *with the benefit of hindsight*. The Pentagon case, however, might be an example of either fortuitous or fortunate data: there are a host of factors that weigh in on whether it is merely data fortunate for the accepted conspiracy theory or, as 9/11 Truthers would have it, fortuitous. This indicates that if we are going to distinguish between fortunate and fortuitous data – between data that is lucky and data that is so-lucky-it's-not-true – then we need to either focus on the centrality of the said data to the proposed explanation or look for patterns of fortunate data that suggest the data is suspicious (and thus fortuitous).

There is another response: if the stronger thesis were true, then we should expect clever conspirators to ensure no fortuitous *or* fortunate data is in the evidential record, since fortunate data might get mistaken for fortuitous data and thus make people suspicious that a conspiracy exists. As such, the presence of fortunate data in the evidential record (whether it is also fortuitous or not) suggests that the conspirators are not that clever, and thus the stronger reading is implausible.

Whatever the case, the fact that we cannot easily (or, in some cases, at all) distinguish between fortunate and fortuitous data means that, contra what Buenting and Taylor suggest, fortuitous data is not useful in demarcating between warranted and unwarranted conspiracy theories. While some evidence may appear 'too lucky to be true', we cannot use that as a reason to suspect conspiracy theories of being bunk, particularly since some of the data cited by official theories might be similarly fortunate.

What can we do?

The concerns we have about the role of evidence in conspiracy theories are really worries that relate to explanations in general. Selectiveness is a pathology of the presentation of explanations, rather than a pathology associated with the presentation of conspiracy theories in particular. If we have access to the evidential pool, then we can at least check to see whether evidence has been selected in such a way as to warrant an otherwise unwarranted explanatory hypothesis. Still, even if we think we can look at the pool of evidence to detect whether the cited evidence is selective, it may still contain disinformation.

So what can we do?

One answer is based in the trust we have in the sources of explanations, which brings to focus the discussion of our trust in public institutions from Chapter 6. However, another comes from the dissection of the adage 'Trust no one!'

Surely, according to the principle of charity, what someone means when they say that is: 'Do not accept an explanation *merely* out of trust in the authorities that put it forward when you can look at the evidence they use to make their explanatory hypotheses look warranted.'

It is reasonable (at least sometimes) to have some measure of trust in an informant. This, on its own, can count as a reason to accept (or, at the very least, not challenge) that informant's view. However, where you have access to the evidence, you should look at it and not let the trust you have in the informant do all the work. As we saw in Chapter 7, while we might have a case for accepting endorsements from academic institutions, we do not seem to have much of a case for accepting them from the political establishment. If we are concerned that explanations are selective, then we should look at the evidence.

However, the worry about disinformation is not so easily overcome even if we do look at the evidence. Inspecting the propositions being put forward is one thing, but being able to ascertain whether the propositions are actually true, which is to say they are pieces of evidence and not disinformation, is another thing entirely.

This brings us to another tricky issue: we have some grounds to be suspicious of the utterances of the members of our influential institutions. Thus, when conspiracies are alleged about them (or when authorities are in disagreement about whether some conspiratorial claim is true), some will claim that the right thing to do is to go and look at the individual arguments and their evidence. However, as we have seen in this chapter, it is not that easy. Sometimes the evidence we are presented with is either distorted or fabricated, and often our judgements about the evidence are informed by who we take to be the right kind of authority to arbitrate on the matter. For example, many of the arguments and evidence for claims of conspiracy require significant theoretical knowledge before you can go and make sense of them, like the various 9/11 conspiracy theories that alleged the Twin Towers collapsed in a way that resembled a controlled demolition. It is hard to know how a layperson can just examine these arguments and the evidence for them.

In this respect, trust really is our only arbiter on subjects on which we know very little (or nothing at all), and this once again raises the awkward question: 'Just how much do we trust the influential institutions in our society?'

10
The Inference to Any Old Explanation

Much of this book has been concerned with countering the common sense but misinformed suspicion that belief in conspiracy theories is irrational. As we have seen, the fact that some theory is a *conspiracy theory* is no reason to automatically assume it is false, or that it is irrational to consider it seriously.

However, the attentive reader will be thinking: 'This is all fine and good, but just because we don't have grounds for a *prima facie* suspicion that conspiracy theories *in general* are bunk, that doesn't tell us that we should believe specific conspiracy theories.' After all, even if we do not have grounds for a common sense suspicion of the class of things we call 'conspiracy theories', surely we are still right to doubt specific claims of conspiracy? As a general rule, anyone saying that some conspiracy has come to pass takes on a significant burden of proof, because, as claims of conspiracy are extraordinary – which is to say that, typically, conspiracies are unlikely compared with other, more prosaic explanations – they require extraordinary evidence to satisfy them.

If there really is a problem with respect to belief in specific claims of conspiracy, then it is likely to be centred around what we might call the 'Inference to Any Old Explanation': sometimes we might infer that a conspiracy exists and ignore other potential explanations, and, even in cases when we can satisfy the claim that there really does exist some conspiracy, we still need to show that the said conspiracy is the salient cause of the event we are seeking to explain. As such, many of the prototypical fears conspiracy theory skeptics have about belief in conspiracy theories turn out to be worries that conspiracy theorists are inferring to *any old explanation* rather than the *best explanation*.

Inferring to Any Old Explanation

When someone commits the fallacy of the Inference to Any Old Explanation, they mistake some arbitrary candidate explanation for the *best* explanation.

Mistakenly inferring to any old explanation happens all the time: politicians often impute malicious motives to their rivals when it turns out someone has simply cocked up; people assume their partners are deliberately ignoring their messages when really their partners are too busy to check them; students assume that the reason it is taking so long for their marks to be returned is that they have failed the course, and so forth. In some cases we infer to any old explanation – rather than the best – because we confuse our own psychological state with that of someone else: I am afraid of failing the course, so I assume you have not notified me of my marks because of the potential embarrassment for all parties. Sometimes we simply make a mistake in our judgement of what is likely and what is not: I might assume you are specifically grumpy with me, and downplay your suggestion that you might just be generally grumpy and having a particularly bad time *today*.

The Inference to Any Old Explanation is a widespread error of the process of inferential reasoning. The worry some conspiracy theory skeptics have about belief in conspiracy theories is that conspiracy theorists infer that conspiracies – rather than more prosaic explanations – are the most probable explanations of events. So, if there really is something to the suspicion that conspiracy theories are typically bunk, then it probably arises out of one or both of the following two objections to a claim that a conspiracy exists:

1. Showing that the conditions for conspiratorial activity have been satisfied is difficult, and
2. Claims of conspiracy are often vague and thus may be unfalsifiable.

These objections do not present an insurmountable obstacle to warranted belief in specific conspiracy theories. In the end, we must judge conspiracy theories on the merits of their evidence. It is also the case that neither of these objections justifies us in taking a dim view of conspiracy theories in general. So, let us look at some examples of candidate explanations for some event that have been put forward as *the* explanation, despite its turning out there is no good reason to believe this particular candidate explanation (rather than some rival) is *the* explanation.

The curious case of Lewis Carroll and Alice Liddell

The mathematician and author Charles Lutwidge Dodgson (also known as Lewis Carroll) based the character of 'Alice' from his novels *Alice in Wonderland* (Carroll, 1967) and *Alice through the Looking Glass and What She Found There* (Carroll, 2005) on Alice Liddell. The real Alice was the daughter of two of Dodgson's friends, Henry and Lorina Liddell, with whom Dodgson spent a lot of time. However, in 1862 a rift formed between the two families, and no explanation was ever given for it either by the Liddells or by Dodgson. This has led some people to speculate that Dodgson's close relationship with Alice was the cause of the falling out, with some biographers even arguing that the Liddells discovered that Dodgson was having an inappropriate relationship with the 11-year old Alice.[1]

The curious case of Charles Lutwidge Dodgson and the Liddell family is an interesting example, because we do not have access to any hard evidence of what caused the rift between the two families: we only have rumour and speculation. The Liddells refused to talk about why they severed contact with Dodgson, and, although Dodgson was keeping a diary at the time of the rift, his sister destroyed the relevant pages after his death. As such, there is no extant record of why the Liddells and Dodgson fell out, just *post facto* speculation. The hypothesis, then, that Dodgson was engaged in an inappropriate relationship with Alice Liddell is the result of an inference that has the following form:

1. We have some event we want to explain (such as the rift between Dodgson and the Liddells), and
2. We have some evidence (such as the missing diary pages, the reluctance of the Liddells to comment on the rift, etc.), and
3. We have some related theories that pertain to the kind of thing we are trying to explain (such as psychological or sociological theories of the mores of Victorian culture,[2] and so forth).

A problem for the proponents of the hypothesis that Dodgson was engaged in an inappropriate relationship with Alice Liddell is that those who endorse it might be doing so solely on the basis that it accounts nicely for the evidence (or lack of evidence, so to speak). If they have not considered alternative hypotheses – such as the Liddells discovering that Dodgson had been engaging in an affair with Alice's governess – which would also account for the same evidence, then it seems that they *might* have an 'inferred to any old explanation' rather than the best. To put it another way, if we are after the truth (which surely we are when we are considering explanatory hypotheses), we want to get the best (here, most probable candidate) explanation rather than any old one.

The worry is that the hypothesis: 'Charles Dodgson had an inappropriate affair with Alice Liddell' might turn out to be an example of an inference to any old explanation. This should be understood as being an instance of part of the packet of issues associated with our understanding of the under-determination of theories by the evidence.[3] In this particular case we have an explanatory hypothesis that provides a link between the known background facts (the silence of both Dodgson and the Liddells about what happened) and the specific event or phenomenon whose occurrence we want to explain (here, the rift). We are often in a position to choose between explanatory hypotheses that fit the available evidence and explain whatever it is we are trying to account for. However, we need to be able to tell a story as to why we would choose one particular explanation from this range rather than some other.

Four possible inferential mistakes

How does this relate to our analysis of conspiracy theories? Well, if the problem with belief in conspiracy theories is that such theories are typically examples of the Inference to Any Old Explanation – which seems to be one of the main drivers behind the claim that we should be wary of conspiracy theories – then elaborating on the kind of problems ordinary reasoners face when inferring to any explanation should explain why such inferences to the existence of a conspiracy might be so troubling.

When inferring to an explanation, ordinary reasoners might fail to consider:

1. The extent to which the available evidence for the phenomenon being explained renders the hypothesis probable (the *posterior* probability),
2. The degree to which the hypothesis is independently likely (the *prior* probability),
3. The likelihood of the hypothesis, relative to the other hypotheses being considered (the *relative probability*), or
4. The possibility that there are some worthwhile hypotheses that have not been considered.

Three of these issues are to do with how we consider the probability of a given hypothesis. The fourth is about the failure of ordinary reasoners to consider *other* worthwhile hypotheses. Even if we end up accurately appraising the probability of rival hypotheses, it is still possible that a worthwhile candidate might not have been considered. This might be due to the fact that we have unwittingly failed to consider alternative hypotheses because of a lack of knowledge about them, or because we have a psychological disposition to ignore some of them.

We should also consider the possibility that we might choose hypotheses for reasons that are not entirely within our control. For example, in a situation of high urgency, when we are being pressed to make a decision, a third party might restrict the pool of hypotheses to force us to choose the best hypothesis available to us. This might be despite the fact that the person who is offering us the said set of hypotheses knows that there is another hypothesis, which, if we had known about it, we would have chosen. Our choice of plausible hypotheses might also be restricted to *what we have been told about* (if we are going to take seriously the worries expressed in the previous chapter about the selection and presentation of evidence by influential institutions).

Whatever the case, it is fair to say that, when we infer to some explanatory hypothesis, we want to be inferring to the best explanation rather than to any old one. If belief in conspiracy theories is predicated on their typically being inferences to any old explanation, then one of the four inferential mistakes outlined above must occur when conspiracy theories are put forward as the best explanation for some event. This, though, seems to be an unusual claim, *unless you assume that conspiracy theorists suffer from some defect of reasoning*. Yet, it should be clear that any reasoner – conspiracy theorist or not – can infer to any old explanation. As we have just seen, the case of Dodgson and the Liddells is an example where people may have failed to consider other worthwhile hypotheses. The next example we will look at is one in which there are serious questions as to whether the available evidence renders some of the hypotheses put forward as even being *probable*.

Irvine and Mallory's ascent of Sagarmāthā

On 8 June 1924, George Leigh Mallory and Andrew Irvine were last seen making an attempt at the summit of Sagarmāthā (aka Mt Everest). Ever since, some historians and mountain climbers have become obsessed with finding their remains, in the hope that amongst Mallory and Irvine's effects there will be evidence as to what happened to them that day.

The only established fact of the matter is that Mallory and Irvine were last sighted at 1 pm, several hundred metres away from reaching the summit. However, this has not stopped some historians and mountain climbers from claiming that Irvine and Mallory died *after* completing their ascent. This would mean that they, rather than Tenzing Norgay and Edmund Hillary, would have been the first people to reach Sagarmāthā's summit.

Various hypotheses have been put forward to explain why Irvine and Mallory did not return to camp. These range from the claim 'Mallory reached the summit alone (because Irvine died earlier in the ascent)' to 'Mallory and Irvine reached the summit together and died afterwards.'[4] These hypotheses are intellectual fancies, however, as there is no evidence whatsoever for them. Given what we know about the traverse Mallory and Irvine chose, according to the records, and worries about the adequacy of the technology available to them, as well as their limited resources, it seems much more likely that they met their demise attempting the summit, rather than descending from it.

Why, then, has this particular fancy been pursued? Well, if it turned out that Mallory and Irvine made it to the summit, that would challenge the established orthodoxy of who 'conquered' Sagarmāthā. As such, while the available evidence does not render this particular hypothesis probable, arguably it has been promoted because, if it were true, it would change our view about the history of the said mountain, and of the pioneers of mountaineering.

However, the available evidence does not render this hypothesis probable. The posterior probability in this case is low, because there is no evidence that Irvine and Mallory completed their ascent. There is only the wishful thinking of some historians and mountaineers. Not only that, but the hypothesis that they successfully made their ascent is also improbable in the *prior* sense, given what we know about the likelihood of their attempt, their chosen traverse and the gear they had with them at the time.

When we consider rival hypotheses, we should want our chosen explanation to be probable with respect to the evidence. Now, it is true that some conspiracy theories are unlikely with respect to the evidence. It is not, however, clear that this is an issue unique to conspiracy theories. Rather, it is an issue with the people who advance theories. Sometimes hypotheses are promoted because it would be interesting if they were true. As such, sometimes people claim a hypothesis is probable *despite the evidence not making it so*. The next example we will look at, drawn from the annals of xenobiology, concerns the relative probability of a candidate explanation with respect to its rivals.

Not exactly life on Mars

In 2005 two astro-biologists, Chris McKay and Heather Smith, argued for the following claim: if it was discovered that there was a lack of expected hydrocarbons on the surface of Titan (one of the moons of Saturn), that might suggest the presence of methanogenic life there. In 2010 a pair of studies were published, and these showed that there was some process occurring on the surface of Titan that was causing the active depletion of two hydrocarbons, acetylene and hydrogen. Chris McKay was asked to comment on whether this indicated that life existed on, or just below, the surface of Titan. He argued that, although the new evidence might suggest the presence of methanogenic life on Titan, it was unlikely that methanogenic life was responsible for the active depletion of those hydrocarbons.

> The existence of methane-based life churning through hydrocarbons and gaseous hydrogen is the fourth most likely explanation ... according to McKay. 'This is a still a long way from "evidence of life",' he wrote. 'However, it is extremely interesting.' (Matson, 2010)

The evidence – the lack of acetylene and hydrogen – renders the hypothesis that methanogenic life exists on Titan probable, but it is not *more probable* than its rival hypotheses. It is true that Titan has some of the necessary precursors for abiogenesis, and is certainly the kind of environment we might think is conducive to the emergence of life. However, the rival hypotheses – there being atmospheric processes transporting hydrocarbons out of the upper atmosphere, or there being some non-biological chemical reaction that is responsible for the depletion of hydrocarbons on Titan's surface – are more probable. If you were to claim that the presence of methanogenic life on Titan best explains the lack of hydrocarbons on its surface, you would be guilty of inferring to any old explanation: you would be failing to notice that the hypothesis is *relatively improbable* compared with its rivals.

Our probability estimates depend on the information available to us, and this varies over time. For example, in the 16th century it was thought that witches, through their magicks, were a significant cause of the unfaithfulness of spouses. This was considered to be a good explanation of infidelity at the time. Here and now, however, it is safe to say that this would not be considered anywhere near as probable, relative to many other available candidate explanations, because, although acts of infidelity still occur in the 21st century, the hypothesis that such acts can be explained with reference to magick no longer fits with our collective understanding of how the world works. As such, when we consider some hypothesis, we need to be aware of how probable it is *compared with its rivals.*

The burden of proof

Perhaps the worry conspiracy theory skeptics most often have about belief in conspiracy theories is that the prior probability that a conspiracy theory is the best explanation of some event ignores the fact that claims of conspiracy are extraordinary, and thus improbable. This argument can be expressed as a burden of proof issue.

> *The Burden of Proof Argument:*
> As a claim of conspiracy must show that all conditions of conspiratorial activity are satisfied, and as the satisfaction of the final condition (that of secrecy) makes it likely that evidence for the satisfaction of the first two conditions will be unusually hard to obtain, the evidential requirement for a claim of conspiracy will be difficult to discharge.

This point is urged by Pete Mandik. As we saw in Chapter 3, he argues that belief in conspiracy theories is *prima facie* irrational because they are too hard to warrant. This is, at least partly, because of the secrecy condition, which puts conspiratorial activity into the category of unobservable causes (Mandik, 2007, p. 207). Explanations that rely on such unobservable causes, Mandik claims, are problematic. Does this, then, justify our common sense suspicion of conspiracy theories?

If someone proposes a conspiracy theory but provides little to no argument for it, then we should be wary, as we would be about any extraordinary claim that is proposed without evidence to support it. We should not, routinely, accept bold claims without some evidence (where that evidence might be documents, an appeal to an appropriate authority, or so forth). Claims of conspiracy are no different.

However, in reply to Mandik's specific complaint, the secretiveness of conspiracy theories does not mean that evidence for them is never available. Indeed, if invoking unobservable causes is a problem, it is one that is not peculiar to the evaluation of conspiracy theories. The same issue arises for scientific explanations that posit unobservable entities, and these explanations are not usually regarded as especially hard to warrant. Indeed, much philosophy of science is devoted to revealing the conditions under which they succeed. So, although we might be tempted to say that warranting a claim of conspiracy will be difficult, because it requires that all three conditions of conspiratorial activity have been satisfied – including the secrecy condition – this does not mean we have a *prima facie* rationale for taking a dim view of conspiracy theories. Many explanations rely on complex or barely understood mechanisms, and it would be strange if we only thought this was a problem for conspiracy theories. That would suggest we hold conspiracy theories to a higher standard than, for example, scientific theories. If there are burden of proof issues with the kind of complex, conspiratorial claims inherent in conspiracy theories, then they are also problems faced by other kinds of explanations that we do not think are faced with *atypical* burden of proof issues.

Another worry the conspiracy theory skeptic might have is that sometimes we confuse suspicious behaviour *that is conspiracy-like* with actual conspiratorial behaviour. This is to say that some, possibly many, events can be explained with reference to behaviour that happens to looks conspiratorial, but this does not mean that the best explanation for the event is a conspiracy theory. This, surely, is the basis for Juha Räikkä's worry about *genuine* conspiracies; some activities may look conspiratorial, but are not examples of plotters conspiring.

Let us, for the moment, assume that there is an easy distinction between something that is genuinely conspiratorial and something that is merely conspiracy-like. If such a distinction can be made, then perhaps our judgement about how conspired our world is (whether 'middlingly so' or 'very') might be overstated, because we might be conflating conspiracy-like (but not actually conspiratorial) behaviours with actual examples of conspiracies. For example, Lee Basham takes it that we live in a world in which conspiracies happen every day:

> There is some prior probability of conspiracy. Most human behaviour is honest and innocent. But conspiracy also occurs at every level of human interaction, from family, romance and sexuality, friendship, work, business, to local, national and international politics. It's the social subspecies of that more basic individual human ability, deception. On most any definition of 'conspiracy,' wherever two or more meet to hide an infidelity, plot a social or business ouster or secretly manipulate a market price, conspiracy is in action. All of these actions and many similar ones happen million [sic] of times a day. (Basham, 2011, p. 59)

So, can we really say we live in a world where conspiracies occur, but with no great frequency? Are conspiracy theories rarely in the pool of candidate explanations for suspicious events? The question, really, is whether we live in a world where conspiracies are so common that this can be considered as evidence that a conspiracy theory – as a kind of hypothesis – is independently likely. Are conspiracy theories, we should be asking, in the pool of independently likely hypotheses that would explain the occurrence of some (suspicious[5]) event?

To illustrate how our subjective assessment of things like secretive or conspiratorial activity is affected by the situations in which we live, Basham uses the example of someone brought up in a Mafia family. For the child of a Mafia family,

> [A]n expectation of betrayal and conspiracy is the norm, and conspiracy theories, having a fairly high prior probability, will animate much of the self-reflection of this family[.] (Basham, 2011, p. 65)

The member of the Mafia family believes that conspiracies occur all the time because they – in particular – live in a heavily conspired world. Yet someone living on the other side of the city might belong to a family that is always open and honest, and so 'conspiratorial betrayal would be an astonishing turn of events, one quickly discovered and retaliated against' (Basham, 2011, p. 65).

Another way to think of it is this: we might very well suspect conspiracies by evil outsiders, but we tend to trust those of us we see as being on our side. As such, we tend to suspect the worst of our enemies and dismiss claims of malfeasance by our friends. Thus, if we hear a conspiracy theory about what 'our side' is up to, we are liable to treat it as extraordinary, since we might just assume that the prior probability of our friends conspiring is low *no matter what we think about our enemies*. The 'insider status' of people in the Middle East, for example, might explain why some of them are likely to endorse the claim that 9/11 cannot have been undertaken by terrorists from the Middle East and must, instead, have been an inside job *despite Al-Qaeda taking responsibility for it.*[6] American intervention in the Middle East is seen by these people as suspicious, and so the USA is seen as the 'bad family'. Who the good and bad families are can differ significantly cross-culturally, or even cross-generationally. This may explain why some conspiracy theories are treated as being more likely in certain cultures or age groups.

The question, then, is: 'Which "family" is most representative of the society in which we live?' Answering this goes some way to diagnosing whether there really is a special burden of proof when it comes to assessing conspiracy theories. If it turns out that we live in a world where conspiracies are just not all that common, we might claim that this justifies having a dim view of conspiracy theories *generally* (even though we would still be obliged to look at the available evidence – and establish its posterior probability – if pushed to justify our suspicion of a *particular* conspiracy theory). However, if we live in a world where conspiracies are commonplace, this surely means that it is at least probable that a conspiracy theory is amongst the candidate explanatory hypotheses for some suspicious event. In such a world, the burden of proof argument – which says that conspiracies are extraordinary and thus we have grounds for a *prima facie* suspicion of conspiracy theories – would be misguided.

How conspired is our society?

This might explain a certain characteristic or pathology (depending on how you view things) common to a certain kind of conspiracy theorist: the seemingly endless litany they provide of prior examples of conspiratorial behaviour on the part of our governments, public institutions and private corporations. If you believe we live in a world where conspiracies are common, but you suspect your audience of believing conspiracies are rare, then what better way to get them onside than by persuading them to change their views on just how common conspiracies are?

This might also explain a salient difference between some conspiracy theory theorists and skeptics. People who think we live in a world where conspiracies are rarely, if ever, invoked in our best explanations are liable to have a dim view of conspiracy theories *generally*. Those of us who advocate that conspiracy theories can be warranted might believe we live in a world where conspiracies are relatively uncommon, but claims of conspiracy must be investigated because of what might happen if they turn out to be true. Or we might think we live in a world where conspiracies are relatively common, such that it is likely some conspiracy is going on here and now.

How do we establish just how conspiratorial our society is? Herein lies an issue: the question of how common you think conspiracies are really depends on whether you think there is an easy distinction between something that is genuinely conspiratorial and something that is merely conspiracy-like. If we limit talk of conspiracies to 'serious stuff' – like political or corporate malfeasance – then, even if we think those kinds of conspiracies are common, they are still restricted to a small number of people and a limited number of incidences. If, however, you think that the organisation of a surprise party is not just conspiracy-like but is a genuine conspiracy, then conspiracies turn out to be common.

Some might argue that adopting such an open definition of what counts as a conspiracy is too radical, and so we should reject such a definition of conspiracy. However, David Coady approaches this issue in a different way. He considers a variety of different definitions of what counts as a 'conspiracy' and comes down on the side of the claim that, no matter how restrictive we make our definition of what counts as a 'conspiracy', conspiracies turn out to be common nonetheless (Coady, 2012, p. 114).

Think of it another way: do we have sufficient reason to believe we live in a world where conspiracies rarely occur, particularly when it comes to talk of corporations and governments? We know corporate conspiracies occur (and are often successfully pursued through the courts), and there are numerous examples of contemporary political conspiracies. From the information leaked by Edward Snowden to the data dumps of WikiLeaks, it seems that any trust we can reasonably have in the political sector is, at best, highly conditional. The evidence indicates that the independent likelihood that conspiracies occur is higher than we previously thought.

If we live in a world where conspiracies are uncommon, then claims of conspiracy will be considered extraordinary-qua-non-typical with respect to certain kinds of events. In such a world, we probably would assign a high burden of proof to any conspiracy theorist who puts forward a conspiracy theory as *the* explanation for some event. However, in a world where conspiracies are common, if there really is a special burden of proof when it comes to conspiracy theories, the burden of proof might be held by those who object to some theory about a conspiracy.

Indeed, there might well be a case for thinking that in some situations the standard burden of proof argument becomes unintelligible when it comes to certain kinds of conspiracy theories. Clare Birchall argues that, as many seemingly implausible conspiracy theories have ended up being true – like the CIA laundering money through the drug trade, and the like – then we may well be forgiven for giving serious consideration to some other, seemingly implausible, conspiracy theories (Birchall, 2002, p. 236). Birchall's argument here is not about the epistemic justification for belief in conspiracy theories. Rather, her argument is a psychological explanation as to why people might be drawn to belief in some conspiracy theories.

If we utilise our analysis of selected evidence, disinformation and the role of officialness with respect to the rivals of many conspiracy theories, then this psychological justification may even warrant some kind of agnosticism about implausible conspiracy theories, especially when we can cite examples of very implausible conspiracies indeed – such as the assassination of Alexander Litvinenko – which, nonetheless, seem to only be explicable via some conspiracy theory.

The death of Alexander Litvinenko is a fascinating story. A vocal detractor of Russian Federation President Vladimir Putin, Litvinenko was poisoned in London back in November 2001. The method of his execution was bizarre: he was poisoned with a very rare and hard-to-produce radionuclide, polonium-210. Although he was administered a lethal dose – 200 times the amount required to kill a human being – it took three weeks for Litvinenko to die. During that time he accused various agencies in the Russian Federal Security Service and Foreign Intelligence Service – the successors to the KGB – as well as Putin himself of being involved in a conspiracy to kill him.

The murder of Alexander Litvinenko is still unsolved (largely because of the refusal of the Russian Federation to allow some of its citizens to be extradited to the UK for questioning or trial), but two things suggest the very real existence of a conspiracy. First, the amount of polonium-210 used in the assassination would have required an exorbitant sum of money to buy, or needed to be produced in a special (and not particularly common) kind of research lab. Both these options suggest the role of some influential institution in the murder.

Second, because polonium-210 is radioactive, and the assassins did not carry it in a hermetically sealed container, the British authorities were able to trace the path of the assassins from the cafe in which Litvinenko was poisoned all the way back to Russia.

Poisoning someone with polonium-210 is an unusual form of assassination, because the sheer logistics of getting access to the radionuclide is so difficult that it beggars belief that the assassins did not use a simpler, cheaper toxin that could have been procured in the UK. Given that his death was so unusual and the method of his execution so bizarre, it seems likely that Litvinenko's demise was the product of a conspiracy. The big question, then, is why kill Litvinenko in this unusual (some might say 'ostentatious') manner? Some have argued that Litvinenko was killed at the behest of the Russian state and the method of his death was a show of power. Others have argued that Litvinenko's long and protracted death – which caused a media frenzy at the time – was ordered by the opponents of Vladimir Putin in order to give them a stage from which to attack Putin and his cronies. Proponents of this thesis claim that either Litvinenko was a willing participant or he was a dupe in the conspiracy to frame Putin for Litvinenko's murder. In either case, it appears that the death of Alexander Litvinenko is most likely explicable by reference to some theory about a conspiracy, one that seems outlandish no matter how you try to phrase it.

Working out the prior probability of what kind of world we live in – a relatively conspired or unconspired one – will, then, sometimes go against our expectations: if the CIA can launder money through drug cartels and people can commission assassinations using outlandish radioactive materials (when a simpler poison would have been quicker and less ostentatious/obvious), then what other outlandish claims should we investigate? How do we assign the burden of proof in situations where outlandish plots are, if not common, at least common enough to confuse matters?

It is tempting to think we can avoid answering this tricky issue by asserting that we should just deal with claims of conspiracy on a case-by-case basis. After all, even if we think conspiracies are really very common, we still have to ask: 'Common with respect to what, exactly?' Are we making the claim that conspiracies are so common in politics that they are routine and standard operating practice, *such that they occur as frequently as non-conspiratorial political activity?* Or do we simply mean that conspiracies occur more commonly than is typically thought? But we do not need to rigorously quantify what is meant by 'common' here. After all, can we not just say that conspiracies occur, and so we should not dismiss a conspiracy theory as being a potential explanation for some event?

We can. Conspiracies are not rare events, even if we do not want to admit that surprise parties qualify as conspiratorial. As such, we cannot dismiss belief in conspiracy theories *generally* because they are extraordinary claims. Conspiracy theories are only extraordinary in the sense that, if they are true, we have uncovered some suspicious activity. As such, there is no special burden of proof when it comes to claims of conspiracy being cited as salient causes of events. We do not have any especially good reason to take a dim view of conspiracy theories in general. This does not mean we have to endorse some version of conspiracism and start seeing conspiracies everywhere. All we need to do is accept that conspiracy theories can be amongst the pool of candidate explanations for particular kinds of events. After all, we still have to look at the evidence to work out whether some conspiracy theory is going to be warranted.

Conclusion

As we have seen in this chapter, sometimes we make mistakes when inferring to a hypothesis. We sometimes fail to understand how the available evidence renders some hypothesis probable – the posterior probability – as we saw in the example of the hypothesis that Irvine and Mallory were the first people to reach the summit of Sagarmāthā. We can also fail to consider just how likely some hypothesis is relative to the other hypotheses on offer – the relative probability – which we looked at when considering whether there might be life on Titan. Sometimes we do not even consider other worthwhile hypotheses, as might be the case with the curious rift between the Liddell family and Charles Dodgson.

The examples we have just looked at demonstrate that there are issues we need to be aware of when evaluating inferences *that purport to be inferences to the best explanation.* It is reasonable to expect, when a hypothesis is put forward as the explanation of some event, that a good argument has been offered. Such an argument will show that the explanatory hypothesis is likely in each of the three senses of probability – prior, posterior and relative – and that other worthwhile candidate explanations have been considered. Thus, when we consider the claim of conspiracy embedded in a conspiracy theory – an explanation of an event that cites a conspiracy as a salient cause – we need to consider just how probable the alleged conspiracy is and whether the conspiracy theorist has considered rival, non-conspiratorial explanations (if they are on offer).

The issue of prior probability, the question of whether it is independently likely that a conspiracy theory will be amongst the most credible explanatory hypotheses for some event, turns out to be the big issue for belief that we should take conspiracy theories seriously. At stake is the question: 'Just how conspired is our world?'

It is obvious that we do not live in a totally unconspired world. Conspiracies occur, and recent events indicate that conspiratorial activity is perhaps much more common than the public typically thinks. However, even if it turns out that conspiracies are common enough to be seriously considered as potential explanations for certain kinds of events, it is another thing entirely to say that some conspiracy theory is the best explanation for this *particular* event. We could, after all, live in a world where conspiracies are common but conspirators seldom or never get what they desire. In order for a conspiracy to be explanatory, we must show that there is a tight connection between the existence of the conspiracy and the occurrence of some event. That is the topic of the next chapter.

11
The Inference to a Conspiracy Theory

It is one thing to be skeptical about whether conspiracy theories can ever be the best explanation, but it is another to be skeptical about the existence of conspiracies. Conspiracies happen in the boardroom, in meetings, in deciding who gets selected as a political candidate, and so on. Not only that, but criminal conspiracies are successfully prosecuted through the courts *all the time*. Conspiracies, it seems, are not altogether rare, and thus a skepticism about the existence of conspiracies seems untenable.

Some conspiracy theory skeptics argue that our suspicion of conspiracy theories *generally* is based upon the claim that they are rarely good explanations. Why do they fail to be good explanations? Often, it is claimed, such a suspicion is justified because conspiracies do not (often) go according to plan. For example, detractors of some political opponent might leak information to the press that the candidate selection procedure is a farce. A member of your department might decide to contact the Dean, and reveal what really happened at the staff meeting, contra to what was reported in the minutes. Whistleblowers might even decide to hold a press conference about the botched safety standards in your factories. Sometimes conspiracies occur *but they fail to achieve anything of note*: political candidates end up being selected on their merits, departments are forced to face up to their mistakes and corporations are required to follow rules and regulations.

This worry, that conspiracies are often unsuccessful, was expressed by Karl Popper in his discussion of the *conspiracy theory of society*. Yet the fact that conspiracies are sometimes unsuccessful does not itself justify our suspicion of conspiracy theories *in general* unless you adopt some fairly weird definition about the ultimate success of conspiratorial activities (as we have already discussed in Chapter 3).

However, we can say this: just because we can show that a conspiracy exists, this does not tell us that some attendant theory *linking the conspiratorial activity to some event* will also be warranted. A warranted claim that a conspiracy existed will only be explanatory if we can show that the conspiratorial activity is *the salient cause* of the event we are trying to explain.

This is an important point. It is possible to point towards groups that, if not outright conspiratorial in their activities, have known and vested interests. Many conspiracy theories about the establishment of a One World Government concern secret societies like the Freemasons, Opus Dei and the like or private think tanks such as the Trilateral Commission, the Bilderberg Group and so forth. The claim of conspiracy is that: 'These secretive groups have a known interest in actively promoting closer economic and political ties between sovereign nations; they are, in effect, conspiring!' In essence, we can show that the conspirators exist, they have a plan and most of what they do occurs in secret. The question we need to ask with respect to these conspiracy theories is whether we can link the existence of these conspiracies (or the existence of a conspiracy involving all these groups) to the occurrence of some event or set of events in the world.

It is not immediately obvious that we can. If we assume that the goal of the aforementioned groups is the establishment of a single, worldwide governing body, then things get messy. Let us put to one side the claim that there exists a single governing body, a 'One World Government' or 'New World Order', of which we, the public, are ignorant. We can look at the more interesting claim (from the viewpoint of the available evidence) that the close ties that now exist between sovereign nations are the result of a conspiracy. However, we do not necessarily need to posit a conspiracy to explain these ties. For example, while it might be the case that there is a conspiracy being run by the Trilateral Commission and the Council for Foreign Relations to create a single governing authority under their control, it might also be the case that our sovereign governments have decided on closer ties for reasons that have nothing to do with the conspiracy. Both theories could be true, of course. It might be the case that sovereign governments have argued independently for closer ties between nations *and* that the conspirators, unbeknownst to the said governments, have stepped in where necessary to grease the wheels of diplomacy.

So, in which case is the existence of a conspiracy the best explanation? Even if we can warrant some claim that a conspiracy exists, it does not necessarily follow that it is part of the best explanation of some event. Warranting a claim that a conspiracy exists only means that the evidence shows there is a conspiracy in existence. It does not follow that the conspiracy is the salient cause of some event. In order to show this, we need to demonstrate that there is a tight link between the conspiratorial activity *and* the event in question. To illustrate this, let us look at some well-known examples of contemporary conspiracy theories, the various explanations for what really happened on 11 September 2001.

The Inside Job hypotheses

Some of the most widely discussed and sneered at claims of conspiracy of recent note are to be found in the set of 9/11 conspiracy theories known as the 'Inside Job hypotheses'. Broadly speaking, the Inside Job hypotheses cite the existence of a group of conspirators within the USA as being responsible for what happened in New York and Washington, DC on 11 September 2001. Versions of the Inside Job hypothesis range from 'Some group in the USA allowed the events of 9/11 to happen' (which is to say that the terrorist attack could have been foiled but some set of conspirators decided to let it occur *for their own purpose*) to 'Some group in the USA was directly responsible for the events of 9/11' (which is to say that the terrorist attack was really a 'false flag' operation – a concept we discussed back in Chapter 9 – run by members of the American political establishment). So, whatever we think about the real perpetrators of the events of 9/11, the secrecy condition of what counts as conspiratorial activity (as discussed in Chapter 3) seems easily satisfied: there was no, or very little, warning of the attacks on the World Trade Center in New York and the Pentagon in Washington, DC. However, some skeptics of the general set of Inside Job Hypotheses have argued that the claims about *who the conspirators were*, and *what it was they intended*, are vague and that this is a reason to take a dim view of these theories.

The Vagueness Argument

Some vagueness might be expected when it comes to making a claim that a conspiracy exists. After all, conspirators act in secret, and the whole point of secretive activity is to avoid being found out. As such, the secrecy condition of conspiratorial activity means that evidence for some of the other conditions might be either entirely lacking or simply inadequate for establishing that some conspiracy exists. Consequently, it will sometimes be difficult to support any precise claim about, for example, who the conspirators are or what they intended. This gives rise to one reason why some might say they are suspicious about a claim that a conspiracy exists: the evidence cited in support of such a claim might be too vague. Let us call this the 'Vagueness Argument'.

> *The Vagueness Argument:*
> Claims of the existence of a conspiracy should be treated suspiciously because the secrecy condition of such a claim means that we should expect such claims to be vague *and we should not expect vague claims to be warranted.*

There is an immediate and obvious problem with this argument. Any precisely formulated theory will entail a vague theory. For example, the explanatory hypothesis that the events of 9/11 were the result of a conspiracy orchestrated by Al-Qaeda entails that the events of 9/11 were the result of a conspiracy. The former explanation – which is precise with respect to who was behind the events of 11 September 2001 – entails the vague, but still explanatory, claim that the events of 9/11 were due to a conspiracy. In some cases we might prefer vague theories over precise ones in situations where the precise theory is implausible but the vague theory is not. For example, before the evidence was in we might have preferred the vague claim that it was a conspiracy that brought the Twin Towers down on 11 September 2001 over the much more precise, but (seemingly) implausible, claim that it was a conspiracy by the British Crown to level the Twin Towers. It was obvious at the time that some kind of conspiratorial activity was behind the 9/11 attacks, even if it was not obvious who the conspirators were and what their goal was.[1]

One philosopher who talks about the vagueness of claims of conspiracy is Steve Clarke. In 'Conspiracy Theories and the Internet – Controlled Demolition and Arrested Development' (Clarke, 2007) he argues that many contemporary conspiracy theories suffer from vagueness. Looking at the development of conspiracy theories on the Internet, he argues that such theories have fared badly, since it does not take long for them to be analysed and subsequently shown to rely upon shaky or shakily interpreted evidence. As such, conspiracy theories online are now phrased in vague and less precise ways in order to avoid being easily falsified.[2]

However, as Keeley writes (on the unfalsifiability of conspiracy theories in general),

> My claim here is that unfalsifiability is only a reasonable criterion in cases where we do not have reason to believe that there are powerful agents seeking to steer our investigation away from the truth of the matter. ... Strictly hewing to the dogma of falsifiability in these cases

would have led to a rejection of conspiracy theories at too early a point in the investigations, and may have left the conspiracies undiscovered. (Keeley, 1999, p. 121)

Consider the Dewey Commission's report on the Moscow Trials. The report claimed a conspiracy had occurred and could have been interpreted as making unfalsifiable claims about the conspiracy, since it predicted the existence of disinformation that would, in turn, discredit the Commission's report. So, while the conspiracy theory the Dewey Commission produced was unfalsifiable, it was not vague: it singled out who the conspirators were and why they were covering up what really happened. It just also happened to provide reasons as to why disinformation might be present in the official theory that would seemingly falsify the conspiracy theory.

Disinformation, as discussed in Chapter 9, is a form of errant data, where the errant data – treated as evidence – appears to falsify some theory. When we are dealing with claims about the suspected deceptive practices of people in positions of power, we might be worried they will only look vague because of the presence of *disinformation* in the evidential record. This is because such disinformation would cast doubt on the claims being made about the said deceptive practices.

Many conspiracy theories predict errant data such as disinformation or false flag campaigns. If it turns out that some of the evidence for a rival theory has also been selected for, the conspiracy theory might also look vague, and go against the 'received wisdom'. However, this would not be because the conspiracy theory is lacking in evidence. Rather, it would be because the pool of evidence for the rival theory is not really evidence at all (or it turns out to be evidence plus some disinformation).

The preceding analysis could be criticised for assuming the existence of conspiracies, and thus amplifying the fears of conspiracy theorists of a certain stripe into the kinds of worries we should all share. However, given the analysis of the previous chapters, we should at least be entertaining the possibility that some of the information that emanates from influential institutions is selective or examples of disinformation. We are, after all, operating with a perfectly general notion of what counts as 'conspiratorial' here, where the deceptive practices undertaken in secret by a group would count as a conspiracy.

So, in a situation where the claim of conspiracy is vague, that should only be considered a reason for being *cautious* about accepting it as part of an adequate explanatory hypothesis. Sometimes we may not have all the details, particularly in cases when the suspected conspirators continue to deny their involvement, but figuring out the deceptive practices of others is not an insurmountable task.

Vagueness is relative: we might not know who, but we might know why (or vice versa). A vague claim is one that we should not accept *if there is no other supporting evidence or background information we can bring to bear on the matter*. However, in most cases the evidence for a theory – conspiracy or otherwise – will likely be a packet of information, which might be vague in parts but must be looked at as a whole. Some of that information might be evidence about how conspired our society is, or claims about other, similar activities the said conspirators have been engaged in. That some of it might be vague is not a *prima facie* reason to reject it.

The various Inside Job hypotheses about 9/11 are interesting precisely because, while they make some vague claims about who was behind it or vague claims as to why 'they' did it, the vagueness of some of these claims is not necessarily a mark against them. So, why do so many people, particularly conspiracy theory theorists (and not just conspiracy theory skeptics), act dismissively when talk of 9/11 being an Inside Job comes up? Well, it is usually because there is a rival theory to the Inside Job hypotheses that accounts for all the known evidence and does not suffer from vagueness. This is the official theory about the events of 9/11, or what we might call the 'Outside Job' hypothesis.

The Outside Job hypothesis

The official theory of the events of 9/11 – that they were the result of terrorist activity by Al-Qaeda – is a conspiracy theory that is quite specific about who the conspirators were and what their desired end was. With respect to the Outside Job hypothesis about 9/11, we have grounds for believing that:

1. There existed conspirators consisting of at least the named hijackers and the named members of Al-Qaeda whom they worked with, and
2. These conspirators desired to commit a terrorist act on mainland American soil, to show that America was not immune to the consequences of its actions in the Middle East,[3] and
3. Steps had been taken to minimise public awareness of the hijackers and their activities, including the use of false IDs and the like.

There is little vagueness in this claim about the existence of a conspiracy with respect to:

a) who the conspirators were, and
b) what it was they desired to do.

The Outside Job hypothesis is a conspiracy theory, and appears to be a warranted one at that. The notion that the Outside Job hypothesis, the official theory of the events of 9/11, is a conspiracy theory flies in the face of many of the intuitions we have about conspiracy theories, as we discussed in earlier chapters, but it should be clear by now that there is nothing inherently wrong with claiming that a conspiracy theory can be warranted, and that official theories can also be conspiracy theories.

What makes the various theories about 9/11 so interesting from the perspective of how we analyse conspiracy theories is that all the explanatory hypotheses on offer are conspiracy theories; they simply differ with respect to the *who* and the *why*.

Now, it turns out that the *who* and the *why* are quite important here, and the evidence that supports the *who* also tells us something about the *why*. Al-Qaeda quickly admitted responsibility for 9/11 (telling us who) and they also explained why they did it (although even without an explicit explanation as to *why*, given what we know about Al-Qaeda and their particular form of political activism, the intention behind 9/11 would not be hard to fathom). It is possible that Al-Qaeda falsely took responsibility for 9/11, so the fact they claimed responsibility is not, in itself, *prima facie* proof of their involvement. However, there are multiple lines of evidence supporting the claim that Al-Qaeda *sincerely* took responsibility for the attacks on New York and Washington, DC. It is for this reason that many conspiracy theory theorists and skeptics think that the claims about the *who* and the *why*, with respect to the official-cum-conspiracy theory of 9/11, are less vague than some of the claims made by proponents of the Inside Job hypothesis.

Not only that, but the type of event – a terrorist act – rendered it independently likely that a conspiracy was the most likely explanation. So, the available evidence – the admission by Al-Qaeda that they were behind the attacks, and the evidence supporting that fact – renders the Outside Job hypothesis as being probable. As long as we have considered all the different possibilities/rival theories about who might have been behind the 9/11 attacks, according to this kind of analysis, the Outside Job appears to be the most probable explanatory hypothesis *relative to its rivals*.

Now, any Inside Job conspiracy theorist worth their salt will point out that the admission of guilt by members of Al-Qaeda might be false (or, worse, faked) and that there is significant other evidence that points towards 9/11 being the product of a conspiracy by members of the US political establishment. This is a live possibility, given the concerns expressed about disinformation, false flag operations and selective evidence expressed in Chapter 9. This is why, while we can say that the example of the Outside Job hypothesis demonstrates how we might warrant the claim that a conspiracy exists, this does not tell us that the conspiracy theory that Al-Qaeda was responsible for the events of 9/11 is warranted. Warranting an inference to the existence of a conspiracy is only part of the story when it comes to demonstrating that some *conspiracy theory* is not an inference to any old explanation. To explain why, it is going to be necessary to discuss Russian presidents, and then my own paranoia about academic peer review.

The kidnapping of Mikhail Gorbachev

In August 1991 the leader of the Soviet Union, President Mikhail Gorbachev, was kidnapped by a select few of his own Communist Party. The State Committee on the State of Emergency (or 'gang of eight': Gennady Yanayev, Valentin Pavlov, Boris Pugo, Dmitry Yazov, Vladimir Kryuchkov, Oleg Baklanov, Vasily Starodubtsev and Alexander Tizyakov) had a simple plan: they wanted a return to the good old days of Russia's particular brand of communism. Gorbachev's recent political and social reforms – *glasnost* (increased openness and transparency in political institutions) and *perestroika* (the reformation/restructuring of the ruling Communist Party) – were leading to both the dissolution of the Soviet Union and a move away from the kind of communism that Stalin had put in place in the early part of the 20th century. As such, the conspirators planned to kidnap Gorbachev and declare him to be ill. Once the people of Russia believed their president was unfit to govern, the Central Committee would reverse his reforms and the status quo in Russia would be re-established.

What happened after the kidnapping, however, was the opposite of what the conspirators intended: the news of Gorbachev's improper detention spread quickly and solidified the public's opposition against the old guard who opposed Gorbachev's reforms. This had the effect of increasing the pressure on the government to continue the reforms, which, arguably, led to the dissolution or collapse of the Soviet Union later that year.

What the conspirators intended ended up being quite different from what their conspiratorial activity achieved. We can say that the three conditions of conspiratorial activity were satisfied in this case of the kidnapping of Gorbachev because:

1. There existed a set of agents, the State Committee on the State of Emergency,
2. They desired to detain Gorbachev, return power to the Central Committee and reverse his reforms, and
3. Steps had been taken to minimise public awareness of the coup by claiming Gorbachev had fallen ill and was no longer able to govern the Soviet Union.

However, this is clearly a case of a conspiracy that *went awry*. The conspiracy, although *causally responsible* for what happened to Mikhail Gorbachev in August 1991 and, at least in part, *causally responsible* for the rapid dissolution of the Soviet Union at the end of that year, did not succeed in re-establishing communist rule over the Soviet Union.[4]

This particular conspiracy theory is a partial explanation of what happened in Russia in the early 1990s. In this case the conspiracy is *a cause* of the event (the dissolution of the Soviet Union), but the best explanation is a story about how the conspiracy went awry. The lesson here is that, if we are to say that a conspiracy theory is *the* explanation of an event, such that what the conspirators intended actually occurred, then we need to show that there is a tight connection between what the conspirators *intended to achieve* and the *results of their conspiratorial activity*. To illustrate this, let me now tell you about my worries about the peer review system, and how knowing that a conspiracy exists sometimes tells us very little indeed.

A paranoid peer-review fantasy

For the sake of argument, let us assume that I have warrant for my belief that there exists a set of conspirators whose plan is to promote the interests of my nemesis, a rival academic. Not only is my belief in the existence of this conspiracy warranted, but I am also of the belief that this conspiracy explains why a recent paper of mine, 'Towards an Ontology of Gaffing', was rejected by the editors of a prestigious journal, the *Journal of Accidental Thoughts*. I am claiming a conspiracy exists because I can say that:

1. There exist conspirators, comprising members of my academic peer community, including the editors of the journal I submitted my paper to, and
2. They desire to advance the career of my nemesis, and
3. Steps have been taken to minimise public awareness of the conspirators and their work, mostly via the secrecy of the peer-review system, anonymous referees, and the like.

Let us accept that I have the evidence to back up my claim that there is a conspiracy against me.[5] The story I have told about the existence of a conspiracy to promote the cause of my nemesis *and its alleged role in the rejection of my paper* is, indeed, one of the explanatory hypotheses in the pool of candidate explanations for why my paper was rejected. Since I know there exists a conspiracy to advance my nemesis's career, I have assumed my paper was rejected because of that conspiracy. However, for all I know, it might be the case that my paper was simply not good enough for publication.

If we accept there really is a conspiracy to advance my nemesis's career, then, if my paper was superior to my rival's, the conspirators would ensure that my paper was rejected (in order that my nemesis's paper could be published instead). If my paper turned out to be inadequate, however, then my paper would still be rejected and my nemesis's paper published (assuming that it is up to the standards of the journal). There is nothing explicit in the evidence available to me that warrants an inference to the conclusion that it is because of the existence of a conspiracy that my paper was rejected.

Unlike the previous example – the kidnapping of Mikhail Gorbachev – in which the warranted belief in some conspiratorial activity can be considered, at least, *a* cause of the event, in this case the fact a conspiracy exists to advance the cause of my nemesis may have nothing whatsoever to do with the event – the rejection of my paper – that I am trying to explain. There is, in this case, no reason to think that there is a tight connection between the existence of a conspiracy and the event in question, and so I might well be inferring to any old explanation *if I have failed to consider other options*.

We might think of this example as analogous to the situation many conspiracy theorists find themselves in. They see evidence of wrongdoing in our influential institutions and they then use the said wrongdoing to argue that some particular activity can be explained by reference to a conspiracy. For all I know, it is as likely as not that the conspiracy against me is the reason my article was not published, rather than my philosophical incompetence. This, we probably should think, characterises much of our epistemic relationship to what Lee Basham calls 'ambitious conspiracy theories' and is part of the motivation for what he terms a 'pragmatic rejection' of belief in such theories (as discussed in Chapter 6). For ordinary epistemic agents like ourselves it will be hard to distinguish between events caused by particularly robust conspiracies and mundane and non-conspiratorial causes. Just because we know people are out to get us does not mean they have got at us. This is why we need to make some tight connection between the conspiracy whose existence we may have warranted and the event we want to explain before we can say our conspiracy theory is the best explanation.

Abstract Expressionism and the CIA

Here is another example showing that resolving the tension between knowing a conspiracy exists and thinking this warrants some associated conspiracy theory requires care.

When people talk about the Central Intelligence Agency (CIA), America's foremost organisation dealing with intelligence about foreign affairs, we tend to think of a secretive group made up of black-suited workers who work long hours, have no hobbies and routinely spy upon almost everyone. However, in the 1940s, 1950s and 1960s CIA agents were a much more eclectic bunch, some of whom liked to drink heavily, write novels in their spare time and collect art. This latter interest led some members of the CIA to develop what was called the 'long leash': the secretive funding of artistic endeavours for the purposes of showing that America was culturally superior to the USSR, with which it was engaging in a Cold War.

One of the art movements funded in this manner was Abstract Expressionism, and so it might be tempting to say that Abstract Expressionism was, in the end, simply part of the CIA's arsenal in the Cold War.[6] However, it is clear from the evidence that the Abstract Expressionists themselves were unaware that much of their funding was coming from the CIA. Nor were they aware that their art movement was being used in a war of culture between the USA and the USSR. As far the Abstract Expressionists were concerned, their art was being appreciated *on its own merits*. Indeed, it turns out the art really was being appreciated on its own merits, garnering critical acclaim from the right quarters, being bought by the right institutions and the like. No matter what the intention of the CIA was in this case, the Abstract Expressionist movement ended up being important in its own right.

So, although the CIA acted conspiratorially to promote Abstract Expressionism for their own ends, the conspiracy also resulted in the mainstreaming of the Abstract Expressionist art movement. In part this must have been a desired end of the CIA agents who ran this particular long leash: the pre-eminence of the Abstract Expressionists at that time allowed Americans to say that their own, homegrown art could compete, culturally, with that of European and Soviet nations. The CIA merely set events in motion: they did not pay off every art critic or secretly buy every painting. In this respect the Abstract Expressionists were lucky to have such secretive patrons, but the success of their art and the importance of the moment were, in the end, the responsibility of the artists rather than of the CIA.

Some might argue that this is hair-splitting: the CIA was a salient cause of the success of Abstract Expressionism, and thus the conspiracy theory that cites the CIA as being behind Abstract Expressionism is warranted. It is. However, it would be a mistake to solely attribute the success of the movement to members of the CIA. The conspiracy theory about the funding of the Abstract Expressionist movement here only partially explains the success of the movement, given that a host of non-conspiratorial factors (both before and after the end of the Cold War) are responsible for Abstract Expressionism making it into the (art) history books.

The conspiracy by the CIA is *a* rather than *the* salient cause of the success of Abstract Expressionism. While there was a conspiracy to help fund the movement, and one of the goals of the conspirators was the legitimisation of Abstract Expressionism – as a way of winning part of the PR war between the USA and the USSR – the success of the movement can also be attributed to the unwitting pawns: the artists, the art dealers and the unsuspecting public.

Conclusion: warranted conspiracy theories

Warranting an inference to the existence of a conspiracy theory requires that we first warrant the claim that a conspiracy exists. As these examples illustrate, it is not enough, merely because a conspiracy is in the pool of candidate explanations for some event, to then assume it is the most probable/best explanation. Rather, we have to make a case for the conspiracy being the salient cause of the event.

In the case of the kidnapping of Gorbachev, we know there was a plan to undertake a kidnapping, which was undertaken by the State Committee on the State of Emergency, who kept their real intentions secret by disseminating a cover story that the president was ill. We can cite the conspiracy both as the explanation of why Mikhail Gorbachev disappeared for several days in 1991 and as one of the reasons for the fall of the Soviet Union later that year. However, this example shows that, although we can show that conspiracies occur, this does not tell us that conspirators get what they desire. Compare this, however, with the peer review example: the evidence for the rejection of my article does not render the conspiracy theory as the most probable explanation, despite the fact that there clearly exists a conspiracy against me. This is why we need to show not just that a conspiracy exists, but that the conspiracy in question is tightly connected to the event we are seeking to explain.

All of these examples are designed to show that a conspiracy theory is only good – which is to say warranted – if we can make a tight connection between the existence of the conspiracy and the event to be explained. Conspiracies are activities undertaken in secret by some group to achieve some end. Warranting the inference to a conspiracy might be difficult: after all, the aforementioned secrecy might make it hard to establish the who, the how and the why of the conspiracy, but claims of conspiracy should not be seen as facing a higher burden of proof than other explanations of complex, social processes.

If there is a problem with belief in conspiracy theories – and this is a big 'if' – then it is the worry that sometimes we infer to any old explanation when we are presented with a choice between rival theories. However, it is fair to say that if we take the concerns of certain conspiracy theorists seriously – that the world features more conspiratorial activity than most of us think – then the independent likelihood that a conspiracy theory will be in the pool of theories explaining some event may be higher than many of us think. All this means is that we should, at the very least, treat claims of conspiracy seriously and ask: 'Is there evidence that a conspiracy exists?' This is not an arduous burden: we simply have to look at the evidence before dismissing a claim of conspiracy out of hand. If it turns out there is a conspiracy in existence, then we should ask: 'Is the conspiracy the best explanation for some event?' If the answer is no, then the conspiracy theory is unwarranted. If the answer is yes, then we have a conspiracy theory that is warranted and thus is rational to believe.

12
Conclusion: In Defence of Conspiracy Theories

We hear conspiracy theories at the breakfast table, at work and in the media. People go around saying 'I'm not a conspiracy theorist, but ...' trying to persuade you that, say, the oil companies are conspiring to keep cheap, renewable energy sources from entering the marketplace, or health professionals discovered the cure for cancer in the 1960s but have kept it a secret from the public. Sociologists and psychologists study why these beliefs are so popular, and also why some of them are only popular in certain communities. Historians look at these beliefs in their historical context, while political theorists ask whether belief in conspiracy theories adversely affects the political structures in our societies. The literature on belief in conspiracy theories grows ever larger (even though it is quite possibly being outpaced by the generation of new conspiracy theories).

The worry, as we have seen, is that a lot – although certainly not all – of the academic literature on conspiracy theories is written from the point of conspiracy theory skepticism. Many of the arguments we have seen – some of which have been endorsed by philosophers – assume that belief in conspiracy theories *generally* is suspicious, if not outright irrational.

The consequence is that many conspiracy theory skeptics do not acknowledge that some theories about conspiracies can be warranted, or, when they do acknowledge that such theories can be warranted, they downplay their importance. This reluctance to deal with examples of warranted conspiracy theories skews the academic debate on the rationality of belief in conspiracy theories. It means that the fears and worries conspiracy theorists have – which are really general concerns about what counts as evidence *and* whether our trust in authority is predicated on good arguments – are downplayed or even dismissed.

So, what does looking at the philosophical literature bring to the table? Well, for one thing, philosophers like Charles Pigden, David Coady and Lee Basham have challenged the view that we should think of belief in conspiracy theories in a dim light. They take it that a conspiracy theory is any explanation of an event that cites a conspiracy as a salient cause, even though their views differ on some of the associated details.[1] This general, non-pejorative definition of conspiracy theory is one that we should endorse, because it helps further the analysis of these things we call 'conspiracy theories'.

In part, these general definitions of what counts as a 'conspiracy' come out of accepting that conspiratorial activity is more common than most people think. If we accept that the most minimal conception of a conspiracy consists of a set of agents who operate in secret towards some end, then it seems we can point towards a lot of conspiratorial activity going on around us here and now. Operating with such a low-level definition of conspiracy might be counterintuitive – after all, it means that surprise parties end up being examples of conspiracies – but, by broadening the scope of conspiratorial activity, we can focus our analysis on what, if anything, is suspicious about theories about conspiracies.

As we have argued, we do not need to subscribe to the thesis of conspiracism – the belief in the existence of conspiracies without good reason[2] – if we admit that conspiracies can (and often do) occur. Indeed, people can keep to a general skepticism of conspiracy theories while operating with a perfectly neutral and non-pejorative take on what counts as a 'conspiracy theory' and who counts as a 'conspiracy theorist'.

Now, many conspiracy theory skeptics will claim that they already admit that some conspiracy theories could be warranted, so what is the issue? Well, it is a matter of perspective: if someone operates with a pejorative definition of 'conspiracy theory' or 'conspiracy theorist', they end up skewing the debate towards the position that we have grounds for suspecting that belief in conspiracy theories generally is irrational. However, if they were to operate with a general and non-pejorative set of definitions, then they could keep their skepticism about conspiracy theories while also coming at particular conspiracy theories from a position of what we might think is a considered agnosticism.

What grounds, then, might we have for being skeptical about some claim of conspiracy?

Well, for one thing, conspiracy theory skeptics are concerned by the kind of evidence that is used to support some claims of conspiracy. Conspiracy theories often feature swathes of errant data or make claims about false flags or disinformation campaigns. Conspiracy theorists are sometimes selective in their presentation of the evidence. Yet the same kind of arguments can be legitimately levelled at other theories. We know, for example, that influential public institutions have engaged in disinformation campaigns and used selective evidence to make their claims look warranted when they might not be. These are not evidential problems that are *specific* to conspiracy theories. Rather, they are part of a packet of concerns we have when dealing with explanations and theories in general.

We might also think that our skepticism of conspiracy theories is based upon the fact that, when we talk to the experts, we discover that most conspiracy theories get pooh-poohed. Many people also believe they have a *prima facie* justified preference for official theories (those that have been accredited by experts or influential institutions). However, we need to be aware that not all appeals to authority or officialness are created equally. Not only that; sometimes authorities speak insincerely but know we will believe what they say *because* of our trust in them.

Our trust in authority is – at least in part – predicated on our beliefs about just how conspired or unconspired the world is. From the Moscow Trials to the NSA material leaked by Edward Snowden, it looks as though conspiracy theorists have been right to worry about that trust. We do not necessarily need to endorse their conspiracy theories to recognise that our trust in influential institutions is much more conditional than many of us like to think.

This recent spate of leaks and whistleblowing has, it is fair to say, led to a great many people reconsidering their trust in influential institutions. Does this, then, provide an answer to the oft-asked question: 'Why are conspiracy theories currently so popular?' If we assume that conspiracy theories are more popular now than they have ever been,[3] then our increasing knowledge of political malfeasance may be a contributory cause for increased belief in conspiracy theories. Certainly, it looks as if the kind of political world many of us live in – at least in the West – is one marked by an increased and justified suspicion that the members of influential institutions are not always truthful when dealing with the public. Now, we may not live in a totally conspired society. Indeed, it might even be the case that our increased suspicion has coincided with a period of reduced conspiratorial activity in the political sphere, since access to the information that drives our suspicion about the members of public institutions might also be leading to more trustworthy behaviour on their part. However, given what we know, it appears that it is not irrational to be at least a little worried.

This may well sound like a ringing endorsement of a certain kind of conspiracy theory. However, just because people find conspiracy theorists suspicious, this is no reason not to consider that the concerns they express might be warranted by the evidence. If we take it that a conspiracy theory is any explanation of an event that cites a conspiracy as a salient cause, we must still provide some argument for believing some particular conspiracy theory to be the best explanation. As such, if we are going to be skeptical, we should have a considered and principled skepticism with respect to specific conspiracy theories. Such a position, however, requires that, if someone presents an argument in favour of some particular conspiracy theory, we must consider it on its merits. This is the principle behind a particularist analysis of belief in conspiracy theories, which we saw defended back in Chapter 3.

Why should we adopt a particularist approach to analysing conspiracy theories? In part, it is because many of the suspicions we have about conspiracy theories are part of a set of worries we should have about explanations *in general*. We need to be careful when assessing the evidence for some claim, especially in situations when we might not be able to check the evidence ourselves to see whether it suffers from selectiveness or is disinformation. We should not accept a theory just because it has some official status. Rather, when we are told something, we need to know whether the teller is trustworthy or an appropriate authority. In this respect, most of the arguments traditionally put forward for the suspiciousness of belief in conspiracy theories point towards us needing to be suspicious, to a certain extent, about any explanation, conspiracy theory or otherwise.

The other part of the answer is this: if someone has an argument for some claim, then we should assess that argument. It does not matter whether it is a radical claim about String Theory or the claim that the president's backtracking on taxing the super-rich was due to the behind-the-scenes machinations of the Illuminati: if an argument has been put forward, we should look at it if we are going to pass judgement. We have a duty to check whether the inference to the existence of a conspiracy is warranted and whether the right kind of connection has been made between the existence of the conspiracy and the event we are trying to explain. When no argument is presented, then, yes, we can be skeptical. Usually, though, conspiracy theorists have reasons for thinking both that a conspiracy exists and that it is *the* explanation of some event. Skepticism in this case would only be principled if we grappled with the said arguments.

In the end, many of the suspicions we have about conspiracy theories are really part of the set of worries we should have about explanations in general: most of the arguments traditionally put forward for the suspiciousness of conspiracy theories point towards our needing to be suspicious, to a certain extent, about any explanation. While some have argued that the term 'conspiracy theory' is pejorative because it refers to explanations that we normally consider to be *prima facie* suspicious, anyone with even a smidgen of imagination should be able to point to some conspiratorial explanation that they consider to be a warranted explanation of an event (whether it is a historical explanation of some Elizabethan treachery, the recent actions of a government hiding trade deals with a foreign nation, or an academic department trying to bamboozle the dean of the Faculty). It is easier, then, to address the question of when it is either rational or irrational to believe conspiracy theories if we take an interest in the *broad class of explanations* covered by the general definition defended in this book.

The analysis of the putative problems of conspiracy theories shows they are actually problems that are shared with other theories and explanations of complex, social phenomena. This is to say that the epistemic issues we normally associate with conspiracy theories are epistemic issues for belief *in general*. So, if people want to continue using the term 'conspiracy theory' as a pejorative that marks out a *prima facie* irrational belief, we cannot stop them. However, we should ask whether they have an argument for that position and whether it can withstand scrutiny.

'They' would ask nothing less from us.

Notes

2 Conspiracy Theory Theories

1. Hofstadter was willing to admit that such paranoid styles could be seen, to a lesser extent, amongst left-wing conspiracy theorists.
2. A point Sunstein has reiterated elsewhere (Sunstein, 2009).
3. Lance deHaven-Smith, who defends belief in conspiracy theories, has argued in his book *Conspiracy Theory in America* that Popper's influential work on the conspiracy theory of society (along with the political writings of Leo Strauss) is the one of the main reasons why conspiracy theories are not treated seriously in contemporary discourse (deHaven-Smith, 2010, pp. 78–80) We will look at deHaven-Smith and his rather conspiratorial view on belief in conspiracy theories in Chapter 8.
4. Lee Basham has also generated an interesting taxonomy:

   [C]ontroversies concerning the definition are common in the philosophical literature:

   1) A conspiracy theory must be contrary to the official story (Coady, 2003; Raikka, 2008).
   2) A conspiracy theory must involve activity that is morally suspect (Pigden, 2006; Keeley, 2007).
   3) A conspiracy theory must be of a historical event (Pigden, 1995; Keeley, 1999; Coady, 2003; Mandik, 2007).
   4) A conspiracy theory must not be widely accepted (Raikka, 2008) (Basham, 2011, p. 53, all citations in original).

   Many of these issues will be covered over the course of the book. In Chapter 7 we will look at whether conspiracy theories must be contra some official theory (and whether they must not be widely accepted). The question of whether conspiratorial activity is morally suspect will be discussed in Chapter 4.

3 Conspiracies and Conspiracy Theories

1. Brian L. Keeley has also made a comparison between God (understood as some version of the OmniGod; at the very least all-knowing, all-powerful) and the kind of conspirators he thinks conspiracy theorists believe in. Unlike the aforementioned theorists, Keeley does not necessarily think that conspirators are godlike but, rather, that God would be the ultimate conspirator, given the powers and mystery typically associated with God's workings (Keeley, 2007, p. 143).
2. Which is surely one of the longest article titles on the subject.
3. Interestingly enough, Icke has a theory as to why we know about the master-plan of our reptilian shape-shifting overlords: they deliberately leave clues for us to find in order to show to us just how powerful they are. In this manner Icke gets to preserve his claim that they are all-powerful and allow 'enlightened' individuals to know about the plan and try to work against it.
4. The Moscow Trials will be discussed in more depth in Chapter 7.

4 Some Problems with a General Definition

1. Typically. The child of a dictator may very well have a surprise party organised for them which costs a tenth of the country's GDP and involves thousands of people. Surprise parties can scale in size remarkably well.

5 Conspirators, and What They Want

1. Or, in some cases, 'they intended for this to occur, but what we got was that!'.
2. Although I owe a debt of gratitude to Charles Pigden for suggesting the term (personal communication).
3. Given that doublethinking is obviously problematic, the informal or humorous past participle of 'think' seems appropriate here, and should be our preferred terminology.

6 The Public Trust

1. An associated conspiracy theory is that both incidents, if not initiated by the USA, were attempts to deliberately provoke the North Vietnamese into conflict in order to then legitimise going to war.
2. So as to prevent the mind-control waves being broadcast from influential institutions from taking over their brains and making them happy, docile conspiracy theory skeptics.

7 The Trouble with Authority

1. Which itself could be taken to be a kind of 'evidence-based policy', if the evidence that members of the political sector are meant to take most seriously is the will of the voting general public.
2. Whether the untrustworthiness is neutralised by the institutional processes is, of course, an empirical matter.

8 Should We Prefer Official Theories?

1. Indeed, in a world that turned out to be heavily conspired, our psychological preference for official theories might well be one of the intended results of an all-embracing conspiracy (a plot point related to the character 'Gag Halfrunt' in Douglas Adam's radio series *The Hitch-hiker's Guide to the Galaxy*) (Adams, 1978).
2. Basham makes the interesting point that every 20 years or so the political slate seems to get wiped clean: we either forget about the institutional problems that led to some scandal or assume that the issues have been sorted out. He writes:

   > History recedes at a terrific rate in contemporary civilization, creating the illusion that we are somehow 'born again' as a society, with a clean slate, every 20 years or so. This blinds us to what are really systemic vulnerabilities to conspiracy and a chronic pattern of institutional bad-habits. Institutions, far from changing, have only become more so in their secretive aspects. (Basham, 2011, p. 60)

   Basham argues that we do not need to insist upon perfect secrecy when talking about the success of a conspiracy, because often conspirators only need to keep their activities secret until they have paid off. We could also add that sometimes conspirators only need to keep their activities secret *until the next scandal erupts*. So, for example, it might be the case that they have been awarding contracts to close family members, but look at what the opposition has just been accused of!

3. More problematically, Räikkä's view brings up another metaphysical quandary. It seems that, in the process of uncovering and publicising a conspiracy, the whistleblower is somehow turning a genuine conspiracy (which is not known about) into something else, like a local conspiracy. This seems odd. Does this mean that, if the whistleblowers discovered the conspiracy *but did not publicise it*, it would remain genuine (presumably because then the prospective whistle-blower would end up being part of the conspiracy)? Or does the very act of discovering a conspiracy mean it was never genuine in the first place (because of a failure to keep the conspiracy perfectly secret)?
4. Lee Basham presents another, related argument against both Coady's and Räikkä's assertions that we should respect common usage when it comes to the terms 'conspiracy theory' and 'conspiracy theorist' by comparing the restricted usage (contrary to some official story) to how we used to claim that rape could not, by definition, occur within the bounds of marriage (Basham, 2011, pp. 57–58).
5. It is quite possible that some people believe a variation of this explanation whereby the actual terrorist act was intentional, but it was not undertaken by Al-Qaeda; they merely took the credit for it.
6. deHaven-Smith is also concerned that conspiracy theorists tend to focus on suspicious events *in isolation* and thus fail to see how conspired and complicit public institutions really are (deHaven-Smith, 2010, p. 799). This seems an odd claim, because it is not clear that conspiracy theorists tend to focus on suspicious events in isolation: some do, but some do not. deHaven-Smith is characterising conspiracy theorists as what we might call 'reverse conspiracists'. He is criticising conspiracy theorists *for not acting as if everything is connected*. A version of the same objection to the thesis of conspiracism (which was argued for in Chapter 2) can be levelled against deHaven-Smith here: we should not characterise the beliefs of conspiracy theorists with respect to only one kind of conspiracy theorist (in this case, the reverse conspiracist).
7. An argument similar to Brian L. Keeley's claim that there is no 'mark of the incredible' that distinguishes warranted from unwarranted conspiracy theories (as discussed back in Chapter 1).

9 Evidence and Conspiracy Theories

1. The idea that Salieri was responsible for the death of Mozart is not original to Shaffer; it first appeared in Alexander Pushkin's one-act play *Mozart and Salieri* (Pushkin, 2003). However, arguably it is Shaffer's play that is the more well-known example of this particular story.
2. Contenders for this title include Don DeLillo's *Libra* (DeLillo, 1989), Thomas Pynchon's *Gravity's Rainbow* (Pynchon, 2000) and Robert Shea and Robert Anton Wilson's *Illuminatus* trilogy (Shea & Wilson, 1998). Each of these books, like *Foucault's Pendulum*, plays with the notion of conspiracy theories as fictive and yet believed/believable.
3. Indeed, the origin of the word 'disinformation' comes from the Russian 'dezinformatsiya', which was used in the late 1930s to describe the views of Stalin's opponents.

4. The most famous alleged false flag operation is the Reichstag fire. When the Reichstag building in Berlin burnt down in 1933, the Chancellor of Germany, Adolf Hitler, urged the President, Paul von Hindenburg, to enable emergency legislation suspending civil liberties, so that the suspected arsonists, members of the Communist Party of Germany, could be rounded up. This had the effect of the National Socialist Party, once the Communists had been expunged, becoming the biggest party in the German parliament. This has led some conspiracy theorists and historians to claim this was all too convenient. Some have claimed that the Reichstag fire was started by members of the National Socialist Party in order to incriminate the Communists. To this date historians are still divided as to who started the fire and just how much Hitler knew about it at the time.
5. While individuals can disinform others, disinformation is best taken to be the domain of influential institutions. The kind of agents who disseminate disinformation need to have the power and influence to get their fabricated 'evidence' accepted as fact. This may or may not be part of a given individual's definition of disinformation, but we can remain agnostic on this issue, as it does not matter for our analysis here.
6. The existence of errant-unaccounted-for data is not the kind of thing we should be *unduly* worried about generally, since there is likely to be data in the total pool of evidence for some event that will be errant to some rival theory. For example, one piece of data about the assassination of JFK is the colour of the President's socks. The official theory makes no mention of the President's socks, nor do any of the conspiracy theories, because it is not salient *with respect to the assassination*.
7. This seems like an unusual example, as disinformation is typically considered as the kind of thing that emanates from influential institutions. However, if we think about it carefully, we should realise that disinformation can emanate from many sources, only some of which will be institutional.
8. Basham advances an early version of this notion of a 'toxic truth' in 'Conspiracy Theory and Rationality' (Basham, 2011, pp. 69–71).

10 The Inference to Any Old Explanation

1. A number of biographies now allege that Dodgson had an affair with Alice, although there is some dispute among the biographers as to whether it was sexual. Morton N. Cohen's *Lewis Carroll: A Biography* (Cohen, 1995), for example, mentions the affair.
2. Such psychological or sociological theories of the mores of Victorian culture might be part of the thing to be explained, rather than part of the evidence to be explained, of course, if we take it that such theories about Victorian behaviour are, themselves, explanatory hypotheses.
3. See W. V. Quine's 'Two Dogmas of Empiricism' (Quine, 1951).
4. The *New Zealand Herald* article, 'Campaign to knock Hillary off his summit', ably summarises these views (Johnston, 2010).
5. Even in a world where conspiracies are so commonplace that almost every event can be explained by them, putting forward a conspiracy theory for certain events – such as why the week-old milk went off – might be considered weird. Thus the 'suspicious' caveat here.
6. In the same respect, members of radical groups within the USA might similarly claim that Al-Qaeda cannot have been behind 9/11 because they fear elements within their government more than foreign terrorist organisations.

11 The Inference to a Conspiracy Theory

1. Lee Basham (personal communication) has pointed out that disjunctive claims about specific conspiracies jointly entail a vague claim that a conspiracy exists. For example, either the conspiracy to destroy the Twin Towers was committed by Al-Qaeda or it was committed by members of the executive branch of the US government. These precise claims, joined as a disjunction, entail the vague claim: 'It was a conspiracy!' As such, the vagueness of a claim of conspiracy might originate from having evidence that a conspiracy occurred but not being sure who is behind it.
2. Either this is due to the evidence for such theories being constantly called into question, thus leading to vagueness, or it is by design: the conspiracy theorist deliberately makes their conspiracy theory vague so as to make it harder to falsify.
3. The success of the Pentagon attacks is the subject of some debate, since it is possible the intention behind the attacks was to show that American soil could be the subject of outside terrorist activity, not that the hijackers thought that their actions would actually destroy the Twin Towers. If this is the case, then the Pentagon attack was successful and the complete destruction of the Twin Towers was unintended but not unwelcome (from the terrorists' point of view).
4. This example differs from the example of a conspiracy that had unintended consequences, the death of Julius Caesar as discussed in Chapter 4. In the case of the death of Julius Caesar the conspirators achieved what might be called 'partial success'. In the case of the kidnapping of Mikhail Gorbachev, what the conspirators achieved should be considered a total failure. Although both these examples feature unintended consequences, the kind of unintended consequence we should be interested in here is one in which the intent of the conspirators is totally at odds with what the result of the conspiratorial activity.
5. And that I am either a foolish academic who submits papers to journals knowing they will be rejected or a courageous uncoverer of vile misdeeds, given that I can use the rejection of my paper to expose the conspiracy!
6. For a good overview of the CIA's role in funding the Abstract Expressionism movement, you could read the article *Modern art was CIA 'weapon'* (Saunders, 1995).

12 Conclusion: In Defence of Conspiracy Theories

1. Pigden, for example, thinks of conspiratorial activity as being morally suspicious (not necessarily sinister), while Coady takes it that conspiracy theories can never be official theories.
2. A conspiracist might have a 'lucky' belief in the existence of a conspiracy, of course, but such epistemic luck would not *typically* count as showing that the conspiracist's belief in the existence of a conspiracy was warranted.
3. This might be considered contentious – it is also possible that conspiracy theories are no more popular than ever – since it might just be the case that it is easier to be informed about them in this day and age.

Bibliography

Conspiracy, n. (2011). *Oxford English Dictionary* .

Aaronovitch, D. (2009). *Voodoo Histories: The Role of the Conspiracy Theory in Shaping Modern History*. London: Jonathan Cape.

Adams, D. (1978). *The Hitchhiker's Guide to the Galaxy*. Radio series.

Arnold, G. B. (2008). *Conspiracy Theory in Film, Television and Politics*. Westport, Connecticut: Praegar.

Bale, J. M. (2007). Political paranoia v. political realism: on distinguishing between bogus conspiracy theories and genuine conspiratorial politics. *Patterns of Prejudice*, 41(1), 45–60.

Barkun, M. (2003). *A Culture of Conspiracy: Apocalyptic Visions in Contemporary America*. Berkeley, California: University of California Press.

Basham, L. (2001). Living with the Conspiracy. *The Philosophical Forum*, *XXXII*(3), 265–280.

Basham, L. (2003). Malevolent Global Conspiracy. *Journal of Social Philosophy*, 34(1), 91–103.

Basham, L. (2006). Afterthoughts on Conspiracy Theory: Resilience and Ubiquity. In D. Coady (Ed.), *Conspiracy Theories: The Philosophical Debate*. Hampshire, England: Ashgate.

Basham, L. (2011). Conspiracy Theory and Rationality. In C. Jensen & R. Harré (Eds), *Beyond Rationality* (pp. 49–87). Newcastle upon Tyne: Cambridge Scholars Publishing.

Basham, L. (Forthcoming). Conspiracy Theory and the Accusation of Cover-up. *Episteme*.

Birchall, C. (2002). The Commodification of Conspiracy Theory. In P. Knight (Ed.), *Conspiracy Nation: The Politics of Paranoia in Postwar America*. New York: New York University Press.

Brown, D. (2003). *The Da Vinci Code*. New York: Random House.

Buenting, J. & Taylor, J. (2010). Conspiracy Theories and Fortuitous Data. *Philosophy of the Social Sciences*, 40(4), 567–578.

Carroll, L. (1967). *Alice in Wonderland*. London: Dobson.

Carroll, L. (2005). *Alice through the Looking Glass and What She Found There*. London: Walker.

Carter, C. (1993). *The X Files*. TV Series.

Clarke, G. & Most, B. (1901). *Does FNORD in reverse spell conspiracy?* Simla: James Clarke Publisher.

Clarke, S. (2002). Conspiracy Theories and Conspiracy Theorizing. *Philosophy of the Social Sciences*, 32(2), 131–150.

Clarke, S. (2006). Appealing to the Fundamental Attribution Error: Was it All a Big Mistake? In D. Coady (Ed.), *Conspiracy Theories: The Philosophical Debate*. Hampshire, England: Ashgate.

Clarke, S. (2007). Conspiracy Theories and the Internet – Controlled Demolition and Arrested Development. *Episteme*, 4(2), 167–180.

Coady, D. (2006a). Conspiracy Theories and Official Stories. In D. Coady (Ed.), *Conspiracy Theories: The Philosophical Debate*. Hampshire, England: Ashgate.

Coady, D. (2006b). An Introduction to the Philosophical Debate about Conspiracy Theories. In D. Coady (Ed.), *Conspiracy Theories: The Philosophical Debate*. Hampshire, England: Ashgate.

Coady, D. (2006c). The Pragmatic Rejection of Conspiracy Theories. In D. Coady (Ed.), *Conspiracy Theories: The Philosophical Debate*. Hampshire, England: Ashgate.

Coady, D. (2007a). Are Conspiracy Theorists Irrational? *Episteme*, 4(2), 193–204.

Coady, D. (2007b). Conspiracy Theories. *Episteme*, 4(2), 131–134.

Coady, D. (2012). *What to Believe Now : Applying Epistemology to Contemporary Issues*. Chichester, West Sussex: Wiley-Blackwell.

Coady, D. (Ed.). (2006d). *Conspiracy Theories: The Philosophical Debate*. Hampshire, England: Ashgate.

Cohen, M. N. (1995). *Lewis Carroll: a Biography*. London: Macmillan.

Cubitt, G. (1993). *The Jesuit Myth: Conspiracy Theory and Politics in Nineteenth Century France*. Oxford: Clarendon Press.

Darwin, H., Neave, N. & Holmes, J. (2011). Belief in Conspiracy Theories. The Role of Paranormal Belief, Paranoid Ideation and Schizotypy. *Personality and Individual Differences*, 50, 1289–1293.

deHaven-Smith, L. (2010). Beyond Conspiracy Theory: Patterns of High Crime in American Government. *American Behavioral Scientist*, 53(6), 795–825.

deHaven-Smith, L. (2013). *Conspiracy Theory in America*. Austin: University of Texas Press.

DeLillo, D. (1989). *Libra*. New York: Penguin Books.

Eco, U. (1989). *Foucault's Pendulum* (W. Weaver, Trans.). San Diego: Harcourt Brace Jovanovich.

Feldman, S. (2011). Counterfact Conspiracy Theories. *International Journal of Applied Philosophy*, 21(1), 15–24.

Fenster, M. (2008). *Conspiracy Theories: Secrecy and Power in American Culture* (2nd ed.). Minneapolis: University of Minnesota Press.

Gelfert, A. (2013a). Coverage-Reliability, Epistemic Dependence, and the Problem of Rumor-Based Belief. *Philosophia*, 41(3), 763–786.

Gelfert, A. (2013b). Rumour, Gossip, and Conspiracy Theories: Pathologies of Testimony and the Principle of Publicity. In G. Dalziel (Ed.), Rumour and Communication in Asia in the Internet Age. Oxford: Routledge.

Groh, D. (1987). The Temptation of Conspiracy Theory, or: Why Do Bad Things Happen to Good People? Part I: Preliminary Draft of a Theory of Conspiracy Theories. In C. F. Graumann & S. Moscovici (Eds), *Changing Conceptions of Conspiracy*. New York: Springer Verlag.

Heins, V. (2007). Critical Theory and the Traps of Conspiracy Thinking. *Philosophy Social Criticism*, 33(7), 787–801.

Hofstadter, R. (1965). *The Paranoid Style in American Politics, and Other Essays* (1st ed.). New York: Knopf.

Johnston, M. (2010). Campaign to knock Hillary off his summit. *New Zealand Herald*, 29 May.

Kaiser, T. E., Linton, M. & Campbell, P. R. (Eds.). (2007). *Conspiracy in the French Revolution*. Manchester: Manchester University Press.

Keeley, B. L. (1999). Of Conspiracy Theories. *The Journal of Philosophy*, 96(3), 109–126.

Keeley, B. L. (2003). Nobody Expects the Spanish Inquisition!: More Thoughts on Conspiracy Theory. *Journal of Social Philosophy*, 34(1), 104–110.

Keeley, B. L. (2007). God as the Ultimate Conspiracy Theorist. *Episteme*, 4(2), 135–149.

Knight, P. (2000). *Conspiracy Culture: From the Kennedy Assassination to The X-Files*. London: Routledge.

Knight, P. (2002). Introduction: A Nation of Conspiracy Theorists. In P. Knight (Ed.), *Conspiracy Nation: The Politics of Paranoia in Postwar America*. New York: New York University Press.

Knight, P. (2003). Making Sense of Conspiracy Theories. In P. Knight (Ed.), *Conspiracy Theories in American History*. Santa Barbara: ABC-CLIO.

Knight, P. (2007). Conspiracy Theories about 9/11. *Centre for International Politics Working Paper Series* (34), 1–19.

Lee, M. F. (2011). *Conspiracy Rising: Conspiracy Thinking and American Public Life*. Santa Barbara, California: Praegar.

Levy, N. (2007). Radically Socialized Knowledge and Conspiracy Theories. *Episteme*, 4(2), 181–192.

Lewandowsky, S., Cook, J., Oberauer, K. & Marriott, M. (2013). Recursive Fury: Conspiracist Ideation in the Blogosphere in Response to Research on Conspiracist Ideation. *Frontiers in Psychology*, 4, 1–15.

Lewandowsky, S., Oberauer, K. & Gignac, G. E. (2013). NASA Faked the Moon Landing – Therefore, (Climate) Science Is a Hoax: An Anatomy of the Motivated Rejection of Science. *Psychological Science*, 24(5), 622–633.

Locke, S. (2009). Conspiracy culture, blame culture, and rationalisation. *The Sociological Review*, 57(4), 567–585.

Malcolm, A. (2009). Breaking: Charlie Sheen demands Obama meeting on 9/11 cover-up: http://latimesblogs.latimes.com/washington/2009/09/obama-charlie-sheen-911.html.

Mandik, P. (2007). Shit Happens. *Episteme*, 4(2), 205–218.

Mason, F. (2002). A Poor Person's Cognitive Mapping. In P. Knight (Ed.), *Conspiracy Nation: The Politics of Paranoia in Postwar America*. New York: New York University Press.

Matson, J. (2010). Astrobiologist tries to set the record straight about extraterrestrial life on Titan: http://www.scientificamerican.com/blog/post.cfm?id=astrobiologist-tries-to-set-the-rec-2010–06–08.

Pagán, V. E. (2004). *Conspiracy Narratives in Roman History*. Austin: University of Texas Press.

Pagán, V. E. (2012). *Conspiracy theory in Latin Literature*. Austin: University of Texas Press.

Pigden, C. (1995). Popper Revisited, or What Is Wrong With Conspiracy Theories? *Philosophy of the Social Sciences*, 25(1), 3–34.

Pigden, C. (2006). Complots of Mischief. In D. Coady (Ed.), *Conspiracy Theories: The Philosophical Debate*. Hampshire, England: Ashgate.

Pigden, C. (2007). Conspiracy Theories and the Conventional Wisdom. *Episteme*, 4(2), 219–232.

Pipes, D. (1997). *Conspiracy: How the Paranoid Style Flourishes and Where It Comes From*. New York: Free Press.

Popper, K. R. (1969). *The Open Society and Its Enemies* (5th ed., Vol. 2).: Routledge and Kegan Paul.
Popper, K. R. (1972). *Conjectures and Refutations* (4th ed.). London: Routledge and Kegan Paul.
Pushkin, A. (2003). *Alexander Pushkin's Little Tragedies: The Poetics of Brevity*. University of Wisconsin Press.
Pynchon, T. (2000). *Gravity's Rainbow*. Penguin Books.
Quine, W. V. (1951). Two Dogmas of Empiricism. *Philosophical Review*, 60, 20–43.
Räikkä, J. (2009a). The Ethics of Conspiracy Theorizing. *Journal of Value Inquiry*, 43, 457–468.
Räikkä, J. (2009b). On Political Conspiracy Theories. *Journal of Political Philosophy*, 17(2), 185–201.
Ramsay, R. (2006). *Conspiracy Theories*. Hertfordshire: Pocket Essentials.
Roisman, J. (2006). *The Rhetoric of Conspiracy in Ancient Athens*. Los Angeles: University of California Press.
Sackur, S. (2011). *HARDTalk*. TV series.
Saunders, F. S. (22 October 1995) Modern art was CIA 'weapon'. http://www.independent.co.uk/news/world/modern-art-was-cia-weapon-1578808.html.
Shaffer, P. (1979). *Amadeus*. Play.
Shea, R., & Wilson, R. A. (1998). *The Illuminatus Trilogy*. London: Raven Books.
Sunstein, C. R. (2009). *Going to Extremes: How Like Minds Unite and Divide*. Oxford: Oxford University Press.
Sunstein, C. R. & Vermeule, A. (2009). Conspiracy Theories: Causes and Cures. *Journal of Political Philosophy*, 17(2), 202–227.
Swami, V., Chamorro-Premuzic, T. & Furnham, A. (2010). Unanswered Questions: A Preliminary Investigation of Personality and Individual Difference Predictors of 9/11 Conspiracist Beliefs. *Applied Cognitive Psychology*, 24, 749–761.
Vanakin, J. (1991). *Conspiracies, Cover-ups and Crimes*. New York: Paragon House Publishers.
Wood, G. S. (1982). Conspiracy and the Paranoid Style: Causality and Deceit in the Eighteenth Century. *The William and Mary Quarterly*, Third Series(3), 401–441.
Wood, M. J. & Douglas, K. M. (2013). 'What about Building 7?' A Social Psychological Study of Online Discussion of 9/11 Conspiracy Theories. *Frontiers in Psychology*, 4, 1–9.
Wood, M. J., Douglas, K. M. & Sutton, R. M. (2012). Dead and Alive: Beliefs in Contradictory Conspiracy Theories. *Social Psychological and Personality Science*, 3(6), 767–773.
Zonis, M. & Joseph, C. M. (1994). Conspiracy Thinking in the Middle East. *Political Psychology*, 15(3), 443–459.

Index

Lightning Source UK Ltd.
Milton Keynes UK
UKHW022116300322
400850UK00004B/144

9 781137 363152